ANCESTRAL MOUNDS

ANCESTRAL MOUNDS

Vitality and Volatility of Native America

JAY MILLER

Foreword by Alfred Berryhill

University of Nebraska Press
Lincoln and London

© 2015 by the Board of Regents of
the University of Nebraska
All rights reserved
Manufactured in the United
States of America ♾

Library of Congress
Cataloging-in-Publication Data
Miller, Jay.
Ancestral mounds: vitality and
volatility of Native America / Jay Miller;
foreword by Alfred Berryhill.
pages   cm   Includes bibliographical
references and index.
ISBN 978-0-8032-7866-0 (cloth: alkaline paper)
ISBN 978-0-8032-7899-8 (pdf)
1. Mounds—Oklahoma. 2. Indians of
North America—Oklahoma—Antiquities.
3. Ethnology—Oklahoma. 4. Indians of
North America—Funeral customs and
rites—Oklahoma. 5. Indians of North
America—Oklahoma—Religion. 6. Indians
of North America—Oklahoma—Social life
and customs. 7. Community life—Oklahoma.
8. Monuments—Social aspects—Oklahoma.
9. Oklahoma—Antiquities. 10. Oklahoma—
Social life and customs. I. Title.
E78.O45M45 2015
976.6'01—dc23   2015013576

Set in Garamond Premier by L. Auten.
Designed by N. Putens.

Gratefully dedicated to
the Felix and Minnie Franks Gouge Family
and
Sanger Sullivan Clark
$\alpha \sim \Omega$

Raised up in song
Packed down in dance
Vital communion with the volatile cosmos

CONTENTS

Foreword
ix

Preface
xi

Acknowledgments
xxiii

Conventions
xxv

Archaeological Time Frame
xxvi

Kinship Codes
xxvii

Graphic Codes
xxviii

1. Mounding Up
1

2. Breaking Ground
23

3. SEeing Mounds
61

4. Modern Mounding
91

5. Mounds in Full
119

Notes
131

Bibliography
157

Index
183

FOREWORD

We Creeks are proud of our tradition of mound building. In our homeland (today's Alabama and Georgia) each ancestral town (*etvlwv*) had its own mounds, large and small. Every year at the Buskita Green Corn some were renewed along with the earth. Soils and mementos of these mounds were carried west to Oklahoma when we were forced to move away. From these heirlooms, new smaller mounds were started in our new towns. These mounds of today contrast in size to the huge ones of our past. Their size called for special techniques and abilities, which faded. In the hope that all Creeks will soon come together to build a modern great mound, our basket makers relearned the art of making weight-bearing baskets with strong rims. Expressing shared effort, community wellness, and beloved heritages, this project moves forward.

Today about a dozen towns maintain ceremonial grounds and mounds, while other *etvlwv* have converted into a Methodist or Baptist church keeping the same name. Both communities have camps and arbors focused on the East, with the church in the central place of the fire. Hymns in our language hold us together, along with fellowship and communion.

Our towns and churches honor fours, such as the directions and seasons. At ceremonial grounds the foursome of soil, song, stomp, and spirit are especially vital. *Ancestral Mounds* helps to explain why this is so and why they will continue until the end of time.

Mvto,
Honorable Alfred Berryhill†
Past Second Chief (*vpoktv* ~ "Twin") of the Creek Nation
Cultural Preservation Office, Muscogee (Creek) Nation
Okmulgee, Oklahoma

† Rev. Berryhill went across on 31 August 2013

PREFACE

Mounds have motivated me in recent decades, vital to my increasing grasp of Native North America. Imposing and ubiquitous across the Americas, mounds have always been a prime interest of Americanist research, though lacking any comprehensive understanding. In my own case knowing members of communities who are still building small mounds each summer has spared me from thinking they are only for burials or that the separate mound builders were anything but a political fiction by land-hungry settlers trying to assuage their conscience or assert a moral defense for their own taking of Native land. Founders of the United States hoped mounds would help to define national style and character. With more than an envious glance toward European tumuli, Thomas Jefferson had one excavated. George Washington and his officers invested heavily in mound-filled Ohio lands.

In academia centuries of scholarship (and an archaeology monopoly) have been devoted to basic questions of mound research, especially who, what, where, when, and how, but as yet there has been no serious investigation of a basic *Why?* As argued herein, the source for that answer has to be today's Native mound builders, particularly Native southeastern towns driven to Oklahoma almost two hundred years ago, in combination with reliable ethnographic and archaeological reports. Sometimes, to fill gaps in these data, resort must be made to best-case comparative information from other sections of the Americas, where fuller instances, examples, and quotes provide better illumination.[1] Space limitations, however, severely cut these comparisons, but they are noted for the record.

Because I wished to be comprehensive, my manuscript on mounds kept increasing. Academic presses in the Southeast declined it. Nebraska's editorial review suggested concentrating on the southeast materials, those most associated in the popular mind with mound traditions, now and in the past.

Divided into halves, the remaining trans-American mound comparisons will later appear as a companion book about aggregated fates.

Indeed what happened to Native America was more than a shattering of lives and cultures; it was a violent outward explosion, leaving tiny bits and pieces of traditions scattered across the continent. To make coherent deductions about their original widespread themes and variations therefore requires reassembling best cases selected from the entire continent. To fill in gaps, judicious comparative use can also be made of global examples that illustrate particular features of the human condition. The intent is to reassemble from these explosions not a flat jigsaw puzzle but instead something like a whole pot after it has shattered into many far-flung pieces. From best-case telling fragments, its designs, shape, and function can be determined in outline if not in detail.[2] Some of these exemplars exist in prior printings, some in memories, and some in actions, which must be experienced to be comprehended.

While childhood tours of archaeological sites exposed me to the variety of mounds throughout the East, it was as an adult researcher that I discovered, sometimes with embarrassment, how extensive mound distributions were for all the Americas. Even more important, coming to mounds so personally means I backed into the turf monopoly claimed by American archaeology and was (mostly) spared its frontal assault.

Further, crucial linkages for my research were forged in Chicago, at the Newberry Library, far from the Southeast. Instead it was specialists of the caliber of Ray Fogelson, Bob Hall, Jim Brown, and other researchers well connected with Creek and Cherokee communities who opened the way for me, provided a general understanding, and supported me with food, housing, and good thoughts. As a linguist I was also interested in working with a community with many Native speakers since I had already outlived several speech communities. At seventy-five thousand members with thousands of Native speakers, the Creek Nation will long survive me.

Once my eyes opened to mounds, they were everywhere. In the Pacific Northwest coast my own intimate knowledge, musings, and personal chagrin revealed obvious mound images. Throughout the Northwest human-made piles of dirt served as defensive forts or flood protection (Miller 2011), though they once seemed not to have the sacred, burial, or spiritual aura of mounds elsewhere. Instead cultural emphasis was devoted to arts, crests, and treasures descended from the ancestors, both human and spirit. In Puget Sound, despite my authoring three relevant books concerned with local Lushootseeds, I overlooked any evidence for mounds until I glanced at my own *Shamanic Odyssey*, with illustrations drawn by my own hand, and groaned. At the base of each one of the protecting planks sheltering a shaman, there is a black half circle that is explicitly said to be the earthen mound serving as the home of a being called a Little Earth, one of the spirits who are said to "own" the earth (Miller 1988, 1999b). Thus here is artifactual evidence for a mound as a safe "holy home" for a powerful earth spirit. If I had not personally traced that mound at the base of each plank diagram based on museum photos, I would have been even slower to see the link. It remains unclear whether these hills or outcrops were specifically built by immortals or by natural forces, though they are probably one and the same. In the few instances where this place-name has been recorded near Seattle, it refers to a hill that looms over a natural spring.

The need for such earthy massiveness is supported linguistically. The Lushootseed word for earth is *swatix*ʷ*təd*, indicating outwardly expansive motion, as "something that fully takes care of spreading everything around."[3] Its further extensions mean both forest and these same earth-owning spirit immortals (Little Earths) who live in those hummocks near springs. Thus their earth, like life, is inherently dynamic if unstable. To gain stability, the earth, or a portion of it, must be held safely in place in a way that stands out and up from the uncertain landscape. Moreover it is now clear that mounds are not attested only in Salish rituals and mythology. Archaeologists have indeed found burial mounds at sites just to the north and south along major rivers (Ames and Maschner 1999: 190–91; Carlson 2001: 36).[4]

Strong respect for tribal languages, especially in cooperation with fluent elders, encouraged me to coin a few new terms (see "Conventions") to better reflect Native concepts. Key among these are *powha* for the mindful energy in the cosmos; *tysic* for the nexus of the Time Space Center; the use of ~ to indicate nuanced similarity, likeness, or interlinkage; and the equals sign = for translations. Tysic was coined to provide cultural parallels to the linguistic term *deictic* (from the Greek "proven") to indicate words simultaneously conjoining concepts of identity ~ space ~ time from the standpoint of participant(s), such as *here, there, now, then, this, that, former, latter*. More debated is my use of *Indien*, for those of the Indies instead of India, to better reflect the preferred self-identification of most tribal peoples of the Americas. Though my interest is most concerned with the past, it must be informed by the present.

Reverence for mounds continues. My current visits to mound sites often include seeing fresh offerings left there, such as once at Aztalan and many times at Cahokia, starting when Monk's Mound still looked down on a suburban street grid with split-level houses. A sense of mounds as monuments soon expanded my interests to include other types. During a trip to the Big Horn Medicine Wheel, the sounds of walkie-talkies between rangers alerting each other to the arrival of a Native family with offerings remain particularly vivid.

As I have worked throughout Native America, including three decades among southeastern peoples who were driven from the South (Dixie) to Oklahoma almost two hundred years ago, I became increasingly fascinated by indigenous analogies that crisscross the Americas. In particular, as part of a larger agenda to bring the North Pacific Coast back into pan-American scholarship, I want to draw attention to ways the Northwest can help us to understand the Southeast.[5] Both traced kin through strong matrilineality among ranked chiefdoms, heavily supported by carefully tended natural resources (fishing for both, farming for the Southeast), which were enhanced by elaborate rituals.

There are also striking historic differences.[6] Major ceremonies are held inside during the rainy winter in the Northwest but outside during the blistering summer in the Southeast. Most communities in the Northwest, especially in Alaska, remain in their own diminished homelands, dynamically involved in their own place-based ecotraditions. The southeast peoples, by contrast, were mostly relocated to the West but sustained themselves as farmers relying on the later trinity of corn+beans+squash after these embellished the early eastern domesticates such as sunflowers, sunroots, sumpweed, and amaranth.

Focusing on mound vitalities and their cultural ramifications, this book marks my own coming to terms with the last of the four quarters ⊕ of Native North America (SW, NE, NW, SE), as understood through place-based rituals with cosmic meanings. In hindsight my work has been in terms of diagonals, starting in the Southwest with Keresan Pueblos and then adding the Northeast with favored Delawares (Lenapes). While several articles have made it into print, the book-length treatments of Keres and Lenapes have not survived peer review.[7] In sharp contrast my research in the Northwest, where I am more deeply involved as a resident among Salishans and Tsimshians, has seen friendly support and ready publication. Now, with the southeast materials presented here, that other diagonal is broached. Though an avid interest of most people, fieldwork in the Plains has never attracted me. Instead reading its ample publications has served to provide necessary comparative data already rich in detail. Moreover both Delawares and Creeks living in Oklahoma (on the southern Plains) visit many neighboring Plains tribes, so I have not escaped some involvement as a guest at Powwows, bundle openings, Sun Dances, and other bison-fed rites.[8]

Finishing this book brings enormous relief. Throughout I often struggled as a ruggedly independent scholar, choosing between either time or money. Time always won out, fostering a rogue scholar status. Applying for grants or currying favor would have taken time away from my sustained efforts and tribal involvements. Trial papers at conferences and meetings might have sped final drafts and tested peer review, though adding more distractions. Moreover entrenched professional turf defenders make a fair hearing unlikely where mounds are concerned.

The writing went well, but printing out long drafts strained resources. Unlike Native friends who shared my condition, however, I could draw on assets they lacked. I put my "free" time and PhD to good use. I had ample opportunity to read, write, and attend ceremonies, though I could not provide abundant gifts. I was driven to finish what was started as well as compelled to download (or purge) a brain obsessed with figuring out this immense cultural puzzle. Full employments have both drawn out the process and eased stringencies along the way. There were times, however, when being simultaneously between jobs and an active scholar seemed as abysmally lonely as being a "mustee," the last survivor of a southeastern tribe "erased" by disease or slavery.[9]

I always had a vital sense of supportive community. A close continuity from the ravaged Mississippian past (reigning over several hundred years in the Americas) still enriches many Native communities affiliated if not fluent with a variety of languages. In Oklahoma alone these include the Caddoans such as Caddos and Pawnees, Algonkians (Algics) such as Delawares and Shawnees, Muskogeans such as traditional ("stomp ground") Mvskoke Creeks, and Siouans such as the Osages. Though many today are Christians, all still "look up to pray." Indeed their churches are built upon Oklahoma hills to make this easier, as their temples were once set upon mounds (Miller 1996).[10] Those rural churches at crossroads similarly evoke the ancient and continuing religious orientation of the crossed logs (+) of a sacred fire and the Sun at the nexus of the heavens.

Native conflicts and (necessary) secrecy have not helped the process of public understanding. To be sure, many of the modern-day mound-building people have long and greatly suffered from the criticism of their Southern Baptist kin and unkind outsiders. Talking openly about what they do in worship has never been beneficial. For as long as visitors have been asking, therefore, these Natives have denied any knowledge of mounds in terms of who, when, or why. In worship they act rather than analyze—to re-create is more important than to ponder or expose.

Yet they live every day with mounds and continue the devotions that they have always been obliged to perform for the sake of the vital security of their portion of the world. I have lived and learned from them. My role has been to help, to participate, and to listen, rarely asking questions or seeking explanations. Instead, as I was steeped in the past literature and dialogue with colleagues (Natives and others), the occasional act or remark (fleeting in the course of routine or arduous religious activities) would open whole vistas of understanding. The pages that follow are inspired by what they have said and done to stir me, though their reluctance to reveal much detail will be fully and carefully respected. On the other hand, generalities are inescapable in the human condition, and much that remains useful has been published over the centuries and can be cited.

Preface

A succinct, spontaneous comment will be pregnant with meaning but go unnoticed because outsiders, especially academics, lack any fuller sense of cultural context. A telling example is the remark by Barney Leader and Turner Bear, Creek Busk officials (below), that the low mounds at modern square grounds are called *taco fi•ki* [~ *tvčo fi:ki*],[11] which James Howard translated literally as "mound heart." But these words are more inclusive, indicating the larger "square ground" + "heart," and encompass the heart at the core of the male precinct of the ceremonial square, particularly that near the vitalizing fire (Howard 1968: 146).[12] Therefore in addition to the mound's function as a bulging bulk holding an area safe, stable, secure, and steady, it also was aquiver with pumping or pulsating heart-like actions that sanctified, honored, elevated, charged, and vivified that vital space inhabited by men and women ~ males and females.[13]

Throughout a modern-day Busk Rite (Green Corn of Mvskoke Creeks) soil is a deep and abiding concern. Enormous effort is spent cleaning and clearing the ground, as well as moving around soils of appropriate colors and consistencies. Sometimes it is more a matter of taking soil from the appropriate direction rather than anything more visually or geologically obvious. Some soil is mounded up, some spread out, and some applied to other surfaces. In the way of farmers across the world, land (soil, dirt) matters in all possible forms, both seen and unseen, today as in the past. Always the weeding out of grass to clear off the square and the cutting down of live trees for support posts involves asking forgiveness and giving thanks for their lives. Firewood, by contrast, is usually deadfall limbs, after the new fire is laid—using four sections cut from the same living tree that have been reset in the shape of a cross (+) and ritually fed with maize ears and beef tongue.

Thus my fieldwork has been in the nature of a seminar in the field rather than anything like direct questioning or interviewing. Written notes or direct questions are never allowed inside the ring or in public space. Instead, during lulls in the night-long stomp dancing, a small group of us, including Creeks with bachelor's, master's, and doctoral degrees sometimes dubbed "the Varsity," engaged a topic that arose during the daytime rituals or that is mentioned in the classic ethnographies, particularly by John Swanton, or at a recent professional meeting or tribal event. Mvskogee speakers provide insight based on their fluency. Rarely, early in the morning when keeping awake is more of an effort, a square leader or elder might join us to add a detail or explain a feature to keep thoughts lively. By etiquette and protocol nothing can be written down at that time because the modern world is taboo during the Busk, lit only by the central fire. Electric lights, common in the camps, are forbidden on the square ground, as are papers, pens, cell phones, cameras, and other media intrusions. At night, on the edges, the two night deacons ~ *takpa:la* = land-lenders (Martin and Mauldin 2000: 114, 115, 263), who invite each stomp leader and his following dancers onto the bare ground around the fire, shine the dancers' way to the edge of the clearing with flashlights. Later, after a day of sleep and slow recovery, more so with age, I follow up on our night-long seminar far away from the ceremonies by referencing professional publications, grammars, and dictionaries and begin jotting notes (often communally at breakfast) to fill out our observations and conclusions from that session.

Discussion and debate is also facilitated by the long drives, often several hours, to attend dances, reciprocating other towns for visiting and leading dances at your own town's Busk. Another night begins another seminar, exploring the subject of Creek traditions and their unconscious motivations. During visits to Cherokees, talk shifts to compare and contrast, with the Creek winter rotunda highly praised on cold nights. The overall result is a consensus of what makes sense in terms of what is being done now in terms of evidence, reports, or echoes from the ancient past. Indeed, in thought and deed, the past lives today.

For those who follow traditional beliefs, mounding today is a devotional exercise with many sacrificial ramifications. Its origins are as ancient as humans and relate to obligations to the landscape, concerns with security, and vital communion (Creek = *anogechka* ~ *vnokeckv*) with the cosmos in up/down balance (Chaudhuri and Chaudhuri 2001: 101). Understanding worldview is fundamental. In the Americas in particular it can be traced from the caches of finely made Clovis blades,[14] through the carved stone offerings deeply buried along precise alignments at the Olmec center of La Venta, down to the food still buried on the vast tundra by Yup'ik Eskimos of coastal Alaska as offerings to thank and feed their living homeland. In all instances digging down has left behind a mounding up, like any act of planting. Scale, however, distinguishes the huge Mississippian efforts, as animal effigies do later ones. Digging down and piling up are balanced aspects of a whole, the halves of a globe, the sky dome and sea bowl, the complement of microcosm for cosmos.[15] Moreover the final engendered bulk applies bulging pressure to hold in place a safe vitality on the thin skin of the Earth.

Most especially I want to provide models and analogies for mounds that are firmly based in Native beliefs and traditions. Too much of what goes on in present-day academia, especially archaeology, reflects unapologetic Eurobias. A distressingly greedy consumerism, instead of grateful sustainability,[16] asserts an overly generic, competitive, grasping assortment of individuals, assembled from comparisons carelessly drawn from all over the map of the anthropological world at the expense of the Native Americas. Yet there is no denying that scientific research, experiment, and testing is a European asset. Scholarship benefits from the tests of time in ways that mortal, all-too-human scholars have not.

In hindsight this book emerged in the best possible progression from my study of Southeast sources while living in the Northwest, my direct experiences in Oklahoma, and, last of all, my residence in the academic and natural climate of the South and Ohio. Positioning myself to teach in prime mound areas, the most obvious aspect of mounds occurred (9 October 1998 at 9:30 p.m.) while I was surrounded by the density of effigy mounds in Madison on Lake Mendota at the University of Wisconsin (Birmingham 2010). Three years later I published my preliminary findings in support of such instilling in a Native studies journal, with the enthusiastic help of the late Robert Hall, a skilled archaeologist unlike any other. His *Archaeology of the Soul* continually informs and sustains my own work.

When I could find no word for *mound* in the many dictionaries of Cherokee, I asked for help from Barbara Duncan, who consulted with speakers in North Carolina, texting me that the word is *ugwelvtvi* "it's bubbling up," according to Wiggins Black Fox in consultation with Roger Smoker, Eastern Cherokee–speaking elders.[17]

Working closely with archaeologists at Ole Miss in 2004–5 proved startling on several occasions because of my Oklahoma-ingrained cultural expectations of mounds and associated ritual behaviors, derived from personal experiences at modern Creek grounds. A variety of culture shock, it eventually led to the label of "mlm = martin luther moments" when Native beliefs were cast into clarity by a few remarks by archaeologists that seemed sacrilegious from a born-again Mississippian perspective.

Primary among these Oklahoman assets was a sense of the cosmos as a whole—a willingness to look up and about as well as out and down. Too much time digging a hole, staring down, took the wrong toll. A chance remark denigrating the use of aerial panoramas of sites like Cahokia set in stark relief the importance of always considering the viewpoint and motion of the Sun (a solar being) during any southeastern ritual. Participants, especially men, do indeed cast their thoughts to emulate those of the Sun looking down on the square ground during a ritual such as the Busk, praying to win favor.

Similarly the vital importance of dualities, particularly moiety membership, for defining core being is lost to the archaeological record, as in the consistent reference to the main burial at Mound 72 at Cahokia as that of a man on a bird-shaped cloak of shell disk beads. In fact a pair of burials, head to feet, facing up or facing down, offset by 10 degrees, share the beaded cloak between them. The Siouan Earth/Sky moieties come immediately to mind for ethnologists and Natives and are indeed mentioned in the exemplary excavation report (Fowler et al. 1999: 183–89).[18]

While scholarship in the Southeast is commendable for a willingness by its academics to link archaeological complexes and colonial documents with modern-day merged tribal survivals—more easily done than in other regions because these coalitions are so huge—the chilling absence of most Native people from their very homeland has created a range of gaping holes in the methodologies and publications for this culture area. Such lapses, however, are also an aspect of the historical record of the South. In Dixie it was frequently better to overlook a problem for as long as possible rather than to address it.

In the Southwest, where stone pueblos occur both archaeologically and ethnographically, a more comprehensive understanding is the rule (Kane 1989). While less willing to identify prehistoric complexes with modern communities, except in general ways, the Southwest shares this appreciation of cultural traditions and diversity, alive and well in a richly multicultural milieu, where many tribal members now engage academia and earn advanced degrees in linguistics, anthropology, history, and physics.

Throughout the Americas all Native languages, especially in their grammars, emphasize verbs over nouns—process over products. This inherent sense of dynamism is close to the outlook of geophysics, of a universe made up of moving molecules and plate tectonics instead of stolid locked-in-place landforms that, while reassuring to human frailty, are clearly against the grain of nature and the forces of the cosmos.

In all, mounds mimic the Earth, as a microcosm built and maintained by human hands, tools, sweat, and prayers, paced by rituals, songs, and dances. Built of earth, strengthened with internal architectural ingenuity, and ritually consecrated by men and women who are atoning, praying, singing, and dancing, they weigh down upon the greater Earth to secure a safe place. Because the world is extremely volatile and dangerous this is necessary, especially when agitated by human faults. Through their obvious bulk mounds atone for these faults and serve as stable, safe, anchoring beacons during both calm and troubled times.

Specifically, ancestral mounds are secure weights set upon the earth and are necessarily composed by the labor, song, dance, and prayers within communities of men and women to be safe havens in a volatile world ever vengeful of grievous human faults. Each mound therefore engenders human atonement, creating instilled safety for a community over time. The bigger the mound, the greater its obvious stability, especially during times of crises such as flood, attack, and traumatic tumult.

More generally, while the dynamic analogy for a mound by an insider is a heart in a torso with an air duct, filled with song and prayers, by far the best analogy for an outsider to understand a mound is that of a safe = a heavy, hollow, hoard symbolic of security, protecting family gems of men and women, who renew its vitality by singing and dancing from the top down once they have built it from the bottom up. The main difference, of course, between mound and safe is that most activity takes place on top rather than inside, though mounds once supported temples whose interior mirrored underworld vaults within its rooms.

ACKNOWLEDGMENTS

Oklahoma provided the backdrop for this study, which soon cascaded across the continent and the world as connections to honor earth grew out of my lifetime of Americanist research. I would like particularly to thank fellow backbenchers Blue Clark, Ray Fogelson, Bob McKinley, and Ted Isham for sustaining concern. Blue deserves special thanks, as always, as a constant source of documents, encouragement, and meals. Thanks too to Sherry Sullivan, Sanger Clark, and John, Luceen, Peggy, and Stella Sara Dunn. I am most grateful to Mikkos Barney Leader, Cal Leader, and Jeff Fixico, as well as the devoted Felix and Minnie Gouge family. Through them I realized the continuing importance of localized song and dance for amassing power ~ energy (*powha*) within revitalizing mounds.

Before he undertook a heroic review of this manuscript, Robert Hall experimented with his Christmas digital camera to provide interior views of the wonderful Pawnee Big Doctoring diorama that explained what the texts could not. In its wisdom the Field Museum soon took it off display, proving once again that it is best to plan for uncertainty.

Thank you to Dr. F. Kent Reilly III, who gave permission to use the "hypothetical model of the Native American cosmos" drawn by Jack Johnson.

For technical, factual, and emotional support I am grateful to John Swanton, Erna Gunther, Viola Garfield, Clara Sue Kidwell, Vic Kucera, Tom Steinburn, Astrida Blukis Onat, Lona and Claude Wilbur, Phil LeTourneau, Janet Pollak, Harvey Markowitz, Marilyn Richen, Tammy Jackson, Vi Hilbert, Bob Walls, Laura Dassow Walls, Ann Richel Schuh, Kurt Reidinger, Patt O'Flaherty, Mary Laya, Donna Ellefson, Julian Baumel, Sally Anderson, Monday Nite, and Ashland Annuals. Geoff Keyes, a blacksmith and computer wiz working at both ends of the tech scale, saved the day many times. The YOLFs made their own backhand contributions.

Acknowledgments

At Ole Miss, the Sociology and Anthropology Department, especially Jay Johnson, Janet Ford, Ed Sisson, Robbie Ethridge, and Gabe Wrobel, as well as the Center for the Study of Southern Culture, were all gracious, even when they unfailingly stopped me in my tracks with yet another "mlm." Robbie was a sometime miner's canary ~ guinea pig for testing the climate of the academic South. Maureen Meyers kindly loaned Lamar site materials. At Ohio State grudging support came from Jackie Royster, Linda Schoen, Richard Shiels, Rob Cook, Mike Sherfy, Tina Bergsten, Phil DeSense, Brian Joseph, Newark Earthworks Center, and American Indien Studies (Indies, not India), as well as kind and helpful Brad Lepper, Jeff Gill, and others struggling against that awful Ohio time warp. The near final draft basked in a Fogelson Beneficence within the *powha* of Nikwasi (North Carolina) and Southeastern penumbra.

Meticulous editing and proofreading of the final version became a new skill for Amelia Susman Schultz, the last PhD student of Franz Boas, a longtime friend, and a dynamo at the age of one hundred. Thanks, Amelia.

Mounds, as banked havens of stability in a precarious universe, have an amazing continuity over millennia, testifying to the saving grace of soil and stone as pledges of security and immortality in bulge, bulk, body, and ballast. To those of the past, who still teach us, mvdo vcululke.

To all, Mvdo, Yakoki.

CONVENTIONS

Over the years the frustrations of trying to discuss Native America using standard English have led me to publish certain usages based in Native understandings. In the global context I use the European (French, Italian, Danish, etc.) convention of spelling *Indien* with an *e*, for the Indies, instead of *a* for India. Two vital concepts are expressed in translation by the words *powha* (= for the all-pervading cosmic vital energy, cosmic mind) and *tysic* (= for t̪ime + s̪pace + c̪enter, with vowels pointing down and up, that is its multidirectional intersection as well as source and summary nexus, within a circuitry that is very like a global spider web ⊛ with rings and rays). Both terms derive from crucial concepts embedded in Native languages. Cosmic energy is termed *pow-* in Eastern Algonquian and *puha* in U.S. Numic languages; hence *powha* serves as a better conjoined variant of words for "power." What linguists call deictics, from Greek, refer equally to time and space, as tysic does in graphic fashion.

The names of spirits are in capitals, such as Bear, Coyote, Raven, in lieu of the ordinary species of bears, coyotes, ravens. Native words are in italics, with proper nouns both italic and underlined. Direct translations are marked by an equals sign (=), followed by the term in single quotes (' '). Equivalences or synonyms are linked by a tilde (~), while those in a series are separated by commas.

Dates will usually be presented as CE/BCE (= current era / before current era), though some will appear as AD/BC. At the moment this chronology seems to be involved in a reanalysis that has doubled the earliest dates of some mound features yet continues to provide a general sequence of events.

ARCHAEOLOGICAL TIME FRAME

PALEO INDIENS +15,000–9,000 years ago
    Pioneers: Foliate, Stemmed, Fluted
ARCHAIC Settlers, Tenders 9,000 BCE = before current era
    Early 9,000–7,000 BCE
        Windover, Dalton ~ pecans
    Middle 7,000–5,000 BCE
        Watson Brake ~ mounds
    Late 5,000–3,500 BCE
        Poverty Point
WOODLAND Founders, Intensive Tillers, Pottery 5500 BCE
    Early 3,500–2,000 BCE
        Adena-Cresap 3,685–2,020 BCE
    Middle 2,500–1,500 BCE
        Hopewell-Kolomoki (BC 1,650–1,250 > AD 350–750)
    Late 1,500–300 CE
        Fort Ancient, Oneota
MISSISSIPPIAN 1,200–270 CE maize farmers, > AD 800
        Cahokia > Natchez (shattered AD 1731)
PROTOHISTORIC 500–300 CE disease, epidemics, slaving
HISTORIC 400 CE >

KINSHIP CODES

To deal with kinship more precisely, lone capital letters are used for primary kin, emphasizing a proper matrifocus for the Southeast. Thus eZetD = elder sister's eldest daughter.

C = child(ren)
Cz = cousin
ego = central point of reference
e = elder / y = younger
et = eldest / yt = youngest
+/− generations, up/down from ego
G = grand, great

GM = grandmother	+2	GF = grandfather
M = mother	+1	F = father
A = aunt	+1	U = uncle
Z = sister	0 = ego	B = brother
W = wife	0	H = husband
D = daughter	−1	S = son
Nc = niece	−1	Np = nephew
GD = granddaughter	−2	GS = grandson

GRAPHIC CODES

= equal, equivalent to, same as, translated as
~ similar, related, comparable, variant, overlapping, parallel, linked, also known as
' ' direct translation
+ plus, add, conjoined
> transposed, changed to, becomes

ANCESTRAL MOUNDS

1

Mounding Up

Mounds weigh on the earth, as they do on the curious mind. From this basic and very obvious fact follow more complex associations, derivations, uses, and functions that have long challenged scholarly research. This touchpoint truism is enacted every summer as soil is piled up at Native harvest ceremonies, but this weighty activity has been overlooked by those who view the earth as inert and unaware. A mound instead is a steady microcosm of the dynamic world.

Mounds are often misunderstood, mostly because of disjuncts between living traditions and erroneous yet popular presumptions, as in these examples. A giggling girl runs down the slope into her grinning father's arms, shouting, "I'm running over dead Indiens."[1] A park ranger begins his campfire talk, "Parents wanted the best for their children so they all came together to build these pyramids made out of earth." An archaeologist at a meeting of her peers begins, "The one thousand cubic feet of soil in this construction were deposited by seven discrete labor-intensive stages." A mother packs their car with kitchen supplies and food, reminding her children, "We'll be keeping the family camp and feeding guests at the square grounds, while Dad prays for us all during the Green Corn Poskita."

Such, then, are some of today's mound-related remarks, with usual misunderstandings that most Americans have about the "inert" ancestral "Indian" mounds that once abounded in the U.S. East before they became casualties of farming, extraction, and sprawl. In contrast, simultaneously, those surviving monuments that are still sitting across our entire continent are venerated by their Native descendants, who find meaning and purpose in their presence as monuments of heaped-up earthen platforms (rarely used for burials) well blended on and into the organic landscape. Moreover the all-important songs and dances that revivify mounds during today's rituals are ignored by academics in favor of a truly sterile understanding. Clearly a disjunct, hinting at a latent sense of winner's gloat, has hampered any understanding of a Native cultural perspective on these ubiquitous vitalized bulges throughout the American landscape.

Indeed we should readily grasp that mounds mimic the Earth, as a microcosm built and maintained by human hands, tools, sweat, and prayers—paced by rituals, songs, and dances that are very specific to towns and genders. Built of earth and strengthened with internal architectural ingenuity, they weigh down the greater Earth to hold some of it safely in place for men, women, and other beings. Because the world it(her)self is extremely volatile and dangerous, this is necessary, especially when agitated by human faults. Via their obvious bulk, mounds atone for these faults and serve as stable, safe, anchoring beacons during calm or troubled times.

This book is concerned with the dynamism of mounds, their core meaning and obvious physicality, across the Americas and wider world, informed especially by their present-day use and significance among tribes driven away from the U.S. Southeast and now living in Oklahoma. I argue that mounds, underlying many other purposes and uses, are foremost and primarily an obvious, vital, bulging bulk (ballooning bubble, according to their Cherokee name) poised for both raising up and weighing down a safe haven in the volatile world. Each one provides a surface tension of security, sanctuary, "honored earth," and "blessed ballast" in a very uncertain world.[2] Their immediate physicality of size, shape, mass, density, and distribution reflects local conditions, but the basic intent is the same: common security drawn from community vitality concentrated and consecrated in a raised monument by engendered efforts, often in atonement for confessed human faults. The soil inside mounds is special, composed of specific textures created by wind and water, and colors taken from certain places and directions in particular ways by designated people. Some inclusions, including burials, help to feed its vitality. Height, weight, size, and mass add to their bulging effectiveness along with prayers and rites of song and dance.

More specifically ancestral mounds, bulging in substance and weight, are monuments of all-embracing vitality, which is enhanced by tribal rituals, added soils, songs, and dances that are specific to each builder community and locale.[3] They both anchor their environs in a world made unsteady by human faults and provide a bank (safe ~ charged deposit) and beacon to dispense vitalizing power (*powha*) flowing through tubes and networks.[4] Vitality itself is global, dynamic, impersonal, and immortal, with a range that includes general health, success, beauty, goodwill, and fertility (though limited to the mortal and sexual).

Regarding mounds as static has skewed scholarship. While there are clear instances of disturbance—"If enemies reached [the temple on] one's mound, then disaster of the first magnitude occurred [and] desecration of mounds by invaders undermined elites' right to rule" (Gallay 2002: 26)—mounds are believed to be resilient, holding reserves of power much like a charged battery releasing vitalities over eons. While generations of builders may pass on, the life of a mound continues in perpetuity, even to lingering stains in the ground. Today's ongoing reverence for ancient *Nanih Waiya* by Choctaws and *Giduwah ~ Kituwah* by Cherokees recognizes this vitality.

Vitality resides in mounds, with built-up residual reserves. Today, during summer in Oklahoma, the visible vitality of the central fire of a Native town (Creek *talwa*) has to be extinguished once a year to sink into the ground and thereby "forget" the offenses and crimes of members and prepare for the renewal of a new year. Similarly in ancient times, when enemies destroyed the town temple atop a mound, its eternal fire sank down so the rebuilt temple could be revived from the spiritual vitality retained in the substructure mound below.

Mounds energize communities. According to Seminoles, in the beginning, after mound building began, four enlighteners (*hiya yalgi*) came to the people from, in order, the north, east, south, and west. They taught four tenets: primary reverence for life and Life Giver, healing arts, ceremonies to stay "wise and powerful and healthy," and rituals "with the signs and images [and] symbols of their learning and their constancy" (Wickman 1999: 40–41).

At an archaeological milestone, derived from his lifelong research at Poverty Point, with a security shield of earthen rings maintained by its newly named Tamaroha ("Mound Cave") people, Jon Gibson (2006: 311, 315, 320) wisely noted this perpetual vitality: "Mounds were permanent fixtures on the land, conspicuous vessels of lived history and attachment to place [as] Navels of the Earth [with] an enduring traditional, if not direct ancestral, connection between [ancient] and later groups. . . . Even after falling into disuse, mounds continued to evoke emotion, history, and identity (as material memory)."[5] The initial spark of this continuity, underappreciated by scholars, was ~ is the importance of song and dance, the pulsing mechanisms that complement the actual piling of the dirt to vitalize the whole construction while it lasts.

The nearest some archaeologists have come to this dynamism is a concern with the ramifications of the actual construction process: "Doing and experiencing of life almost always has a material and spatial dimension. Archaeologists have direct access to this dimensionality through artifacts, spaces, and places [to] track the continuous culture making of people through the histories, trajectories, or genealogies of things, spaces, and bodies. . . . Mound and mound building were the [societal] institutions *coming into being*" (Pauketat 2007: 2, 42).

As this study concludes with appropriate prepositions (across, into, inside, above, under, for) in reference to mounds, so it begins with a brief consideration of interrogatives. Mound research struggled with the who, where, when, and how, though giving little regard to the why and what, in part because traumatized surviving Natives usually denied knowledge of their builders. Once scholars had resolved that the builders were ancestral Natives (who) of the East (where) piling up dirt by the basket load (how) for over seven thousand years (when) and safeguarding food surpluses at polity centers (what), mound practicalities were thought to be solved. *Why* they were built or *what* they meant ~ mean were avoided questions that hence become my focus in this book, with dynamic answers based in song, dance, ritual, and cosmology that take mound study out of the limiting clutches of archaeologists (who can't sing or dance).⁶ Private and sacred aspects of mounds will be respected by avoidances.

Mounds represent calm order, bolstered by the vital regularities of song, dance (sometimes with trance), and speech as pleas and prayers against tumult and volatility. By means of blowtubes and stomping feet, the town-specific songs, beautified breath, are pumped into mainstays such as fire, medicines, and land, where they can bubble up as mounds. To retain the vitality of these religious efforts, mounds and other ceremonial objects were periodically recapped because "all the medicine is always sealed" (Lewis and Jordan 2002: 53, 100; cf. Conley 2005).

All surfaces (skins) associated with mounds receive careful attention. A passageway under the mound site is opened by removing topsoil to allow, like opening a valve, for its inflation, giving its substance added weight, and then, while in use, its banked vital bulk is periodically expanded by rituals and again resealed.

> Before mound building commenced, the upper dark soil horizon was sometimes removed. The mound fill that was subsequently deposited often consisted of small lenses of earth corresponding to separate basket loads. Blocks of sod were also stacked up, generally with the grassy side facing downward [upside down]. . . .
>
> In the mid-continent—from the Ozarks to the Ohio Valley—it was not at all uncommon for the mounds to be associated with great amounts of stone. In some places, rough rocks were simply piled up. Elsewhere, stone platforms or simple structures made of stacked rocks were built, often covered by earth. . . .
>
> But these events all involved the use of carefully prepared surfaces that were periodically renewed by the addition of more soil. Sometimes these layers were of different colors. Moreover, the ceremonies held on these surfaces, regardless of their specific form or purpose, involved lighting fires and erecting posts. (Milner 2004: 67, 73, 110)

Every mound poises a microcosm anchoring and mirroring this dynamic world, which is composed of a sky dome above and sea bowl below, with the island of living earth floating between them. Carefully and prayerfully constructed and re-covered, mounds are an obvious expression of beliefs about this layered cosmos. In the Americas Natives know their universe to be alive, volatile, precarious, and moving (as it really is) rather than based on a popular but false premise of security that the world is somehow reliable, permanent, and static.

Overall the Native American Earth is precarious: a vengeful living being, with thin skin and hollow heart, floating on a vast sea. Periodically it is imbalanced by human faults. Its denizens, especially their spirit leaders ("bosses"), are shape-shifting, active, and judgmental. Decent people have the moral responsibility to make conscious choices that provide security for all beings by performing rituals of propitiation, giving thanks, and acts of protection. They also use humor as a coping strategy, like that captured herein by the sometimes playful tone of this manuscript—which is also intended to encourage Native readers.

Every summer in Oklahoma over a dozen mounds are remantled (covered anew) by Native people at their ceremonial grounds. Recently as well a few mounds have been reclaimed in ancient homelands of the Southeast. They continue a tradition both global and ancient (thousands of years old): seeking to renew and strengthen the skin of the precarious world under conditions of prayer, joy, fasting, and sacrifice that culminate in feasting. Serving as altar, shrine, beacon, and refuge, these amassed forms of vitality endure to safeguard against uncertainty. Today, however, the predictabilities of hard science and modern comforts have overshadowed the much more realistic (reality-based) traditional cosmologies, relying on watchfulness against the real threat of impending doom.[7] Microcosm mirrored macrocosm, extolling the virtues of such ritualized remounding (via song, dance, chant, and gesture) to assure a similar still, calm, safe, and quiet haven within a perilous, chaotic universe. Paradoxically these older beliefs about an uncertain, unsteady, and ever tumultuous world—under a taut surface skin—are close to tenets of modern physics. Unlike whirling atomic particles adhering to universal laws, however, it was and is rituals enacted by humans, in Native belief, that keep ~ kept everything in balance. During extreme conditions the greatest sacrifices are required at the most desperate times of world upset. Instead of biblical injunctions imposing dominion over nature, humans, weak in terms of inherent natural defenses and abilities, have the responsibility to assure healthy coexistence among all beings.

This universe is active, alive, fragile, and therefore precarious—aptly derived from a Latin word meaning "pray" because it depends on the capricious will of others. Comfort and succor are seen in the ordered regularities of the sky, both stars and planets, helping to schedule rituals and events. Comets, asteroids, eclipses, and lightning bolts, however, provide reminders of sudden change that can strike from the sky, often imagined as dragons, snakes, and others emerging from the underearth abyss. For Creeks, "the slitherings of debris from the top of the giant earth turtle in the creation legend is the source of all evil and pollution [and] can take the form of a great horned snake" (Chaudhuri and Chaudhuri 2001: 130).

Mounds occur worldwide, the result of human intent and placement. They make many vital claims to the built-up landscape. Yet they remain distinctively American as a topic of intellectual curiosity. Concern with mounds, their makers, and meanings have long occupied America's savants, including such towering figures as Thomas Jefferson. After thousands of years, moreover, bulging dirt blends deceptively with the grassy landscape. Bare soil reseeds and soon merges with the landscape, disguised as hills or rises, though still serving as an obvious reminder (to those aware of what they are) of ancient ties of vitality among their builders, users, and adherents. By passing on this memory, others can renew their sense of place, of geo-identification. Both the emplaced earth and its engendered builders belong to and mix with (especially after burial) that very land. Throughout land sustains being, nourishing the senses, souls, and the body, which returns the favor. Mounds are its productive embodiment of vitality, rising up and pressing down, simultaneously leavening and leveling, as "the seen of an unseen source" (Lewis and Jordan 2002: 118).

Today Native Americans keep this thoughtful bond very much alive, even though many of them (because their families were relocated by force) now live thousands of miles away from where their ancestors added such beacons to their southeast homeland. Their return pilgrimages by plane, boat, and car continue to overcome the daunting challenge of bridging these great distances in time and space. Once again, affirmed by such vehicular proximity, this bonding among people, place, and presence is passed on across generations, though now usually in a Christian context.

Standing atop a mound triggers many cultural and emotional associations, physical as well as symbolic and spiritual.[8] A person can enter into another persona, place, and time via this ancient, human-built environment strongly evoking the ancestors, when "digging sticks, stone hoes, clamshells, and shoulder blades of deer and elk served as implements for loosening the earth [to be placed into a burden basket]. The individual offerings then were carried to the mound and added together to the growing heap" (Shetrone 1930: 43).

As a reverential term for this Earth, Turtle Island has gained currency. Indeed the Delaware (Lenape) and the Creek worlds rest on a primordial Turtle (Miller 1974b). But this phrase is not exclusive nor entirely apt. As shown so well by the Mi'kmaw Snake Dance, the Earth can be embodied by any of those crawling on or in its skin. These include lizards, turtles, spiders, toads, and even dragons, but most especially snakes. Some of these species live in mounds of their own making, others in caves set into the earth, and a few share human abodes. Some like the dark, and others the light of day. They can move quickly, sometimes dangerously so, and might cause harm.

In ancient Ohio the fractured terrain ("crypto-explosion geology") around the famous Serpent Mound called for special propitiation to hold down cosmic turmoil.[9] Built about CE 1066, its inspiration probably was the same comet that provided an omen for William at the Battle of Hastings.[10] A precise cosmogeometry of triangles served to position the three twists of the snake's body, as well as the nose and the coiled tail. Each of the loops in the body is pointed to a lunar alignment, while the head faces summer solstice sunset.[11] A line from the center of the coiled tail to the triangle in the head points to true astronomical North. Microcosm aligns with the cosmos, the precision of lines praying for calm and order in the world.

Harmony, balance, and respect are watchwords across the Americas. In this book, however, I will be arguing that there is a basic bottom-line response to negative threat, terror, and dread that served ~ serves to motivate whole communities, not just responsible members, who routinely and willingly work for the common good. Activity to produce the obvious, huge mound to enshrine a safe bank of ballast weight at a particular location combines devotion for most and threat for the rest. Mounds are raised by prayer, sweat, and effort and keep their height because inflated by song and (stomp) dance.

The greatest threat, beyond police or armed forces, is the painfully personal (and, by extension, familial) danger of attack by the geophysical violence inherent in the planet. These hostile energies are subject both to universal laws known to specialists and to moral outrage caused by human faults and breaches that ripple through a community and into the world. While there are many reasons for building mounds, the basic one is to produce an obvious safe bulging battery pack of vitality as a plea for place-based cosmic safety and protection. Community pride, well-being, atonement, public works, and haven also have roles, but as complements to the sitting earth composed of building, banking, and ballast for holding up and weighing down localized community vitality.

Among those holdout Cherokees, Choctaws, and others who remained in their southeast homelands, reverence continues for the Earth and its varied soils. In recent decades small-scale mounds have been renewed. A mound-building ceremony opens the Fading Voices Festival at Snowbird Cherokee (North Carolina) as each person adds to the low mound by pouring out a turtle shell full of dirt taken from their own yards. "It signified a gathering place. Every person brought dirt from their home to add to the mound, and that meant they were coming together as a people" (Duncan and Riggs 2003: 136). Similarly a video at the Eastern Cherokee section of the Museum of the American Indian in Washington DC shows a family adding earth to their ancient mother mound at *Giduwah ~ Kituwa*, recently purchased by the Qualla Reserve (North Carolina).

Sometimes, though rarely, bits of cultural insight have been preserved in early histories written by land usurpers. Such is the case, as supported by other citations to follow, with what seems to be a garbled account from Tennessee, listed under "Civil Traditions": "They [Cherokees] have a fabulous tradition respecting the mounds, which proves they are beyond the events of their history. The mounds they say were caused by the quaking of the earth, and great noise with it" (Haywood [1823] 1959: 279–80).[12] Though faulty, this remark shows that Judge Haywood had some contact with Cherokees but lacked proper attitude and understanding to fully comprehend what they said. Cause is confused with cure, and cosmology is misunderstood. In Native traditions, the world is multilayered, populated by a variety of beings and immortals of varying power (*powha*), while the Earth itself is sapient, active, and notoriously "thin skinned"—making it precarious. It (she) vents with trembling and tumult, often due to continuing human disrespect, harmful misuse, and selfish greed.

The earth is mindful, vital, and thereby powerful, as Creeks articulated:

> The world and all that it contained were the products of mind and bore everywhere the marks of mind. Matter was not something which had given birth to mind, but something which had formerly been mind, something from which mind had withdrawn, was quiescent, and out of which it might again be roused. This mind was visibly manifested in the so-called "living things," as plants, and, still more, as animals. Nevertheless, latent within inorganic substance no less than in plants and animals, was mind in its highest form, i.e., human mind.... Not that mind was attributed to one individuality, but that it was recognized as everywhere of the same nature ... but not in all cases equally powerful.... Unembodied ... power could be invoked by the use of charms and repetition of certain formulae ... imparted to medicines ... four times.... "By a word" wonderful things could be accomplished. (Swanton 1922: 142–43)

Set against this vast inclusiveness, for much of the 1800s mainstream America insisted on a disconnect between large mounds and their true human progeny. Fictitious people called "Mound Builders" were conjured up for the Ohio River drainage, a region well-stocked with huge mounds of many types, and local tribes were thereby denied their ancestry. Popular folklore sometimes repeats this error today, but academia has confirmed this direct link after long debate, testimony, and research. Unfortunately, with the fragmentation that is encouraged by academic hyper-specializations, archaeologists have focused more and more on the supposed political and economic aspects of mounds (cycling rise and collapse of "chiefdoms"),[13] ignoring that today in Oklahoma Native communities building mounds strongly emphasize their instilling religious purpose. Another kind of disconnect has developed as mainstream American values and precepts are erroneously projected backward by archaeologists.

In the years after Hernando de Soto swaggered and staggered through the South in the mid-1500s, great chiefdoms collapsed during horrendous and desperate times. Soto's forces spread both disease and famine in their wake. Their constant, shortsighted demands for food from their captive hosts probably ate up crop seeds as well as surpluses. Epidemics,[14] caused by these Europeans and their (misnamed) livestock, slaughtered vast numbers of Native people. Ironically bison moved into the depopulated prairies of the South, providing a new and needed food source. In the 1600s a "shatter zone" motivated by massive slaving, selling victims to Caribbean (Barbados) plantations, destroyed already damaged communities and tribes.[15] Fashion styles encouraged later animal slaughters: deerskins killed with muskets for men's gloves and breeches in the 1700s, egrets and other showy birds by shotgun for women's hats in 1880–1910.

Along rivers survivors regrouped, clumping together for mutual safety and eventually merging into confederacies supported by memories of their faded glory. By coalescing they survived brutal onslaughts from the native henchmen of many European nations, which were demanding their lands, their labor, and their souls. One of the most chilling details (for me, showing how awful times were in the South, especially after British planters founded Charleston in 1670 to market enslaved Natives) is the use of the word *mustee* for someone who was a lone Indian survivor without any kind of supporting family or tribal community (Forbes 1993). In time such orphans joined the doomed fate of tiny unallied settlement communities near colonial cities, in contrast to those families that did survive in huge confederacies, though later driven far to the west.

WIDER PERSPECTIVES

The earliest mound excavation on record was in North Africa, as reported in Plutarch's account of Sertorius, who captured the city of Tangier in

Mauritania (Morocco) in 81 BC and heard that Antaeus was buried nearby inside a huge mound. Doubting its prodigious size, the general had it opened, revealing a "body, in effect, it is said, full sixty cubits long [so that he was] astonished, offered sacrifice, and heaped up the tomb again" to establish a local cult of worship (Plutarch 1932: 683). The report, contents, and associations confound the physical and mythical, though both are very soil-centered on proven vitality. While the site was probably a Libyan royal tomb (26.6 meters long) at Larache, Antaeus himself was the giant son of Gaea (earth) and Poseidon (sea) who became a famous wrestler, drawing his strength from direct body contact (mound-like touch point) with the Earth. Herakles won by lifting him off the ground to strangle him, then subsequently had a son by the widow (Tangier) who founded the royal line. The excavation therefore had the political consequence of strengthening dynastic claims, reinforced by Roman might. Both in antiquity and the present, mythology, religion, labor, and politics work well together. One result is monuments, both of earth and, in metamorphic form, of marble.

The horrific trauma and destruction from Europe and Africa visited upon the Americas shattered any coherent record, though glimpses can be assembled from best-case examples to argue for a basic safe vitality rationalizing mounds and mound building. While the thinness of the hollow Earth was long assumed (and desired among many Native communities, until geology and earth science dominated classrooms), the best report comes from remote South America, where the Barasana of Colombia regard their boy's initiation (into the HE house) as a triumph of continuity over change: "As the generations succeed one another, or, as the Barasana view it, as they pile on top of one another like the leaves on the forest floor, human beings are in danger of losing touch with the beginning and source of life, the world of myth.... [So] the object of the HE house is literally to squash the pile so that the initiates, described as people of another pile (*gahe tutiana*), are brought into contact with, and adopted by, the first HE people" (Hugh-Jones 1979: 139).

While the sustained focus of this book is on the Southeast, its position in the Americas recalls allied views, such as that of Barasana, of initiation piles providing contact with ancestors. Indeed a North American vortex was the Pawnees (and other Caddoans), who also built mounded graves and ritual spaces into historic times (Bushnell 1927: plates 36, 37).

The actual backbone for such broad comparisons is ideally the trunk of the Mississippi River and its main branches: the Ohio from the east and the Missouri from the west. This interflowing crux was the cradle for the Siouan language stock, which can be expanded into Macro-Siouan to include Iroquoian of the northeast piedmont. The Ohio network saw the early blossoming of domed mounds, avenues, embankments, and earth constructions in the archaeological complexes known as Adena and Hopewell. Later namesake Mississippians, living along this main trunk and building blocky temple mounds, belonged to several language stocks and traditions, which are still echoed today in living rituals and tribal beliefs.

Along other waterways other regional traditions emerged, flowering under the same broad rubric of the Mississippian, but my interest remains the overall pattern. Impressive research has helped to clarify the development of these local complexes, and it should be consulted by interested readers (see the bibliography). Most interpretations, though, are based in European notions of individualism, self-interest, and false permanence instead of a Native one of sharing something safe and obvious to stave off precarious uncertainty and of moral obligations to the larger whole of all living and thinking forms. Where academics see the tools of political competition and control playing out on solid ground, Natives teach of a stockpiled means to survive in a very unsteady world by means of concerted community-based action done in a prayerful manner to provide elevation, blessed ballast, and assured banked vitality.[16]

FAITH ~ HOPE ~ GENDER ~ ROUTINE

Before the invention of ever more probing scientific technologies opened the way to viewing molecular structures and subatomic particles, humans relied on what they saw and knew to work (most of the time): the body, the day, the seasons, the waters, and the skies. Obviously food nourished a body to grow and age. In midlife men and women begat children, who renewed these (re)cyclings. Genders and procreation therefore figure prominently in rituals as a way to assume (and assure) vital bulging continuity. The seasons moved through regular yearly and longer cycles, mirrored in the appearance and behavior of plants and animals. Spring sprouted seeds and welcomed other newborns. Honoring these species renewals assumed continuities.

Waterways, both rivers and oceans, varied in their flows by season and by geographic climate. Long residence in an area taught people about ten-, twenty-, fifty-, and hundred-year floods, and leaders kept careful count between these periods to provide warnings, as Soto survivors learned (see chapter 3). Those living in tidal areas were aware of simultaneous pulls in moon and menstrual cycles, including women's physiological changes within their ritual patterns, often set apart by distinct taboos. The proven power of women's blood, believed to be the kernel of a fetus, made it dangerous to the flowing of other energies, especially those of men and immortals.

Fixed observatories, such as stump seats and rock piles on elevations, allowed specialists to make sustained records by watching along skylines for the orderly movements of the heavens and to show predictabilities in the orbits and transects of stars and other sky phenomena (Miller 1992b). The rising and setting of the sun marked each day, as its movements toward the north and south tagged the solstices (farthest standstill) and equinoxes (midpoint) of a year. The moon's phases traced each month, while its risings and settings around the skyline fulfilled an 18.5-year cycle. Meteors, eclipses, and other calamities shook public confidence in these regular observations, although some routine irregularities may have been anticipated by well-versed observers.

For rituals to partake of full communion with the cosmos, some part-for-whole (metonym) equivalences were invoked to reduce these enormities to human scale. Hair, blood, and bone, especially tubes, stood for the body and genders, while seashells and water-filled pots reflected the aquatic world. The sky itself was mirrored in the shiny surfaces of mica, copper, and rendered oil. Threading these together were pivotal links among the heart, the hearth, the tribal ~ temple holy fire, and the sun, pulsing with song.

SONG ~ RHYTHM ~ ORDER

Songs provided rhythm and order to the universe, enhancing its powers and beauty. "Traditional Creeks speak of gulfs and distances in the earth being brought together by the vibrations (songs) and movements in the earth.... Singing and chanting would accompany the ever-present blowing on the patient and into the medicine pot. The myriad healing songs are intended to engage the spirit and build the energy of the patient so that he [or she] can be restored and reconnected to the flow of universal energy" (Chaudhuri and Chaudhuri 2001: 35, 123).

For Creeks, songs have many uses, including charming "game so that it could be approached and shot," compelling affections, weakening enemies and blinding "the eyes of their warriors," curing illnesses by bubbling into steeping medicine "between the stanzas of certain songs which go with the herbs constituting the formulae" (Speck 1907: 108, 114, 118, 121–33). During the Busk (Green Corn) Ceremony circumscribed songs revitalize the community. Via stomp dances they are pumped into its lands, entering its mounds to sustain them for another year as songs and dicta are blown into Busk medicines. At Creek churches hymns now have an analogous role.

This ritual use of rhythmic song, dance, gesture, and breath infuses a specific place with steady vitality and counters threatening disorder: "The beat of the drum is said to represent the earth's heartbeat.... The drum and the beat, therefore, connect dance participants (drummers/singers, dancers, and observers) to one another through common descent from the first people [who brought fire] and with the earth to which they eventually return" (Sabo 2003: 426). Such regularizing actions highlight the making of medicine both for a patient and for town members at an annual Busk Ceremony. Using a cane blowtube, the medicine man (*heles haya ~ hilis haaya*) "pushes song" into the medicine by bubbling it while reciting dicta and singing songs specific to that locale. While he does this, absolute silence reigns so that only these sounds enter the "herb water." Once prepared, the container is sealed until the medicine is used, in order to retain its full benefits. Similarly the blowtube is plugged when not in use.

The stomp dancing that fills the night and some of the day acts as a bellows, infusing town-specific song and prayer into that ceremonial ground. Song and dance together superbly capture the up-down and male-female tensions inherent within the mound itself: "Stomp Dance songs are performed in a kind of shuffled time by shell shaker rattles which accentuate an even, rhythmic, downward attack upon each 'downbeat' and an upward attack on the 'upbeats' of the Stomp Dance singers" (Taborn 2004: 7, 62, 84, 97).[17]

Protective rhythm also appears in Choctaw reports on their ball game. Six or so of their medicine men are charged with both protecting their own team and jinxing the other side. Songs are sung the night before to invigorate (vitalize) the team and its goal posts, but during the actual game only whistles and drums are used to focus on the team itself. As a tube, the whistle concentrates breath and dicta (talking), while the drumbeat represents the pulsing of the heart. The goal posts, anchored into the ground, transmit vitality into it: "On the night before a ball game, the whistles [*uskulushi*] are blown by the [team's] medicine men [*alikĕi*], there is 'talking' in which it is asserted that 'You are going to win the game,' and the song for success is sung. The whistles are blown during the game, and the medicine men beat on their drums, but there is no singing while the game is in progress. The sound of the whistles during a game was referred to as 'the noise made by the [conjurors]'" (Densmore 1943: 128).[18] The ball itself represents the Earth and other planets, with the spent energy of the players transfusing into the world to help sustain it: "The ball was a sacred object not to be touched with the [bare] hand, and has been identified with symbolizing the earth, the sun, or the moon" (Culin [1907] 1975: 484).

Human rituals provide calm and order to the world, while human faults destabilize it and call for atonement.

QUIVERING WITHIN ~ TREMBLING WITHOUT

Throughout this book the Americas are regarded as potentially volatile and precarious—a very unsteady, unsure, imperfect, and unstable place. This universe is sapient, alive, fragile, and thin-skinned—an accepted fact of coexistence, viewed with eyes wide open and watchful. Flux and flow are its hallmarks of vitality. Human settlement "clings to the skin of a planet involved in the elemental forces of creation—ever-changing, never at rest.... During an earthquake the fertile soil can suddenly absorb liquid from below, become fluid, and flow like a river. Forests can crash to the ground, geysers of sand, coal grit, and water spout from the earth, lakes become dry, and rivers run backward.... Civilization exists by geological consent, subject to change without notice" (Chappell 2002: 16, 18, quoting the Illinois geologist Christopher Schubert quoting the historian Will Durant).

The cosmos is engendered and webbed within a pulsing flow of power-vitality-force-energy (*powha*), which concentrates into tubes ~ pipes and can erupt in ways that are dangerous, destructive, and disruptive. Only continuous and sincere effort keeps it precariously banked, ballasted, balanced, and stable, as mounds hold the earth in place to provide security, heart, and soul for their community—most intensely symbolized by the holy fire burning inside a temple atop (sometimes inside) the mound.

The circuitry of this webbing includes channels that are tube-like. To add interest and protective force, the most common embodiment of this shape is that of a serpent. Symbolically within the greater graphic universe, of course, male snakes are usually portrayed as angular and females as sinuous, regardless of their own biological indicators.

Sudden shifts—such as writhing, trembling, and quivering—are its lurking attributes. Aptly snakes and their images are never far away, often embodied as rivers and waterways as well as lava flows and earthquakes. Coiled inside a domed mound they are weighty and wary, striking at full length they are blazingly dangerous, curved into an arc they are protective, and writhing they are volatile and terrifying.

Such belief is widespread, from Creeks to Inkas. In the geologically active Andes, Inkas knew that when the Earth became imbalanced, the result was *amaru*: "Taking the form of a serpent, it would erupt from beneath the earth, causing destruction in its wake, in an attempt to recreate balance when relations of equilibrium were broken ... in the social and natural universe" (Silverblatt 1989: 316). Snakes are also an aspect of the tube, an image at the core of being, like the spinal column and heart, a microcosm of the hollow Earth.[19] Around and through it everything pulses, sometimes violently, with vitality.

Comparison across the continent also insists on fundamental duality, most often based in gender, such that lines contrast with curves as males with females. Yet the Earth is itself a whole, combining both opposites. Usually it is conveyed by the image of the circled cross ⊕, as well as other curve and line forms. As expressed in various topologies, the outer shape will often be a circle (if female) or a square (if male), sometimes expanded outward; the inner cross can be narrowed into the central fire on a huge bare plaza or stretched to end at shrines set toward the four edges of the world. Variant examples include the following: ⊕ ⊗ ⊚ ⌘ Ψ ♂ ♀. Yet it is the crossed circle ⊕ that is the most basic form, whose expressions include that of a huge snake positioned along the edge of an enclosing C-shape formed around a sacred precinct. This encircling provides the ground plan or template underneath many mounds, enclosures, and community plazas.

For Cherokees, contra Bartram (below), according to Swimmer's testimony to James Mooney ([1900] 1982: 297, 396; 1889), "When they were ready to build the mound they began by laying a circle of stones on the surface of the ground [set a fire at the center, and placed the corpse of a chief or priest nearby] 'together with a Ulunsuti [blazing diamond crystal] stone, Uktena [horned snake] scale or horn, a feather of the right wing of an eagle or great tlanuwa [bird], which lived in those days, and beads of seven colors, red, white, black, blue, purple, yellow, and grey-blue.'" Once in place all these were conjured with protective magic to slay any enemies who dared attack the townhouse atop the mound or breach the defenses of the town itself.

Women brought basket loads of dirt to build up the mound, leaving an open space at the fire in the center until there was enough elevation to insert a long, hollow, cedar log (tube) over and around the fireplace. Its top projected above the floor into the townhouse that was built atop the finished mound. Before any dance or council was held, a special firekeeper kindled a flame from this inner perpetual ancient fire by uncovering the tube and inserting long fleabane stalks. Heat traveled up the stalks to inflame powdered lichens and punk at the top. With this flame the central fire was relit. Then, after the event, the firekeeper closed the opening and covered the top with ashes.[20]

ISLAND WEIGHTS

Along the Mississippi River, among nations of the Midwest, the traditions of the Hochungaras or Ho-chunks (called Winnebagos by Algonkians) of

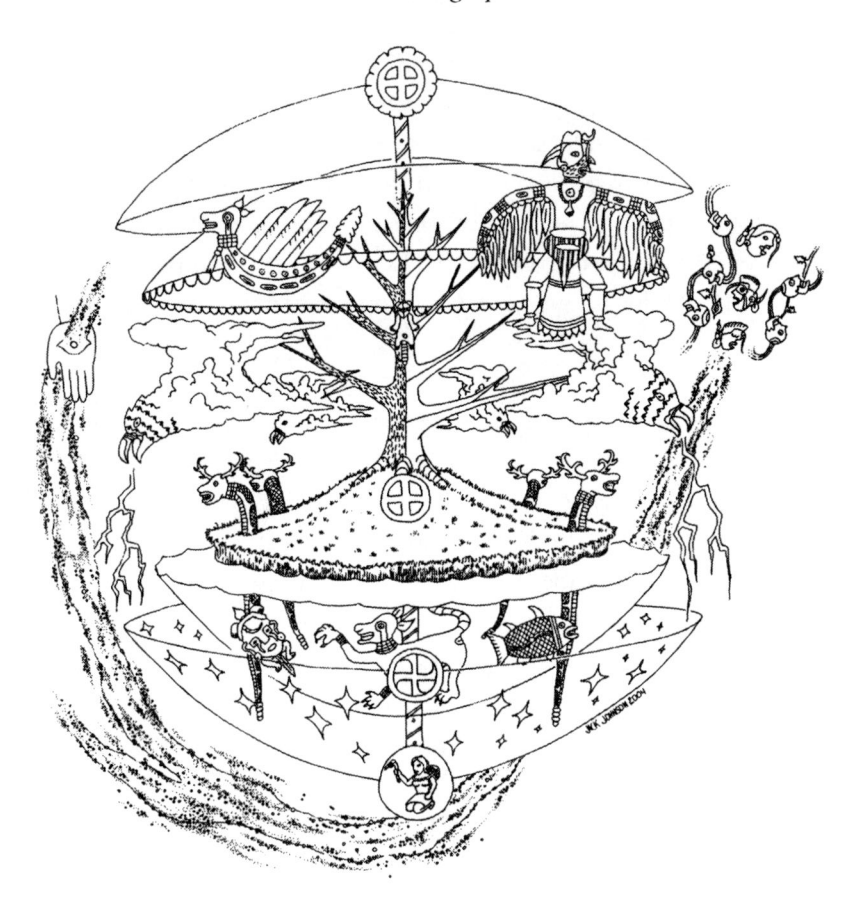

Composite Mississippian Cosmos with a mound at the center. Reproduced by permission of F. Kent Reilly III, drawn by Jack Johnson.

Wisconsin illuminate mysteries of snakes, turmoil, earth, and the world.[21] According to their creation epic, after *Ma'una* (= Earthmaker) placed the land, it was never still (Radin [1923] 1990: 302; Smith 1997: 19).[22] Its constant spinning kept things from rooting and growing, so it remained entirely bare. Anything that tried to settle down slid off into space. Only barely anchored spider webs floated above its surface. Eventually, after he got grass to grow, Earthmaker sent down trees, but everything still spun.

At last he had four Island Earth Weights, brother water serpents, pin themselves tail first at the corners of the four directions, all facing east and the sun, to stretch, steady, and hold the Earth. But the Earth still trembled, so he scattered rocks (regarded as females), and the weight of these finally made it quiet. The name used for these snake stabilizers in ordinary usage derives from *sewe* "to be quiet, to reduce to silence, to press, to press down."[23] Thanks to Copernicus and others, we have come to know that the Earth does indeed continue to spin, but thanks to Earthmaker and all his efforts to slow, weight down, and quiet it, this rotation is now imperceptible.

AFFIRMING EARTH

In a nutshell, drawing on far-flung references and best-case examples, the American Earth is seen as precarious—a dynamic living island of thin soil and hollow heart floating on a vast sea, which is consistently imbalanced by human faults. The sky dome is above and the sea bowl is below, with the earth hoop (and tube axis) floating between the hole and the heap. All life forms are humanoid at home or under the outward cloak of their species and exist around tubes (spinal columns), often filled with concentrated light, life-force, and *powha*, which pulsates, like the Earth itself, in rhythms attuned to harmony, though these can transpose suddenly into a violent trembling that endangers all. Snakes, among other ground dwellers, epitomize this full range of extremes, while spiders, with their webs, embody *powha*'s patterned flow along rings and rays of vitality.[24] In fact and fear, faults within places and by people cause earthquakes and other raging disasters.

Periodic world renewals fix the harm caused by these human faults of disrespect, while bulging mounds, taut rings, and other weighted masses hold high and steady a spot of haven and safety on the tense, thin-skinned land surface. Mounds themselves, moreover, are banked, blessed, and ballasting microcosms of all these engendered aspects of the vital universe, as revealed by considerations of time and of space—according to what is, arranged by prepositions: outside, inside, over, under, of, for, and upon them.

This unsteady world is bolstered by four assurances: fire, tube, mass, and height. Each provides security in terms of one of the four elements (fire, air, earth, water) of the Earth. Fire lights the way to safety; tubes enclose vitality, breath, and air; charged mass and raised bulk weighs down to stabilize a portion of the Earth's skin; and height safeguards against flood waters and quake to bulge above. A mound, such as that of the ancient Cherokees with a central column of layered fires, provides a microcosm of and for their macrocosm for as long as it stands or leaves traces on the land:

> The mounds at major sites were built at different times, and seem not to have been used for the entire period that these settlement were occupied. But even abandoned mounds fixed the basic structure of a site because they were such prominent features. The mounds, used or not, might have been linked to stories about important events or specific ancestors or lineages, much like the monuments of more recent societies elsewhere in the world. If this were so, then the mounds—in fact, the entire settlement layout—served as a visual representation of the history and structure of these societies (Milner 2004: 117).

Above all, and under all, all mounds weigh on the Earth, keeping that spot steady and safe.

2

Breaking Ground

Mounds, assumed to be inert, are not. Indeed mounds, mound building, and mound builders, after centuries of speculation, remain compelling questions of Americanist research.[1] Despite wholesale destructions, hundreds of thousands of such earthworks, large and small, still dot much of the East, with particular clusterings in the Southeast. Explanations for this impulse toward earth moving, mound building, and imposing bulk have been in the manner of blind men describing an elephant. Each has merit but does not include the whole or even major aspects of it. Such basic data as specific dating have also needed to be constantly revised. Nowhere outside Native communities is any recognition given to their primary goal as blessed, ballooning ballast weighing on the honored Earth and vitalized by the rhythmic songs and stomps of men and women living in an unsteady world.

A burial mound is "an 'inverted' grave" providing both interment and "a fitting and a lasting monument [that] reverses the operation of excavating a receptacle beneath the surface level by heaping the covering of earth above the surface" of the grave (Shetrone 1930: 183). In many instances an offering will be placed into the ground before mounds and other structures are built up to consecrate, dedicate, and bless that location.

Among the earliest of these inversions seem to be ritual caches, probably made as offerings to the Earth and its dwellers. Colored earths, especially red ocher, define these caches as sacred, in both the past and the present. Lived-in spaces also serve as offerings. The earliest dated U.S. mounds bury the remains of a prior dwelling with the intent of both memorializing and renewing it in community sentiment. By removing it from view it is also transported to another world or realm of existence, often that of spirit immortals with their own vitality. By re-covering it, the exact place can be reused over a span of time.

I now turn to such key theories, stories, remarks, and experiences in the U.S. record to provide an overview of perspectives, focusing on key thinkers.

TRIBALS

Chicora

While Spanish and French writers described mounds in active use in the Southeast, English sources for usage in the Northeast were vague.[2] Under the onslaught of epidemics, diseases, and missionaries, most Native sages withheld any esoteric knowledge concerning the mounds to avoid ridicule, insult, martyrdom, and destruction.

Centuries before, Peter Martyr d'Anghiera (1457–1526), an Italian at the Spanish court, similarly reported the use of a mound by a Native orator at a reburial. While a dinner guest, Francisco Chicorana ~ Chicora, who had been seized a few years before by an expedition sponsored by Lucas Vasquez de Ayllon, described three festivals among his own coastal Carolina tribes (Quattlebaum 1956). The third rite involved the reburial of a skeleton in a "tomb [when] the chief priest addresses the surrounding people from the summit of a mound" with a eulogy about the afterlife (d'Anghiera [1912] 1970: 2: 258, 264).

Chitimacha

The Western Chitimachas near Charenton, Louisiana, despite pressures from French Catholics, maintained a temple and a mound on a bay of Grand Lake.[3] Surrounded by a picket fence, the temple (dance house ~ *maison de valeur*) was twelve feet square under a pointed roof. People canoed there on the day before the new moon, which they honored the next day with a monthly ceremony "in honor of Kut-nähädh, or the Noon-Day Sun" (Gatschet 1883: 154–55). Leaders carried long wands or poles (tubes) as men danced, wearing red body paint, a breechclout, and feathers stuck in ribbons encircling the head; rhythm was set by shaking gourd rattles and rasping on alligator skins. During the summer this rite lasted longer, with men dancing and fasting for six days before they gorged on water to vomit as a final purification. Everyone then feasted.

Just before the usual monthly ceremony at the temple, occasionally memorial rites were held at the time that was closest to marking the year anniversary after a death. Families were ranked as either nobles, who eventually became conjoined in their tribal mound, or commoners, who were buried in separate graves at their home village. After the remains of a chief or captain had decomposed, their bones were exhumed by turkey-buzzard men (*ramasseurs d'os ~ o'sh hätchina* = 'buzzards picking up'), who removed any lingering flesh, wrapped the bones in a new "checkered mat," and took the bundle into the temple. Led by the widow and sons, everyone walked six times around a blazing fire, then buried the bundle in the nearby tribal mound. The last such mound burial was the child of a noble family in the 1920s, long after they had become Roman Catholics.

Atakapa

Neighboring Atakapas of coastal Louisiana, famous cannibals, described an archetypal grave mound (*imō'c mak ~ imō'š mak*) that included a hole in the top to permit passage of the heart+soul. (Elsewhere this hole is a column above the founding fire of the mound.) The phrase is derived from *mōc ~ mōš* = to dig, to bury + *māk ~ maak* = knot, knob, lump, bump, forehead.

Text 8 *Himō'c ~ Himō'š* (Burial) includes this sentence:

Imō'c	mak	mā'ñ	ká	ya	hóxp	ná-ulat	có	itáxne
Grave	mound	long shaped	they made	and	hole	they left over	spirit+ heart	to come out

"They made a long grave mound and left a hole at the top to enable the spirit + heart to come out."

While only a single mounded grave is indicated in this text, the association of the word for mound with forehead, brow, and Adam's apple ("lump in throat") strengthens the range of anatomical images and adds details about a spirit tube at the grave and a range of grave goods that increased with the rank of the person. At death the home of the deceased was burned down, and the family moved a few miles away (Gatschet and Swanton 1932: 18–19, 78, 82).

Chickasaw

Among the very few recorded Native explanations of mounds to survive, that of the Snowbird Cherokee "gathering place" is quoted in the introduction. Older statements are usually garbled, like this classic one from a Chickasaw agent: "The large mounds that are in Mississippi, the Indians have no idea of; they do not know whether they are natural or artificial. They were there when they first got to the country. They are called by the Chickasaws, navels. They thought that the Mississippi was the centre of the earth, and those mounds were at the navel of a man in the centre of his body" (Schoolcraft 1855: 310).

Though "earth shrines" are known as "earth navels" in the Pueblo Southwest, only this report from the federal agent to the Chickasaws equates mounds with navels (*ittihalbish*), presumably on Mother Earth, though the analogy here is to a man, not a woman.[4] The description furthers the argument that mounds were sometimes regarded as a chest or torso filled with winds and songs to provide a vital nexus. That there are so many of them suggests that each community on Mother Earth was also a body unto itself intertwined with others. Because of their rich farming soil, the Chickasaws occupied the least territory of any southeast Native nation yet raised the most corn. These bountiful lands in the Black Belt were much coveted and, by default, became the cradle of King Cotton after white (Anglo) plantations took over.

James Adair (2005: 117), the trader who wrote his book on the Southeast while living with the Chickasaws (at modern Tupelo, Mississippi), reported that they called "their old round earthen forts, *Aiambo Chaah*," combining words signifying "clay bason [basin]" and "high," while a stockade or wooden fort was "Hooreta."[5]

Chickasaw society became more organized at its lower levels than other southeasterners.⁶ Families belonged to a "House" ~ "canton," which joined others within a named clan that was ranked within a moiety. During recent centuries Chickasaws have ignored the red and white moieties and clans, while relying on House members during their forced move to Oklahoma in the late 1830s (Paige et al. 2010: 134). Functioning moieties, last observed about 1700, had a "peace chief" named Fattalamee, living at the mother town of Hallechehoe, and the "war chief" Oboystabee. Accordingly they were divided between White ~ peace ~ domestic ~ harmony ~ internal and Red ~ war ~ diplomatic ~ slaving ~ external. Concentrated around present-day Tupelo, White towns were scattered on Town Creek's Small Prairie, and Red towns on Kings Creek's Large Prairie (Ethridge 2010: 223–31; Johnson 2000; Swanton [1928] 2006: 18–41). Later, in Oklahoma, the moieties were known as Tcukilissa "empty house" living peacefully in timber or as Tcukafalaha "long house" living warlike on prairie. The former included matriclans of 'Minko' ~ Chief, Raccoon, Panther, 'Muclesa,' Fish, and Squirrel ~ 'Fani.' The 'Fani Minko' = "squirrel king" once specialized in representing other tribes at council meetings. Red clans, appropriately "fierce," included Panther, Wildcat, Alligator, Wolf, and Fox.

Natchez

Mound lore regarding the Natchez is virtually unknown, despite their role as the last functioning Mississippians. In a Natchez tale Thunder blasted apart a human with lightning and hung the body parts in his house. He was away so much that a big Frog maintained his fire, which also served to smoke this meat. While waiting between tasks, Frog burrowed into the floor. Sometimes, however, this meat got angry and shouted back. Then Thunder had Frog bury it. "In that way he had made mounds of earth" containing human remains (Swanton 1929: 239–40; cf. Natchez text 10, "Thunder"). Mounds therefore are here associated with loud noise, violence, cannibalism, and bulging frogs burrowing in the earth. The Natchez word for 'mound' *putkop lekup*, with a variant of *čomotkup*, derives from that for 'mountain' = *putkop* (Van Tuyl 1979: 93).⁷

Delaware

When some Delawares, already Christians, moved into Ohio in 1772 to reestablish their earlier Moravian missions, they repeated traditions to their clergy of their ancestral conflict with the gigantic Tallegwi that also served to bolster a prior claim to these lands, which they supposedly conquered on their way to their Atlantic homeland and thereby retained the right to reoccupy them.

Moravian Rev. John Heckewelder ([1876] 1971: 48, 49) reported that this "very powerful nation, who had many large towns [with] regular fortifications and entrenchments ... called themselves Talligewi," since applied to the Allegheny River and Mountains. Described as giants, they buried their warriors in large flat-topped mounds, which dotted the land.

A colleague, the famous Moravian missionary Rev. David Zeisberger ([1910] 1990: 30–31), provided the first description and explanation of impressive Ohio Hopewell earthworks in English: "Along the Muskingum ... embankments, still to be seen, were thrown up around a whole town [with nearby] mounds, not natural, but made by the hand of man [when Natives were] far more numerous." Atop each mound was a hollow where wives and children took refuge, and "great blocks" were stockpiled to roll down the slopes during attack. After a battle slain men were buried in a pit "and a great mound of earth raised above them, such as may even now [1779–80] be seen bearing in these days great and mighty trees."

The unconverted Delaware majority, in Ohio from the 1750s, were careful to also receive sanctioned permission to settle from resident Wyandots, who long hunted the region as members of the Huron Nation before they settled there as refugees after Iroquois assaults, especially the 1649 slaughter on Christian Island. Central Ohio was Shawnee homeland, under a deity addressed as "Grandmother" (see note 32).

Tutelo

Frank Speck, the great comparative Algonquianist, mused about the role of "mound clusters" as dramatic stages, using the example of the Tutelo Spirit Adoption and Reclothing Ceremony. This rite maintains the spiritual strength and names of the Tutelo nation (Eastern Siouan speakers), banished from the Carolina piedmont and given refuge among Canadian Iroquois. Each of its personal names is renewed a year after the death of the prior holder, when someone of the same gender and relative age is garbed and feted during a long night. The renamee, wearing newly made clothes over a string of beads hung diagonally from the left shoulder across the heart, hosts the spirit of the deceased for ten hours, until its final departure on the rays of the sunrise. Paced by orderly repetitions of songs, intermissions, and feasts at the start and end, the renamee, a drummer, and six singers are attended by deputies, escorts, helpers, and stagehands as well as an audience of mourners, guests, and visitors.

Rattles and water drum provide music during the first set of songs, replaced by split-stick clappers at the actual transfer (embodying) of the name. The renamee with escorts periodically processes and recesses to gift strung beads (seventy-two loops), ribbons, fabric, and other soft goods to the singers, usually tossed (rained down) on their shoulders. Tobacco offerings are burned in the fire, and, at the end, the clappers and drumstick are also cremated. The drum itself is taken apart to release its potency, returning its pulse to the vitality of the wider world.

Overall, though now "decadent legacies," such "reduced ceremonies [testify to] mass performance of the cult of the dead . . . being fitted to sacred-shrine precincts of wide and ample ground space . . . of earthwork structures, elevations, enclosures, and the like which mark so conspicuously the endroits [qualities] of aboriginal settlements in the whole southern area [and survive as] fugitive derelicts of mammoth institutional cults" (Speck 1942: 8, 80, 81).[8]

CAUTIONS

Thus early naturalists like William Bartram and his father, John (Bartram and Bartram 1957), and proto-archaeologists like Cyrus Thomas (above), agreed to the continuous use of mounds to cover the dead, much like the Neolithic and later tumuli across most of Europe that marked the graves of warrior heroes (Bruce-Mitford 1964).[9] Thomas ([1890] 1980: 32, 43), after noting the overlap between ancient mound sites and historic Overhill Cherokee towns, quoted James Mooney that such mounds were built during Green Corn ceremonies. The irony is that Mooney was made aware of this connection by Postmaster Terrell of Webster, North Carolina, and only later confirmed it with Native Cherokee elders such as the man named Tsiskwaya. Even more intriguing, Thomas said that Alice Fletcher saw mound building during a secret ritual of the Winnebago (Hochungara, in their own language).[10] Fletcher ([1893] 1994: 31) herself mentioned hearing the song of a famous Omaha warrior while standing beside his "mounded grave" along the Missouri River.[11]

Today's public sharing of knowledge, especially Native astronomy, starkly contrasts with the private possession of esoteric lore, especially cosmology, which was once a defining criterion for elite membership throughout the Americas. The metaphoric, poetic, and obscure usages given to ordinary Hochungara words in the epic of their Medicine Rite serves as a useful reminder as well as a check on misguided research. As one example, Marion Mochon (1972) tried to find words for Mississippian farming, commerce, society, polity, and worldview by searching through meager dictionaries of five languages variously belonging to the Muskogean (Choctaw, Creek) and Siouian (Osage, Ofo, Biloxi) stocks. Of note, she found many more Muskogean than Siouian examples and accordingly argued for heavy Muskogean participation in the Mississippian period.

Conversely, a decade later James Springer and Stanley Witkowski (1982) argued from the internal branching of the Siouan linguistic stock, especially Central Siouan, to connect them with the archaeological complex known as Oneota, which had a mound-building aspect that grew out of earlier Effigy Mounds. At Blood Run, Siouans (still combined Omaha-Ponkas) were inspired by Ioway to build hundreds of mounds into the early 1700s (see Betts 2010).

In all likelihood, however, mounding required esoteric terms, especially by the Mississippian priesthoods.[12] Few of these adepts survived the collapse of these chiefdoms and the decimation of their ranks by fatal diseases or legal executions when blamed for misfortunes. These terms would not have been common nor public knowledge. If many members of the communities were not privy to this information, it is even more doubtful that it would have been provided to outsiders. Only a Native with an intellectual outlook would have seen the virtue of saving some of this knowledge for posterity. Such was the Osage priest named Saucy Calf, who began the recording of the complex Osage initiation rites with Francis LaFlesche, the Omaha-speaking ethnographer, only to die in the suspicious burning of his home (Bailey 1995).

Height itself was always a factor, representing the elevated status of leaders, especially during times of heightened concern, such as successions. The later earthen platform mounds, as the "quintessential artifacts of the prehistoric chiefdoms . . . represented the 'navel of the world' from which sprang the town's (if not the entire chiefdom's) people sometime in the remote mythical past[, who] built these mounds in successive stages, most likely during periodic episodes of rebuilding that occurred when new chiefs were installed as rulers. . . . A mound likewise served as literal symbol of the chief's elevated status, as his or her private dwellings and other sacred buildings were routinely built on the summit of such earthworks" (Hahn 2004: 15, 162).[13] Such residences moreover placed leaders closer to their own founding ancestors, who came from the sky, as famously claimed by the Natchez Suns, while other, lesser classes of people came out of or were made from the earth. Intermarriage, clanship, and town memberships helped to forge the full multidimensional community relying on such ongoing vitality.

Kinship is often evoked in explaining mounds (below, on Creek matriclans), specifically the labor mobilized for their construction. For the much earlier period the archaeologist Martin Byers (1996) has referred to the central mound in an Adena-Hopewell enclosure as an "iconic warrant" between living and dead kin. In his review of Florida archaeology, Jerald Milanich (1998: 48, 71) insists that, through constant use, especially sequential funeral stages, "mounds are tied to kinship as corporate monuments of, for, and to clanship; while rituals cleanse and restore the world to balance, normality, and stability." Yet in his study of the Florida Spanish missions, he noted, but did not directly connect, that Guale and Timucuan converts gave up "charnel houses and interment in lineage-maintained mounds" for burial "in the floor of the church nave," a practice that had been discontinued in

Europe for centuries (Milanich 1999: 138). Also, in violation of Church dogma, both types of graves included artifact offerings. Both dispositions assured security for these ancestral remains by having been placed within a sanctuary defined by weight and height such as mound or sanctified (church) walls. Yet it is as though, with the end of mound building, Native leaders took refuge inside buildings, either huge council houses or, later, churches.

Discussing Timucua chiefdoms of North Florida, which did not build temple mounds, John Worth (1998: 1: 12) summarized that mounds were ~ are "physical symbols of social rank ... their height a visual reminder ... of distinctions in status [and] of the generational time-depth of noble matrilineages and the hereditary succession of the chiefly office ... constructed ... in episodic stages ... frequently in association with the deaths of chiefs and the succession of heirs to the chiefly office ... a powerful legitimization for chiefly rank and ... an integral part of Mississippian culture."

HISTORICALS

In sharp contrast to these ethnospiritual concerns, American archaeology professionalized by specializing in the reductionist analysis of mounds, with Thomas Jefferson and U.S. federal projects leading the way.[14] Sorting out patterns within the locations, types, and diagnostic artifacts added clarity, though their exact dating long remained problematic. Instead geographical patterns were easier to plot. This research agenda included debunking racist cant by settlers about the Mound Builders as a prior (superior) race destroyed by cruel ancestors of Native tribes, strengthening Americanist continuities and providing reliable insights into the prehistory of the Americas.

By the late 1500s Spanish and French adventurers actually saw mounds in use, but the English ignored their monumentality in favor of asserting their own claims to making "better" use of the land. Jefferson, as noted, thought mounds both important and "American" enough to excavate one. Today scholars still debate—according to intellectual stances, interests, problems, and fads—how to characterize the role of mounds in chiefdoms and the import of the urban hub at the megasite of Cahokia, near modern St. Louis at the heart of the continent (Young and Fowler 2000). Many do this, however, from very Eurocentric understandings, wrongly focusing on individual greed and self-interest.

Brief mention of mounds occurs in early colonial histories. The ill-fated John Lawson ([1709] 1967: 28), writing of the Carolinas in 1708, two centuries after the enslavement of Chicora (above), noted that a mound was built as a "sepulcher" for each of the Santee River "kings," piled higher or lower according to his own "Dignity."[15] Citing a January 1796 flood that crested the Alabama River at forty-seven feet, the Indian Agent Benjamin Hawkins determined that any mound, called in Creek *o-cun-li-ge*, "literally, *earth placed*," (see chapter 4) was a "place of safety to the people, in the time of these floods" (Hawkins [1848] 1971: 38–39; Hawkins 1916: 42–43; cf. Henri 1986; Ethridge 2003).[16] In the same work he described an eight-day Green Corn or Busk much like those of today (Hawkins [1848] 1971: 75–78).

This notion of being lodged or situated on the earth also remains basic to the Creek concept and term for clan, in this instance a matriclan. The word is *em vliketa* ~ *im-a-leyk-ita* from *em* "they" + *liketa* = "to sit, be situated, exist; to settle, live (in a house, place), reside (of one)." A traditional greeting to a visitor was *likepvs che* "Welcome," literally "have a seat" (Martin and Mauldin 2000: 24, 26, 71, 213). That both mounds and clans share morphemes for location strengthens the association of some mounds with kin groups, especially a clan.

William Bartram, privately financed to describe, sketch, and collect plant specimens from the newly British-governed Southeast, relied on the hospitality of his Native hosts.[17] He duly noted mounds and earthworks as an ancient feature of these landscapes, musing that they were "public works [of massive labor for] ornament and recreation [with] some religious purpose, as great altars and temples [or] look-out towers." Drawing direct analogies between his host's Native towns and these sites, he proposed distinct types and functions such that stone mounds were sepulchers for the dead, replaced by earthen ones when stone was not available; that platform "tetragons" were fortress foundations; that conicals were "high places for sacrifice"; and that sunken places served for captive torture sacrifices, with embankments for seats during "games, shews and dances" (Waselkov and Braund 1995: 73, 84, 131).

Of note, to his inquiries elderly Cherokees denied any knowledge of or ancestry to their builders, whom they said were succeeded by a second nation before they themselves arrived in the Appalachians. Yet both Bartram and Adair described Choctaw funeral practices in which a body was exposed for several months, defleshed, and its bones placed inside a kin-based charnel house. Bartram added that when it was filled, locals "repair to the bone-house" by family, take up their kin, and march by seniority to "place the coffins in order, forming a pyramid; and, lastly, cover all over with earth, which raises a conical hill or mount" (Waselkov and Braund 1995: 129). Adair (2005: 212–14n) wrote that graves were usually marked by stone piles, or, lacking rocks, by earthen mounds.

Thomas Jefferson

Mounds early on became an aspect of American character, as they long had been for Europeans themselves, as the mound on the Hill of Tara was linked to Irish kings.[18] A keen intellectual, Jefferson set a strong course for the popular understanding of the Native peoples of the United States and North America, spurred on by nationalist pride. While he wrote voluminously, Jefferson's only published book is modestly titled *Notes on the State of Virginia* ([1785] 1972).[19] Its chapter titles were phrased as questions or queries.[20]

Query 11 looks at the Natives of Virginia, briefly discussing political, cultural, and linguistic differences among the Powhatans, Mannahoacs, Manacans, and their neighbors. But Jefferson expressed the cultural biases and bigotry of his times, though, sagely, he noted these Native lands had been acquired by Euro-Americans not by outright conquest but by legal proofs of purchase such as treaties. Rather than appreciating the farming skills of these tribes, however, he repeated the distortion that these people lived "on the spontaneous productions of nature." Seeking evidence of worthy large-scale labor in "monuments" to compare with Europe, he hoped for something like a common ditch maintained by an entire community for draining farm lands, but instead settled on local "barrows" or earthen mounds.

Curious about these mounds throughout the landscape, Jefferson excavated (by slave labor) one about two miles from his Monticello estate. While much legend and fantasy was and is associated with such mounds, including the apocryphal Mound Builders, he correctly concluded that local Natives had built and used them for burials, wisely noting return visits by living Saponi to strengthen his argument. Much ahead of his time, he was guided by a sense of stratigraphy—that older layers were naturally below younger ones, that older was deeper. With this insight he laid the foundation for future American archaeology, though others were slow to follow his lead.

To understand the origin and distribution of Native tribes, moreover, Jefferson thought it was best to look at language, particularly the names for common objects, noun and verb inflections, and principles of regimen and concord (that is, syntax ~ grammar). At the end of his chapter is a chart of known American tribes and their estimated populations for 1759, 1764, and 1768. (Culminating these thoughts, he drafted the guidelines used by Lewis and Clark to collect natural and ethnographic information during their exploration of the newly acquired Louisiana Purchase, which began American expansion into the Middle West as well as providing eventual new homes for eastern tribes deported from their ancestral homelands.)

While single low mounds were easily attributed to existing tribes, it was the geometry, astronomy, scale, and interconnections of the multiacre earthworks that suggested that these were monuments by populous and "advanced" civilizations. Local tribes—traumatized, diseased, disowned—hardly seemed capable of such feats. Yet it became increasingly clear to open-minded European visitors that they had indeed been the builders. With the ability to date and analyze these landforms came the realization that they had been constructed over centuries and millennia, providing the New World with a remarkably ancient past.

Simultaneously, in contrast to these scholarly advances, Natives were losing their lands and being forced to relocate to the homelands of other tribes, supposedly for their own good. At the center of these conflicting efforts, ironically, was Jefferson, who left the White House with examples of many Native vocabularies collected by himself and others, including Lewis and Clark, to be analyzed in his retirement, but the stout trunk holding them was stolen from the Potomac dock. Since a few pages later washed up, it became evident that the thieves, disappointed that the lock protected mere papers, tossed these unique documents into the river.

Roger Kennedy (1994) reviewed the hope of many U.S. founding fathers for a new beginning that was distinctly American in the Mississippi (and Ohio) River Valley, then a wide-open frontier. Many of these thoughtful men sought freedom and appreciation for all races and classes, especially Natives and Africans, so the complex array of massive indigenous earthworks throughout this region captured their imaginations. As they Americanized, Washington, Jefferson, and others had their slaves and gardeners build paired mounds into the landscaping of their estates. In Ohio politicians such as Thomas Worthington built their mansions atop mounds or positioned them to view earthworks. Albert Gallatin, a Jefferson ally, politician, diplomat, banker, and scholar of Native languages, sold window glass for these new mansions from his factory south of Pittsburgh (below).

William Faulkner

Of note, mounds also feature in William Faulkner's complex portrayals of the human condition set in the South. His ("postage stamp") county's local history begins with its original Chickasaw owners (led by Issetibbeha), but then concentrates on the plantations and homesteaders, both white and black, who replaced them. In the short story "The Fire and the Hearth," during complex marriage negotiations, George Wilkins hides his own still inside a freshly excavated trench into "a squat, flat-topped, almost symmetrical mound rising without reason," so he can safely expose the still of Lucus Beauchamp, father of his fiancée Nathalie, to make him vulnerable and willing to consent to the wedding. Finding a gold piece in the mound, however, sets off an obsessive search by Lucus, using a connived metal detector that further strains family relations (Faulkner 1940: 37).[21] Mounds here are associated with origins, kinship, and treasure.

In *The Wild Palms*, with parallel plots of a physician's tragic love affair and the 1927 flood of the delta, a convict rescues a pregnant woman from a tree, but their boat is swept away. Finally a swimming deer leads them to "an acclivity smooth and swift and steep, bizarre, solid and unbelievable; an

Indian mound," where the woman immediately gives birth. They share this muddy space with other creatures and many snakes (Faulkner 1939: 176).[22] "The Indian mound on which they land is the earth in the reptilian age, emerging from the waters. Here, in this prehistoric world where the snake predominates, the human female fulfills her childbearing function, and the male assumes the vital responsibility of caring for mother and infant" (Volpe 1964: 224). This mound, writhing with life, new and old, male and female, provides a haven barely above treacherously rising waters. Once all are rescued, however, the warden adds to the convict's prison time as punishment because his baffling absence and fierce protection of the borrowed rowboat—scrupulously doing his best—created a morass of paperwork.

In the middle volume of the Snopes trilogy, *The Town*, Faulkner (1957: 307) muses about the new "tyranny [of] incorrigible and unreconstructable Baptists and Methodists [who] had heired from . . . usurped and dispossessed . . . Episcopal and Presbyterian churches and Issetibbeha's old mounds in the low creek bottoms about the country." Like the earliest churches of the "old religions," these mounds represent the antiquity of the land and religion itself, transformed, outdated, and mutated but still arising before their believers and heirs.

REGIONALS

Regional understanding was achieved by local efforts. Jefferson's Swiss-born secretary of the treasury (the first to balance the national budget) Gallatin followed up on his work and produced an early linguistic map of the eastern United States, using the love of detail famous among the watchmakers of his native Geneva. John Wesley Powell later made such careful linguistic mapping an early goal of the Bureau of American Ethnology (BAE), founded in 1879.[23]

Bureau of American Ethnology Mound Research

Though not part of his original plan for the BAE, Powell was soon directed by a financial stipulation from Congress (due to an Ohio effort) to devote a portion of his annual budget to the study of the earthen mounds across the eastern states. Over decades a growing sense of the complexity of mound types, dates, and associations coincided with the increasing recognition of the linguistic diversity of Native America. It no longer was possible to talk of *the* mound builders or *the* Indien language because, for any given time and place, many differences had now been revealed. While stereotypes continued in popular imagination, a better sense of America's prior diverse complexity began to emerge among concerned scholars.[24]

Cyrus Thomas ([1894] 1985: 28, 29, 33), a naturalist from Illinois who oversaw these mound explorations and excavations, defined three types of "monuments": (1) fixed or local antiquities, (2) movable antiquities, such as relics and remains, and (3) paleographic objects, supposedly ancient writings (another indication of the biases of those times). The prime example of fixed sites was and is mounds, which he divided into conical, elongate or wall (rampart), pyramidal, and effigy tumuli. Other fixed features listed were refuse heaps (middens), house sites or hut rings, cairns, enclosures (which could have walls and embankments, excavations, canals and ditches, pits and caches), graves and cemeteries, garden beds, hearths, trails, pebble outlines, and mines for copper, flint, and mica as well as lead, zinc, and colored ores.

Thomas stretched research funds by keeping excavators working year-round, moving them into the South for the winter and the North in the summer. A main goal was to prove whether mounds had been built by a distinct race or by the ancestors of modern Indians. Writers without any Native contacts assumed a stereotype of the "restless, roving, unsettled, unhoused, and unagricultural savage, wherever found, as we have learned to consider him in modern times...judging [their] character...erroneously by their life after they had been disturbed by the European settlements" (Thomas [1894] 1985: 529, 611).

European metals, jewelry, tools, and religious medals found in the top of mounds were intrusive and inconclusive, but those at the bottom were compelling evidence for the link. Chronicles—left by Spaniards with Soto, by French among the Natchez, and by early Americans such as Bartram and Adair—clearly saw Natives actively using mounds. Without a coherent timeframe, however, age could not be assigned to excavations, continuing confusion.

Understanding that there were varied types and distributions provided cautious controls. While burial mounds were almost always assumed, exceptions were made for the obvious. One (#2 at thirty-eight feet by eight feet) of the two mounds at McAndrews farm on the Hiawassee River in Tennessee was identified as a likely signal station (Thomas [1894] 1985: 405). Features such as spiral ramps around mounds, reported as common by Squire and Davis, proved rare—seen only at Rembert, Etowah, and Lamar in Georgia; and Troyville in Louisiana (Thomas [1894] 1985: 300, 315, 588).[25]

Mass graves suggest the magnitude of past trauma. Near Sheboygan, Wisconsin, a mound consisted of many historic skeletons above "a mass of rounded bowlders aggregating several wagon loads, below which were some 40 or 50 skeletons in a sitting posture, in a circle, around and facing a very large [two foot] seashell." Similarly at Dunleith, Illinois, inside a stone-walled vault under Mound #16 were buried eleven sitting bodies—six adults, four children, and a babe in arms, all facing toward a central shell cup. At the Lindsay Mound near Raleigh, North Carolina, skeletons lay in a circle with heads toward the center like spokes of a wheel, faces to the left, with those buried on the west side arranged five layers deep. Another mound in this region held radiating skeletons on their left side, each head toward the center beside a pot graded by size, bigger for older, according to the age of that person. At Allen County, Kentucky, a stone-lined shaft, ten feet deep and feet wide, held layers of slabs between burials at two-foot intervals (Thomas [1894] 1985: 42, 51, 94, 111, 116, 582).

Stone or clay work occurred within some mounds.[26] Under the Rev. T. F. Nelson Mound along the Yadkin River in North Carolina beehive-shaped stone rings covered seated bodies facing the center, where a boulder dome covered a standing skeleton and cut sheets of mica.[27] Though this mound stood only eighteen inches high, these vaults were set on a floor dug three feet into the ground, while the central vault had been excavated down six feet to accommodate the standing body. On Long Island in the Holston River in Tennessee, Mound #3 held four skeletons, each seated at the corner of a square and facing the middle, where a sundried clay basin, nine feet long by four feet wide by fifteen inches deep, held a prone body with a kneeling stone figure at its head (Thomas [1894] 1985: 334 fig. 207, 335, 359 fig. 239).

One of the most elaborate burial tableaux occurred at the Kanawha

County Poor Farm in West Virginia, where, buried three feet below the top of Mound #31 (318 feet by 25 feet) within a ten-foot shaft, were a pair of facing prone skeletons, while ten feet below were two facing sitting skeletons

> with their extended legs interlocking at the knees. Their hands, outstretched and slightly elevated, were placed in position to sustain a hemispherical, hollowed, coarse-grained sandstone slab, burned red and brittle. It was about 2 feet across the top, with a cavity or depression filled with white ashes containing bones fragments (cremains) burned almost to coals. Over it was placed a somewhat wider slab of limestone 3 inches thick, which had a hemispherical or cup-shaped depression of 2 inches in diameter near the center of the underside, but this bore no trace of heat. Two copper bracelets were on the left wrist of one skeleton, a hematite celt [ax] and lancehead with the other.

At the base of the mound, twenty-five feet deep, was an altar, measuring twelve by eight feet, burned brick red and covered by a foot of fine ashes (Thomas [1894] 1985: 432).

A few mounds could be dated by historic events. During the 1800s an Osage chief died in Missouri while most of his village was away hunting, so his burial was modest until everyone returned and heaped a large mound over his remains. Nickasaw, a Wyandot leader, was buried under a mound at the spot where he was murdered in Summit County (Akron), Ohio. Along the Des Moines River in Iowa, slain Ioway warriors were buried in low mounds, as were Potawatomi in another section. In 1836 the Sac warrior Black Hawk, sitting up and wearing a uniform given him by Andrew Jackson, was buried nearby under his own mound surrounded by a picket fence (Thomas [1894] 1985: 658).[28]

In all, therefore, evidence—from excavations throughout the East and Midwest finding European goods deep inside mounds, chronicles tracing decreasing population and mound size, and attributions by name and tribe within recent decades—all proved the continuity of Native usage, discrediting any claims to a separate and superior race of mound builders. The huge scale of these prehistoric remains had been confusing, particularly when compared to the few traumatized survivors of these nations. Another century of scholarship would pass before the full magnitude of epidemic diseases, slaving, and despair was factored into Americanist understandings of what had horrifically happened to Native peoples.

Shapes and Colors

Testing at Watson Brake in northeastern Louisiana almost doubled the prior dating of earliest mounds, to 5500 BCE. The site itself is not a single mound, but rather eleven mounds with connecting ridges that enclose an oval whose diameter is 916 feet (~ 280 meters) long. Gentry mound ("Big A"), the tallest, is 7.5 meters (26 feet) high, and the others are between 3 and 4.5 meters high. In reporting these new dates, the journal *Science* noted, "Archaeologists once thought mound building was linked to agriculture, which created food surpluses and tended to lead to more permanent settlements and more complex societies. But because there is little evidence of agriculture at places like Poverty Point, many researchers thought that these mounds arose as a result of extensive trading networks, which fostered societies complex and prosperous enough to build them. Trade did not seem to be a factor at Watson Brake, however, as the artifacts found were all made of local materials."[29]

Last, Watson Brake had remantling on the north-side mounds but almost none on the south-side ones, as though these were abandoned or off-limits after the mounds were finished. This walking away from a major construction project to leave behind raised bulk and banked bulge should loom large in any rationale as to why mounds were built at first, and then regarded afterward. As noted by the excavator, Joe Saunders:

> Save mound K, all of the mounds on the north half are multi-stage construction. I would call it addition and not rebuilding. There is evidence of occupation on the intermediate surfaces; so they built and occupied, then added another stage and lived on top of that. In contrast, the south ridges and Mounds E, G, H, were single-stage mounds (perhaps F, we are not sure yet). Also, they lack midden deposits under the mounds, in contrast to the thick middens under the north mounds. There is a light scatter of charcoal under Mound E, which suggests that they planned

to build the mound there from the get-go—because the charcoal under Mound A is the same age as charcoal at Mound E.

So, the plan may have existed from the first mound, but remember, they lived at the site for years before the first mound was built. So it was an important place, later marked with mounds.

We have done some survey work near the mounds for years. All we are finding are very ephemeral sites, no large camps around the great mound site, as I expected. Instead it looks like they were living at the mound site—hunting and gathering for food, bringing it directly back to the mounds and subsisting.[30]

From the Archaic into the Woodland period, *conical* mounds for the dead served as regional ingathering locales, filling the lands along Ohio River tributaries as manifestations of what archaeologists have called the Adena, overlapping with later Hopewell earthworks made in huge geometric forms. Eventually platform temple mounds, also gracing much of the drainage of the Mississippi River, became occupied by leaders, living worshippers, and ancestral dead (Silverberg 1986).

Mound caps were often color coded. For example, the large and small Snodgrass sites were built on a ridge that is now an island in the Guntersville Reservoir of the Tennessee River in far northeast Alabama (Krause 1996; Mainfort and Walling 1996: 54–63; cf. Pursell 2004).[31] The Snodgrass largest mound changed the color of its cap seven times (every 28.5 years) between AD 1150 and 1350. The Snodgrass small mound showed alternating layers holding round and square buildings and mantle caps of red or blue-gray clay.

Mounds were ~ are communal expressions. Instead of viewing a mound as the tomb of an individual, Richard Krause (1996) argues that a mound embodied those aspects of authority based in a corporate identity acting in the public domain. Therefore a mound is "both a cenotaph and icon, both an empty tomb, a monument honoring an important person or event, and a holy place—a contact point (*note bene*) between the sacred and the secular, a tangible visible representation of the continuity that joined the past with the present, which did so despite human mortality and the discontinuity wrought by death" (62–63).

West of the Mississippi River, the divide between Early and Late Caddo was AD 1250–1300 (Schambach 1996). Early mounds included deep shaft graves and venerated icons, while Late ones, such as Battle Mound, the largest of earthen Caddo monuments, had buildings (temple houses) set into their tops. Between Early and Late, attention shifted from individuals (such as shamans) to buildings (maintained by priests). In southwest Arkansas the Ferguson site (AD 1300–1500) was vacant of living debris except for the tops of its twin mounds. Its supporting residents lived scattered among nearby farmsteads. Mound A was topped by a pair of buildings (ten rebuilt on five levels). At each layer one building was round, with thatched walls for summer use; the other was square, with wattle-and-daub walls for winter.

Excavation revealed many construction details because the building materials were carbonized by fire. Each level was burned in the same manner: sand was piled over the fireplace and against outer walls, the roof was removed, and the walls were ignited until flames raged. Then the walls were pushed in, one at a time, and the whole was quickly buried with sand, smothering the fire and raising a huge plume of smoke and steam that must have been seen for miles (Schambach 1996: 41). Such a smoke plume signaled passage between worlds, realms, or dimensions, alerting the dead and immortals to a shift from physical to spiritual conditions.

Ohio Geomancers

William Romain (2000: 167, 186) reintroduces the term *geomancers* for the builders of the huge Hopewell earthworks covering acres and miles and argues for their coordinated planning of these sites, using a standard measuring unit of 1,053 feet (321 meters) based on an arm span of 2.1 feet, or 25.27 inches. Comparing consistent measurements, he has found "families" of earthwork squares that form a systematically internested series (called an icosatwist). Equally intriguing is the seventy-mile Great Hopewell Road diagonally linking Newark with High Bank at Chillicothe, with an octagon and square set at right angles to each other at either end. While Newark has been well preserved, High Bank is an open field where tell-tale compacted earth reveals to GIS the subsurface configuration.

Other regularities include placement on the second terrace above a river on distinctive soils (friable Fox series) near vital resources such as water confluences, ancient trails, and gifts from the earth.[32] Among these linkages are the proximity of Newark earthworks and gem flint, Tremper and pipestone, Seip and ocher, and McKittrick and salt (though the salt seems to have been open to all willing to dig it out). Each location tapped into a concentrated flow of cosmic *powha*, which extended from the sun in the sky to the heart in a body, according to a Prairie Potawatomie quote: "Our hearts are only wind and water moving" (Skinner 1924: 221).

Each Hopewell construction is a microcosm of the combined universe in which the circle = earth, square = sky, and a central mound is a mountain mimicking the shape of an actual peak in the local landscape. The axis of each site is aligned to the seasonal path of the sun, moon, or stars. Consistent with Native cultural practices, mounds built over charnel houses for the preparation of the dead usually have lunar alignments because of associations of the dead with the night and dark underworld. At the Newark Octagon, the eight phases of the 18.6-year lunar cycle are each indicated by a gap at an angle marked by a gateway mound. Such a blocking feature consists only of soil and occurs only at linear earthworks like squares and octagons, suggesting continuity for the ethnographic belief that spirits can travel only in straight lines. An octagon's bends were also probably used to track the moon's eight monthly phases (new, waxing crescent, first quarter, waxing gibbous, full, waning gibbous, last quarter, and waning crescent).

Consistent mythic and ritual references recalling these Hopewell sites are the Earth Diver epic, in which a hero brings up earth from the bottom of the primal sea, and the Busk of the Southeast, a world-renewal rite historically celebrating the corn (maize) harvest. Since corn was a rare crop at this time, a bountiful harvest consisted of farmed indigenous plants like sunflower, amaranth, and others. While the actual Earth Diver varied across the Americas and Asia, depending on ecologically appropriate species, Romain suggests that for Hopewell he was shoveler duck or roseate spoonbill, though they could have as easily worked together.[33]

Interesting inclusions in mounds suggest the encouragement of heightened awareness during rituals through the use of tobacco, indicated by hundreds of shattered pipes and, in at least one instance, a copper sheathed model of a foot-long mushroom that is probably *Amanita muscaria* (fly agaric), famously psychotropic. Of note, the sheen of the copper mimics that of the natural species. Both sheets and bits of shiny mica occur in some burials in mounds, which are usually cremations (cremains), providing shiny surfaces also useful in meditation.

Specific parallels with the modern Busk, celebrated by traditional towns of Creeks now in Oklahoma (see chapter 4), include the event known as "going to water" in which participants purify by washing, preferably in running water but more often today in metal tubs. Two thousand years before, sites along rivers often included a graded roadway to the shore that would have facilitated this act, such as the Sacra Via at Marietta, where the Muskingum joins the Ohio River. They also would have facilitated the rolling of canoes out of and into the water, when these craft were the prime prehistoric transport (the Ringler dugout; Lepper 2005: 260–61). River people, such as those of the Pacific Northwest (as well as ancient Egyptians), integrated full-size and model boats into many of their rituals, including graded ramps for moving them about on land. Much of this knowledge was lost historically when the importance of watercraft in Ohio was eclipsed by the adoption of horses.

Cremations

An ancient and recurrent feature of the archaeological record is the incinerating and covering over of a building's remains by one or more layers of soil, renewed and repeated periodically (as with a burial, memorial, or commemoration), either once a year at the Busk, at the decade, or at the end of a longer cycle, such as the fifty-two-year Mesoamerican calendar (Thomas [1894] 1985: 207, 561, 568, 664). Each burning increased the mound's height and size, with classic examples ranging from Watson Brake (5,500 BCE) to Caddo temples (300 CE).

In Vernon Knight's (2004) summary of southeastern mound archaeology, the layering impulse is traced to the covering up (and sending off) of offerings. Over time one of these mounds rose to visually dominate the place and eventually become paired with another across the plaza. Such construction intervals occurred about every twenty-five years, and alternating colored cappings served to highlight contrasts in successive overmantles, making the sealing off of a prior surface both assured and obvious.

This thorough enveloping assured that the integrity of the mound would be maintained by the internal pressure of the compressed songs it held. Such human effort deliberately sent mementos onto parallel other-world orbits and held them there, either by cremating them or by burying them under an earthen seal while continuing to make them useful and energizing in the human world. The Creeks systematically burned, to cleanse and purify, discarded personal clothing, utensils, and building materials and cyclically burned over used-up fields and structures so that new, shared cycles of vitality would begin (Chaudhuri and Chaudhuri 2001: 114).

Of particular concern was the manner of signaling so that this transfer could be done safely across existences. Giving thanks and showing respect serve to obligate immortals to mortals, who exist in separate parallel worlds—except for moments of crux, approach, or overlap during rituals, when their intervening barrier becomes thin. At the Yuchi Green Corn of today, before their Bead and Ribbon Dances, deceased kin and others are invited into the square by throwing beads into the air. Men never step across benches in the arbors so as not to jostle or displace visiting ancestors sitting there invisibly but observant (Jackson 2003: 254).

Usually an initial building was burned down, with the first layer heaped on to smother the fire to raise a huge plume of smoke. Fundamental to understanding this action is the role of human intention in keeping the world in motion and other parallel worlds distinct from each other. Mounds bulge from internal pressure, not solely by packed dirt. In particular they are inflated bubble-like by the songs in rituals and the pumping-like step of the stomp dance that represent order and stability.

In the past the huge plume arising from a smoldering temple would be even more obvious as a visible *axis mundi* across layers. Sent high into the air, its whiteness would be seen by witnesses such as birds acting as messengers between these worlds, as well as immortals themselves. The effect was to let them know that bulk ~ body was being transmitted into their own world, and thus they could avoid possible harmful irritation during that displacement. Since qualities, times, and conditions were usually reversed between these parallel worlds, the burned building would be whole in its new abode, while any mortal remains took active human form. Similarly broken pots became whole, and burned offerings appeared intact. Noises reversed such that whispers became shouts, yawns became speech, and yells became caresses. The pan-being values of sharing and respect were upheld in public, cosmic, and obvious ways.

An overlooked aspect of this reversal, moreover, may have been that the multiple layers formed by successive rebuilding of the temple at that very location fused into a single building representing an ideal. Understanding these public, ritual acts requires a grasp of Native cosmology and needful pan-being reciprocity and respect between parallel orbits or existences. Most easily passing between them are songs, prayers, offerings, blessings, and witnesses such as emblematic birds, snakes, tobacco, and fire. Thus burning down temples served both to fuel the mounds and to transmute them beyond mortal time and space, as cremation did for bodies.

Time-space is a larger issue, especially from a Native perspective. By their very nature, artistic renderings of these parallel worlds seem static. A classic example is the five rings around a central dot ◎ used by Yup'ik to represent their Arctic world. A more dynamic image is that used for the atom, with the suggestion of whirling particles in orbit about the center. Indeed these other dimensions, realms, and worlds of Native America seem to be more like separate orbits. In one aspect, however, these ritual acts create separated train tracks, because human efforts deliberately set places and events onto parallel paths and, ritually, keep them there.

How is that done? Apparently by putting them out of direct sight, either by cremating them or by burying them under a special mantle of earth. Either way they are transformed in ways that continue to make them useful, vital, and energizing to the human world, but unseen. By contrast, the huge smoke plume is an obvious signal to the universe that such a transformation is occurring, warning and alerting those in other worlds that they are about to be intersected by a building, beings, and souls from the mortal world. As such, burning down, mounding up, and cremating are more a launch into eternity than an offering or commemoration from the past or by the present. Repeated cycles of destruction and rebuilding, moreover, allow the continued use of a favored locale over a length of time. Putting a new surface over a cemetery or burned temple enables new graves or a new temple to occupy the same place repeatedly.

INTEGRALS

Lower Illinois

Intense, long-term study of the Lower Illinois River, above its confluence with the Missouri and Mississippi, has identified three loci of interments at bluff crest knolls, at flood plain sand ridges, and at villages beside slack-water lakes.[34] Accretion mounds begin about seven thousand years ago, atop bluffs, with the "sequential additions of bodies [of young and middle-aged adults, tools, offerings] and enclosing sediments." On the floodplain, dotted later by huge platform mounds, at lakeside dwellings, young and infirm were buried in middens without offerings, while sand ridges were used for reburials with a high density and variety of offerings. In all, size and location serve to distinguish an exclusive ancestral ~ political cult focused on knolls from an inclusive so-called earth ~ fertility cult based on floodplain platforms. The former separated out kin units, while the latter integrated whole communities, sustained by these vital mounds (Buikstra and Charles 1999: 208, 212, 216, 218).

Bluff crests are double liminal zones (between the earth/sky and valley/uplands), where these Middle Archaic monuments provided an overview of the living for the ancestors: "Thus began the mound-building tradition." During mortuary rites, carrying bodies or remains across these pitched surfaces, including raised scaffolding, provided each with both a reintegrative cosmological tour and a route for reaching the afterworld. Orchestrated reburials in the sand ridges clearly show the expected reversal between the worlds of living and dead because pottery decorated with raptors is always stacked below that with spoonbills, inverting the natural order of these birds (Buikstra and Charles 1999: 208, 212, 216, 218).

But the study has analytical missteps. For instance, an inference that Burial 8 in Yokum Mound 4 was a shaman because he was buried with four sets of age-graded antlers is ethnographically flawed. Unlike past attempts, such analogies must be drawn from the full spectrum of indigenous Native traditions and not be limited to those decimated, traumatized survivals known to history. Widespread patterns better reflect this full diversity. In this context, therefore, deer antlers remain badges of political office, as they do for Iroquois *royaner* ~ league chiefs. Shamans, by contrast, are usually associated with bears. Thus the man at Yokum is much more likely to have been a chief than a healer.

In terms of overall built environment, moreover, these large and small Middle Woodland monuments re-created the cosmos, both vertically and horizontally, as well as providing a forum for the intense negotiation of power ~ *powha* relations among the living.

Good Knight

In his review of Mississippian religion from the perspective of a broad-based archaeologist, Knight (1986) skillfully looked at sacra (= artifacts and images displaying the sacred) sorted into three icon families, each one characteristic of a respective cult institution (with its own distinctive rituals and adherents). While others have seen the iconographies of temples, crops, and war in the assortment known as the Southeastern Ceremonial Complex (SECC),[35] Knight saw these images and artifacts as concerned with chiefly authority (chiefs), communal fertility (town), and, mediating between these two, priesthoods (priests). Their associated sacra are, for the first (might) = the warriors, werebeings, weapons, and world portrayals, often in defensive zones or levels, that in the past have been regarded (too narrowly) as expressions of the Southern Cult or SECC; second (town) = the mounds periodically covered over with new mantles of earth; and third (priesthood) = temple statuary, especially kneeling, corpse-faced images and figurines (in trance?), at least some of whom were ancestors. For convenience these three cults can be referred to as mighties, mounds, and ministers, defined by internested relationships of markedness.[36]

Accordingly, for Mississippians might is associated with high rank (fusing ages and genders), and so it is inclusively unmarked, while the priesthoods are marked, "clearly having exclusive ritual and supernatural prerogatives distinct from both of the former [and membership] was highly restricted to initiates trained in esoteric arts" (Knight 1986: 681, 683). As public works, mounds receive constant attention from everyone. In particular a fresh layer of soil is added periodically, "an act of burial, a mortuary rite for the mound itself rather than for any individual, sometimes complete with funereal furnishings placed upon the old surface" (676). They are built and rebuilt by the labor of all townspeople under the supervision of the other two cults. In a sense too they were farmed and planted, allowing for other kinds of growth and rebirth. The proper relationships of this Mississippian matrix therefore are expressible either as Mighties (Mounds) Ministers or as ^{Mighties} $_{\text{Mounds}}$ ^{Ministers}, with the mounds always pivotal.

Knight (1989) also provided a masterful summary of what the ethnographic literature says about the symbolism of Mississippian platform mounds. Though he wisely notes the obvious difference in scale between those of the past (dozens of feet high) throughout the East and those of the Oklahoma present (about five feet high), he sees continuity between the two. Intervening in the 1500s was the catastrophic population losses from both epidemics and massive slaving that reduced or wiped out most of the ancient complexity, diversity, and variability of these Mississippians. More recent research and publications help to clarify the meanings and usages of today's mounds.

The earliest reported Mvskoke term (*ēkvn-like ~ i:kan leyki*) given for the large mounds means "earth placed, sitting, dwelling," from *ekvnv* = earth, world, with compound extensions into 'cave, mountain, hill, earthquake' and *liketv* = 'seat, dwelling, residence.' The explicit conjoining of 'earth' and 'earthquake' says volumes about Native perceptions of "natural" stability and thus enforces the sense of "holding steady in place" as banked bulging ballast (Knight 1989: 280).[37]

Knight (1989: 289n1) errs when he relegates to his first footnote another term (*ekvn-hvlwuce*) translated as "hillock," literally "little mountain," because "there is no evidence ... that this term was applied to artificial constructions." Such evidence, however, is definitely insider information among modern Native adherents. Moreover a closer look at this same early dictionary shows a meaning of 'high earth.'[38] The latest Creek dictionary gives for *mound*, in technical spelling, *i:kan-leyki* (archaic) = mound of earth; *lani* = 'mound, mons veneris,' *tachi ~ tači* 'ridge of sweepings encircling dance area,' *tacho ~ tačo* = "area of the ceremonial grounds by the center fire" (Martin and Mauldin 2000: 23, 105, 124, 274).[39] In neighboring Caddo a parallel word means mound, hill, church, because "you look up to pray" (Miller 1996).[40]

Knight (1989: 282) carefully considered Creek Mvskoke mythology, where both Lower Creek "mother towns" of Kasihta (White) and Koweta (Red) mention mounds, serving both for burials and as prayerful offerings, in their origin epics. For example, Kasihta warriors found survivors of an enemy town burying their slain in mounds. Later Kasihta members built large mounds to petition the immortals and to provide a holy platform for taking the all-important Herb Water (*assi*, misknown as Black Drink because of the use of dark roasted holly leaves in the brewing).

Inside of the mounds was a chamber (bubble) that was used for fasting and praying and, for Koweta, waiting to ambush Cherokee attackers. In general, as outer mounds are likened to navels, inner mounds have complex associations of sanctuary, womb, and den subsumed within a chest or torso. Epics about emergence or "coming out" from mounds include notions of regeneration or resurrection from a womb—the pregnant belly of earth mother.[41] As microcosms, like the Earth itself, they are hollow inside and filled with the moving wind-like air of songs, promising vital order and calm.

As the abode of warriors they are dangerous dens where attack and death provide the need for rebirth. Inside the mound of Nikwasi on the Little Tennessee in Franklin, North Carolina, live some of the Nunnehi, a race of spirits fond of singing and dancing. They have other town or council houses throughout the Cherokee homeland. During the Colonial era, in stories, they offered refuge to those Cherokees who wanted to escape hostilities. Anyone willing to accept the help of the Nunnehi joined together in silence inside their town council houses for seven days, until the roar of thunder and shaking ground signaled their approach. Cherokees who cried out were lost, but the others became invisible and immortal when the townhouse was lifted from its mound up to the top of Lone Peak and turned to stone. Nunnehi remained behind after the Cherokees were forced west. During the Civil War they again emerged from Nikwasi to protect a handful of Confederates fighting off a Federal attack there (Mooney [1900] 1982: 335, 337).[42]

Indeed regard for focal mounds as abodes of the dead, and especially as "holy homes" or "hollow hills" of resident immortals, recalls the central chamber described for such mounds as Craig at the important Mississippian site of Spiro in eastern Oklahoma. Such indwelling life was also culturally evoked by references to Ants and Anthills, as at the famous Upper Creek town of Tukabatchee (see chapter 4), which has links to Shawnees (Knight 1989: 281).[43]

Thus among Mississippian descendants "linguistic and traditional material from Mvskoke, Yuchi, Chickasaw, Choctaw, and Cherokee" sources yields the reasonably coherent picture that "mounds possess symbolic associations with autochthony, the underworld, birth, fertility, death, burial, the placation of spirits, emergence, purification, and supernatural protection. They are metaphorical mountains, anthills, navels, or womblike 'earth mother' representations" (Knight 1989: 283). In mythology hollow mounds serve as nests and dens, as well as passages from the underworld.

Before the publication of the new Creek dictionary, Knight (1989: 283) wrongly concluded that modern mounds, four to six feet high, are known as *tadjo* (correctly *lani*) and "appear to be made up partly of dirt from square ground sweepings and partly of fresh dirt dug up nearby. In each case the new mound covers the remnant of the mound built the previous year.... These mounds are distinct from other small mounds formed by successive ash piles from the annually renewed sacred fires." In addition "the low ridge formed around the square ground from repeated sweepings is also called *tadjo* in Mvskoke and Seminole contexts" (284).

Knight found a direct link between Mississippian and historic ritual in the observations of John Howard Payne at the 1835 Tukabatchee Green Corn in Alabama.[44] There, of two mounds, the larger "used as a dance platform during the 'gun dance,' had been given a new coating of earth scraped from the adjacent square ground . . . stunning testimony documenting Creek mound construction in the nineteenth century, involving the addition of an earth mantle (albeit a thin one) to a genuine Mississippian platform mound. The ritual context, moreover, is unambiguous. The symbolism is that of world renewal and purification within the framework of communal Green Corn ceremonialism" (Knight 1989: 285).

Today at Creek grounds, in ironic contrast to all this past and highly public effort, the actual mound building takes place before, as preparations for, rather than at the actual Green Corn Dance. It occurs in the early morning, at a time when almost everyone else is sleeping. In the preceding days or week fresh willows reroof the four arbors and new upright poles replace any of those greatly weakened during the previous year. At dawn before the all-night dance the square is scraped clean of weeds and the refuse is raked outward toward the edge to make a ridge (properly the only *tadjo*), setting off the sacred enclosure that is the domain of fasting men. Women enter it only by special invitation from men officials. Once the area is clean, clear, and packed down again, attention turns to the raised basin in the open center, where the sacred fire of crossed logs $\oplus$ will burn. Its ashes are added to the biggest mound of all, by no means the small ash pile implied by Knight.

Throughout the Americas the ashes of sacred fires have an especially charged status, as in a Delaware story where hero twins are sent to ask help from the Sun to kill an underwater monster. Instead of giving them his fire, which is far too hot and dangerous, the Sun provides them with ash "sweeping," which effectively boils up the lake to kill the serpent (Newcomb 1956: 74).[45]

Reviewing Knight's original source, Payne himself reported that he first saw the 1835 Tukabatchee Green Corn (see chapter 4) while standing on a mound "just outside of one of the open corners of the sacred square." He "was afterwards told that this mound was composed of ashes which had been produced many preceding years by such fires as were now blazing in the center; and that ashes of the sort were never permitted to be scattered, but must thus be gathered up, and carefully and religiously preserved" (Swanton 1932: 179).

Thus one of those two mounds was composed of ashes, as the other was composed of the scraped-up earth noted by Knight. "In the center of this outer square was a very high circular mound ... formed from the earth accumulated yearly by removing the surface of the sacred square thither.

At every Green-Corn Festival, the sacred square is strewn with soil yet untrodden; the soil of the year preceding being taken away but preserved.... No stranger's foot is allowed to press the new earth of the sacred square until its consecration by members is complete" (Swanton 1932: 177). Such "new earth" has strong spiritual associations because it opens the way to the underworld, breaking through the all-important surface tension of the land's skin.

Every summer throughout Oklahoma, as in previous centuries, at the central fireplace of a Creek town (*italwa*, former chiefdom), the old ashes and upper layer of baked dirt are carried off with great care, a shovelful at a time, by a brigade of men who add it as a topping to the five-foot mound that stands toward the east. Another work group goes in a specific direction to gather special soil, often in a wheelbarrow, to add to the small bump in the Northeast that later serves very briefly as a standing place for a young man when summoning "the Birds" before men begin the series of Feather Dances.[46] Indeed these and other dances at the ceremonial ground, all using the distinctively southeastern dance step called the "stomp," provide the means to pump localized songs into the square ground and mounds. In all, at this square, every summer, as for decades prior, three small mounds are remade and blessed, one for the central fireplace, a second for the Birds, and a third topping the decades-old mound of ashes.[47]

This ongoing central Oklahoma pattern, however, might be dismissed as a recent import since, except for Caddoans along rivers draining into the lower southwest Mississippi River, prehistoric mounds are not supposed to occur in the Far West, or so most have assumed. A close look at the ethnography, however, dispels that notion, particularly since mounds, albeit small ones, are still being made during world-renewing rituals in northern California and still appear in Salish art (see the preface).

In Knight's equally masterful summary of southeastern mound archaeology, the initial impulse is traced to offerings of oversized artifacts, especially of chert, shell, and copper, intended for display at and in burials.[48] During the Middle Archaic (4750–3900 BCE), "Oversize Bentons, Cache Blades, Turkey Tails, and Double Notch Turkey Tails" had two forms. One was delicately chipped flint bifaces, and the other was "effigy knives of ground and polished siltstone" that had been shattered ('killed'). Both types contrasted in terms of raw material, knapping, and disposal "even when they were buried in the same cache" (Brookes 1997: 62; cf. Johnson and Brookes 1989). Red ocher covered some offerings, often within female graves, but a burial of a dwarf boy included five stacked blades.[49] The effigy form can be compared insightfully to the *atassa*, the oversize wooden knives to chop up harm that are carried by two lead women every summer in the Ribbon Dance that starts off each Green Corn.

Earth moving and shaping was initially commemorative, sealing off habitation and specialized activity zones with a new, fresh overmantle cap. Often these were large oval embankments under a ring of low mounds, as at Watson Brake. Over time one of these mounds came visually to dominate the site and eventually became paired with another across the open plaza. In all, the five identifiable types of moundings were (1) raised over existing cemeteries to add later burials, as with Copena (derived from *copper, galena*); (2) raised over charnel huts or mortuary crypts; (3) covering secondary burials and cremations placed on a low earthen platform that is capped over with a dirt dome; (4) raised over the central tomb of a special burial, with pots cached along the east side; and (5) raised sequentially over an extended time (Knight 2004: 740). Such construction intervals often occurred every twenty years, and changed colors highlighted the mound fill and the distinct mantles, often in contrasting hues so the sealing off of the prior surface would be assured and obvious to confine its infused songs.

With the ending of burial mounds, the ethnographically known Woodland ritual complex emerged from the segmenting out of world renewal ~ fertility rites such as the Busk, adoption ~ succession ~ rebirth rites such as Calumet feathered pipe(stem) ceremonialism, and mourning observances such as Lakota Ghost Keeping and other forms of ritualized grief (Hall 1997). Ceremonies moved to inside rotunda, halls, and council chambers, sometimes just low protective walls, to further safeguard community vitality.

James Ford

In his comparative analysis of Pan-American and worldwide formative cultures (6,000–3000 BCE), James Ford called attention to early circular villages mimicked in shell rings of the Southeast and sacred circles of Ohio, with later "retention" shown by Plains camp circles and Amazonian round towns. Over time construction efforts became more massive, especially after 3200 BCE, the date at which Ford divided the Formative Period into Colonial (5000–3200 BCE) and Theocratic (3200–2400 BCE) divisions, in lieu of the Early, Middle, and Late eras usually in academic favor. The peak came, according to his perplexing commentary, when, "at various times after 3200 BCE, the Indians in the three Americas began to waste [sic] untold millions of man hours in the erection of tremendous monuments of earth, adobe brick, and stone that served no practical purpose." He then drew comparisons to Egyptian pyramids and Medieval cathedrals to suggest "a religious base, complete with specialist priest-rulers... including architects, engineers, sculptors, and artists" (Ford 1969: 5, 42, 46).[50]

COMPARISONS

Comparisons have also been drawn between regions across the southern United States. Looking at such "constructed eminences," Owen Lindauer and John Blitz (1997) analyzed platform mounds in the Southeast and Southwest. Their outcome is understandably concerned with functions, forms, and politics, without appreciation of the Native religious systems that Ford and modern elders assert were the motivation for these efforts.

In the Southeast, though some platforms occur before AD 800, the majority were built later and served at least four functions: (1) elite ~ chiefly residence, (2) temple ~ mortuary ~ ancestor shrine, (3) council ~ sweat ~ meeting halls, and (4) courtyards ~ stages ~ display in the open, often with a huge central upright pole. At multimound sites each of these functions may well occupy a separate mound top, reached by ramps or stairs up the front. Usually they are built over earlier occupations, resurfaced over time (often thirty-year intervals, one long generation), and then capped by a final seal of colored clay that represents its own enclosed final burial (Lindauer and Blitz 1997: 175).[51]

In the Southwest their three functional forms, whose tops were reached by ladders, include dance, planned, and organic mounds. The first was low and open; the second was built on retaining walls of cell-like rooms filed with rubble; and the third converted prior domestic rooms into a rubble-filled foundation. The last two types had buildings on their summits (Lindauer and Blitz 1997: 177).

In particular, mounds served as observatories, reinforcing elite control of knowledge and reliable predictions. They also provided wider social integration by means of food storage and feasting, invested labor costs, and interdependence among nodes within a diversity of sites. Pottery sherds from the largest vessels are often found atop or beside mounds, as well as in chiefly homes, indicating their larger food reserves and generosity. Labor costs, however, seem to have been spread over time, so that building episodes were not as onerous as single-stage (all at once) construction would have been. Mounds marked administrative centers, coordinating community needs, such as irrigation along the Gila and Salt rivers of Arizona, or farming and raiding cycles in the Southeast (Lindauer and Blitz 1997: 185). Most important, "the repetitive act of covering the symbolically charged older surface with a new episode of construction is a key social dynamic of platform mounds" (192). Such remantling of mounds occurred across the Americas and often used color-coded topping soils to make absolutely certain that the prior surface was entirely sealed to assure the overall integrity of weight and height. As a torso-like bubble, such thick layering confined mound tensions and pressures to assure continued vitality.

Ontario as World

In his review of Ontario mounds, Walter Kenyon (1986: 76–81) notes that, worldwide, mounds belonged to the Neolithic period when crops were being domesticated. This is a useful insight. In other words, once people began actively to work the soil to farm crops, they also raised mounds as another expression of the same interest in vitality. Like Westminster Abbey, they contain burials because they are sacred spaces (weighted honored earth, raised banks of offerings, blessed ballast), closer to the immortals, not because their primary purpose was to be only a cemetery. They were sacred because they were vortices in the cosmos, loci of *powha* maintained by devoted human ritual to atone for faults and sustain life.

Food fueled the system, both on the table and at the altar. Later farming of corn, beans, and squash, however, was only one aspect of the mixed economy of this Great Lakes region. Instead it was the intensive tending of wild rice plots, complete with tagging and binding over their ripe sheaves just before harvest, that acted as a type of natural farming (Child 2012). That these were aquatic resources makes the elaboration of earthen mounds all the more significant since humans obviously live on land not in the water, launching canoes to harvest before cleaning and roasting on shore.

Given usual mound locations on Ontario high points along straight-bank waterways, visibility was a prime consideration in their placement. Similarly Colin Renfrew's study of the distribution of megalithic tombs on European islands, including one of the Orkneys, analyzes the remark by V. Gordon Childe that the location of these ancient tombs was the same as modern farmsteads. The reason is that both were built on what arable land was available. Such tombs served as both *gathering* places and territory markers, in much the same way as the locale of a modern hall, grange, or church fosters a community's identity and cohesion (Hedges 1984: 105).

Ritual, in series or by intermittent felt need, sanctified the mounds and their environs. In Ontario traces and residues of these rites include cremated bones, grave goods, and skulls (as at Hungry Hall) that have beads set as pupils into caked-in eye sockets, holes in the back to extract brains, or scars on the top from scalping.

In all, "we should look upon mound building as we look upon the performance of a ballet or drama in our own society.... Once the mound was built, of course, it would have served, as does a theatre, as a backdrop for other rituals. For, once again, it is through such rituals and ceremonies that human groups are bound together and that individual lives are shaped to accord with ancestral patterns" (Kenyon 1986: 81).

Effigies

Before Effigies were built in the upper Midwest, basic mound shapes probably expressed moieties such that conical mounds are associated with upper world ~ sky, while linear mounds, associated with lower world, evoked snakes. The few cross-shaped mounds represent the Earth itself. In recent centuries intrusive burials were added into these older mounds to "protect the graves of their loved ones" when tribes were being dispossessed of their homelands (Birmingham 2010: 26, 31, 91).

Further, the most encompassing explanation so far comes from Iowa's Clark Mallam, a humanist archaeologist who died in the midst of his insightful research into Effigy mounds. Rich in complex symbolism, mounding was atonement by humans for damaging the Earth while taking a living from it. More than just burials, community projects, or territory markers, mounds represented life's own "cyclical regularity," a microcosm reborn and reaffirmed with each layer (mantle) of fresh earth (Mallam 1976, 1982). Missing from his theory, however, is awareness of the constant threat caused by human faults and the regularity of song and dance in maintaining the bulge of mounds by inflating and infusing their internal tensions to bank up and charge their vitality.

3

SEeing Mounds

Today's Dixie was the homeland of Mississippians who a thousand years ago built mounds of such impressive size that they have long served to define the image of the U.S. Southeast (SE).[1] Other Native southeast characteristics include blowguns; cane basketry; mulberry and moss apparel; feather cloaks; chiefly litters; baby hammocks; a two-stick ball game; an engendered economy engaged in fishing (poisons, weirs, impounds), males hunting (deer, turkey), and females gathering (mast, nut oil, kunti) and farming (indigenous = sunflowers, maypop, goosefoot, maygrass; adopted = Mexican corn, beans, squash; then European grains, melons); totemic matriclans; red and white moieties; towns set around an open square for summer and rotunda for winter with focal sacred fires linked to the Sun; status head-shaping; priesthoods; caffeinated *assi* ~ herb water ~ "black drink"; Green Corn rites to honor successive planting, weeding, first fruits, purification, and new fire; Rabbit as trickster; and orderly Upper and chaotic Lower Worlds with earthen temple mounds poised between.[2]

ECOCULTURE

This region includes three ecozones: swampy lowland of coastal piney scrub forest and the Mississippi River floodplain, piedmont of rolling hills with oak-hickory forest, and worn-down Appalachian Mountains of hardwood forests. While the northern section of the continent was molded by glaciers, the forces of the Mississippi River system shaped most of these southern lands. Particularly distinctive were the majestic, lyrical longleaf pines—with their ecology of wiregrass, scarlet kingsnake, coachwhip pine snake, eastern fox squirrel, red cockaded woodpecker, yellow-bellied slider (a turtle), gopher tortoise, pitcher plant, and Venus flytrap—that were largely obliterated by settlers and their livestock, though their resistance to today's rampant pine beetle infestation has encouraged its replanting on a small scale.[3]

Across the Southeast prehistoric human occupation was dense, with moderate estimates of 250,000 people in 1500 CE, as European diseases began to take their very heavy toll (Smith 1987; Dobyns 1983). Subsequently massive slaving interests attacked, killed, sold off, and scattered many more (as mustee ~ lone tribal survivors). The brutal trek (1539–43 CE), led by Hernando de Soto (below) until he died of infection, provided a last glimpse of many pre-epidemic complex chiefdoms that had emerged after thousands of years of specialized adaptations and local growth. Pomp and ceremony enhanced the elites of these highly stratified societies, sustained by communal labor, trade, and tribute: "Resolute and inspiring leadership was critical for chiefs who had to be ever watchful of rivals at home and enemies from neighboring chiefdoms. Items from mounds also point to an active involvement of key people in a rich ceremonial life. Rattles and scarifiers, for example, must have been used in various rituals and on special occasions, much like they were in later times" (Milner 2004: 139).

Long cycling took these polities through times of rise, fall, and rise. Some developed from simple to complex chiefdoms, supported by vassal towns while escaping attacks by rivals. Most ultimately collapsed under European pressures, though a few small groups like the Natchez survived into the 1700s, when they too were destroyed by French forces, their ethnic soldiers, and other Native allies.

LANGUAGES

Diverse languages were spoken in the Southeast in historic times, with even greater variation likely before these epidemic disasters. Together these languages represent half of the linguistic stocks known for North America. Among them were Iroquoian (by Cherokee, Tuscarora, Yuchi), Caddoan (by Caddo), Algic (by Pamlico, Powhatan, Shawnee), Siouan (by Catawba, Quapaw, Woccon, Ocaneechi, and a subset attributed to the Ohio Valley [Rankin 1996, 2006] before they scattered to become the Biloxi, Ofo, Tutelo, Saponi), and, distinctive of the region, Muskogean (by Creek, Choctaw, Chickasaw, Apalachee, Alabama, Koasati, and Hitchiti-Mikasuki). Often regarded as language isolates are Atakapa, Chitimacha, Natchez, Timucua, Tunica, and Yuchi. All but the last have been joined with Muskogean into a proposed language stock called Gulf, but this is still debated. Yuchi, which survives in Oklahoma, seems to have remote ties to Iroquoian rather than Siouan, as had been suggested earlier. Most survivors speak tongues belonging to the Muskogean language family and Gulf linguistic stock. Other little-known speech communities became dormant (extinct).

Members of elite families were expected to be fluent in many languages, and their children were often fostered out to foreign families for linguistic immersion as part of their training. For everyone else, however, this jargon enabled visiting, trading, and other brief contacts. Captives and slaves taken from other communities also added to the language mixture, serving as interpreters for their owners (such as Lamhatty, the best known mustee).[4] Understandably, escaped African slaves increasingly took on this role during recent centuries, expanding transatlantic linkages.

The ethnographic tribes and confederacies of Frontier and Colonial history were double survivors of both epidemics and massive shatter-zone slave raiding for labor-intensive plantations in the Caribbean.[5] Though he was less aware of the enormity of these cataclysms, these tribes became the life work of John Swanton, a prolific ethnographer at the Bureau of American Ethnology in Washington DC, who published on all the major cultures except Cherokee.

As expected, to facilitate trade across this diverse and increasingly dislocated population, the simplified Mobilian Jargon spread throughout the region, with a distinctive OsV (object + pronominal subject + verb = "book he took") syntax (Drechsel 1997, 2001). This lingua franca, based on Choctaw, explains the many cultural similarities among these diverse speakers. Indeed it must have been a mainstay of a chiefdom's commoners since its distribution matches that of the prehistoric Mississippian tradition (Drechsel 2001: especially 180; Drechsel 1997; Crawford 1978).

For all Native languages of the Americas, verbs are the heart of the grammar, the means of conveying ongoing dynamic processes inherent in the mutating universe. In the Southeast Muskogean was divided into western and eastern branches by Mary Haas, the famous and dedicated linguist first assigned to this stock by Franz Boas and Edward Sapir.

EASTERN	WESTERN
Creek-Seminole	Choctaw-Chickasaw
Hitchiti-Mikasuki	
Alabama-Koasati-Apalachee	

Seminole is the dialect of Creek spoken in Florida by those who left towns in Alabama in the early 1800s. Other Seminoles speak Hitchiti-Mikasuki.

Apalachee was spoken in prosperous towns in northern Florida; the people were smashed and scattered after massive British slave raids in 1704 destroyed their Spanish Catholic missions, sold a thousand into slavery, and displaced thousands of others. Their hub was Mission San Luis at modern Tallahassee, the state capital, a few miles south of the ancestral site at Lake Jackson, where three mounds mark their antecedent Mississippian chiefdom (Hann and McEwan 1998: 339, 403).[6] Another mound site at Lake Miccosukee represented the eastern half of the Apalachees, leading to the historically prominent town of Ivitachuco.

More recently another classification splits into northern, central, and southern branches.

SOUTHERN	CENTRAL	NORTHERN
Choctaw-Chickasaw	Alabama-Koasati	Creek-Seminole
	Apalachee	
	Hitchiti-Mikasuki	

EXPANSIONS

To expand on this southeast overview, the Paleo-Indien era, with beginning Clovis rebounding through the continent, merged about nine thousand years ago into the early Archaic known as Dalton, with an intensifying and self-identifying use of local landscapes. Hunting and plant harvesting (garnering) included a skilled technology to extract oils and meats from pecans, hickory, and other nuts. Thereafter nut oils featured in local foods, meals, and cooking styles. Late in the Archaic a fiber-tempered pottery was developed to improve on soapstone containers, perhaps to transport live shellfish. Many wild plants—such as sunflowers, sunroot (sunchoke), sumpweed, amaranth, and maypop—were domesticated into truly indigenous cultigens of the old farming crop, prior to the spread of maize from Mexico.

All materials that were available locally or via trade were used for the technology. These included stone, wood, shell, clay, and cane. Canoes and watercraft were vital throughout this watery region, and huge vessels transported goods along the wide Mississippi River and into the Caribbean. Leaders often traveled in the equivalent of a royal barge, shaded under an elaborate canopy. Some towns deployed flotillas decorated in matching colors, each canoe manned by ninety warriors seated in three rows along its length.

In addition to bows and arrows, the blowgun was a characteristic weapon also shared with much of the Tropics to the south. Indeed the tube was a potent image throughout this area, serving as a model for the human body as well as that of other beings.[7] Snakes therefore, as flexible tubes, become emblematic of life itself. Native priests, curers, and religious officials had a special cane tube that they used (and, during today's rituals, use) to push place-based dicta, breath, songs, and bubbles into medicines and other sacred potions, as well as to flame up special fires.

During warm weather people dressed merely for modestly. When it was cold, however, men dressed in buckskins and women in doeskins. In Florida the poor made clothes of Spanish moss. In the Carolinas mulberry bark was woven into fabric. Those rich and well-connected also wore elaborate capes woven of overlapping, shingled turkey and other feathers, including flamingos to garb members of the Red moiety.

The many swamps, bayous, rivers, and streams abounded in fish, which were taken with spears, stun drugs, nets, and weirs. Temporary dams facilitated the effectiveness of fish poisons, such as mashed horse chestnuts, that stunned large numbers to float to the surface. Standing in the water, men tossed the limp fish onto the shore, where women and children gathered them up and sliced, dried, and smoked them for storage. Women wove special openwork baskets for use in the fishery.

As tending of local plants intensified into gardening, such greater attention to enhancing growth helped encourage people to stay closer to home and engage in rituals among their transplanted crops. Then, a thousand years ago, the ceremonial farming of corn, beans, and squash was enthusiastically adopted and later developed into huge fields that were planted by both men and women. Certain plots and zones were regarded as tribal commons, and these crops were stored in a public granary for the benefit of the leaders and the community and its guests. "The men perform nothing [sic] except erecting their mean habitations, forming their canoes, stone pipes, tambour [drum], eagles tail or standard, and some other trifling matters, for war and hunting are their principal employments. The women are more vigilant, and turn their attention to various manual employments; they make all their pottery or earthen-ware, moccasins; spin and weave the curious belts and diadems for the men; fabricate lace, fringe, embroider, and decorate their apparel, &c., &c." (Waselkov and Braund 1995: 127). Their pottery had colored, stamped, and textured surfaces, as well as a wide variety of shapes depending on intended uses, purposes, and functions. Basketry, less fragile and more portable, also had and has diverse styles and uses.

Kinship was usually traced through the mother (matrilineally). Children belonged to her clan and were under the authority of their mother's eldest brother (MeB), though they had affectionate bonds to their fathers. Choctaws and Chickasaws observed mother-in-law avoidance as a gesture of respect and domestic harmony. Clans clustered into phratries and, overall, into halves called Red or White. These are usually said to equate with war or peace, though the associations have more to do with foreign relations or local civilians, with defense or domesticity. Unlike the rest of the Southeast, Yuchi divide into patri-moieties of Chiefs and Warriors.[8]

Rank was often obviously and permanently marked on anatomy. Tattooing was an art form that often enhanced status by richly decorating elites' bodies. Boys often had their clan emblem tattooed on their chest or shoulder, making obvious a link that was passed on through women. Creek men strove to win a series of named war titles, and their dandies would cut and stretch their earlobes by wearing heavy ornaments.

Infant heads were molded into sloping foreheads by rank-conscious Natchez, Catawbas, Tunicas, Chitimachas, and Choctaws. Of note, such head-shaping emerged among the Adenas, the first to build mounds in the Ohio. This concurrence of the shaping of heads and of mounds enforces their morphological equation (both have brows, domes), already noted in the ethnography.[9] Birth, naming, marriage, and death were honored with family ceremonies, though those for leaders were much more elaborate. At a wedding each member of the couple was represented by a cane reed (tube) standing together in the ground.[10]

Death started a sequence of funeral rites that marked the successive loss of breath, fluids, flesh, bones, and souls. At each stage in the process, with the increasing loss of less solid parts, the family held feasts and rites until all but the memory of that person was gone. (By contrast, in the Pacific Northwest hereditary names and artistic treasures that were ~ are passed down through generations readily serve to perpetuate the memory of past holders.) When members of the elite died, their sequence of funeral services became more elaborate the higher their rank. Until 1800 the Choctaws observed a lengthy mortuary series (below).

Towns were planned communities, linked to surrounding hamlets. Those located near frontiers between chiefdoms were usually defensively fortified, while those in central locations were palisaded for a more spiritual reason: to enclose and protect community moral unity. The well-being of a "mother town" assured the health and "good minds" of its satellites. Families lived in a range of housing types, more open for the summer and more enclosed for the winter. Those of higher rank lived in compounds where separate buildings, set around the sides of an open plaza (a scaled-down town square), were variously used for cooking, sleeping, storage, rituals, and visitors.

Major towns serving as ritual centers were marked by earthen mounds, temple, and open plaza, collectively known as a "square ground," with a public central (sacred) fire (as well as a private one in the temple) and arenas for team sports. Such games often had strong religious overtones. A tall post topped by a rotating emblem served as the goal for the two-stick ball game (played with a racquet in each hand). Men played against women around this pole, or, with greater fierceness, teams of men played against men surging between goal posts. A long alleyway was once used for chunkey, where a stone disk (*motaka*) was rolled along while men with long throwing poles tried to hit the place where it came to rest. Chunkey seems to have been spread by the outreach of the Cahokia hub, and the stone disks were town, not player, property, enforcing a sense of social cohesion.[11]

Influences from Ohio River mound builders, like Hopewell, and from Mexico, the source for corn seed and maize ritualism, helped to establish the era of complex chiefdoms known as the Mississippian (AD 800–1550). Trade with Puebloan farmers of the Southwest also may have contributed. Its three major cults, which overlapped in support of elite families, focused on the temple, fertile field crops, and warfare (rephrased as ministers, mounds, and mighties). Priests based in temples conducted rites concerned with community welfare and celebrated the growth of the crops in the fields, which were under the primary care of women. Warfare, a man's arena, involved rituals to assure success in competitions held on the battlefield as well as in chunkey and ball games, termed the "little brother of war." During raids of retaliation or revenge in recent centuries, the justification was said to be the "crying blood" of the slain (Adair 2005: 7).

The temple (specifically its fire on a tiny mound inside) was the heart of the chiefdom, often located atop a massive earthen mound. In some cases this was the reuse of a much more ancient mound. In others it was an organic outgrowth of that town, increasingly raised (added to) with each leader's death when the temple that was his or her house was burned down to transfer it into the spirit world. Then another layer of dirt (or mantle) was applied to the mound to cover (bury) it before a new chieftain was installed and another temple built. Sometimes the leader lived atop one mound, and, facing it across the plaza, the temple was atop another. Therein were kept the curated bones or bodies of all past leaders beside the eternal flame of the town, maintained in the temple by special attendants whose lives were forfeit if it ever went out.

Leading families, especially the rulers, were set apart, linked to the sky (such as the Great Suns among the Natchez described by the French). Rarely did they walk directly on bare earth. When such leaders appeared in public, they usually were sitting on litters carried by young men. Often they traced their ancestry to the Sun, the greatest spirit being (more usually its eye) in the visible world. It was the unseen world that was the most powerful. To harness aspects of it, polished and shiny surfaces were used to reflect sunlight onto people and places that were thereby empowered, enlightened, strengthened, and vitalized. Copper, mica, shell, and freshwater pearls were important trade items because of their sacred mirror-like, radiating, and iridescent qualities. Such nacreous items featured prominently in the caches placed inside mounds and temples, subsequently found by archaeologists.

Though the temple served community-wide needs and functions, it was particularly devoted to this cult of chiefly ancestors. Hereditary priesthoods managed temples in large towns. Each day, as well as at all ceremonies, men drank a special beverage, after it was brewed by such religious leaders, that infused many of the helpful plants and medicines. It was known to outsiders as Black Drink (for its tea-like color); Natives often call it 'herb water' and sometimes White Drink for its peaceful and communal associations.[12] In a variety of contexts, all members of the town can drink it, though women and children need to be more cautious in their usage (Hudson 2004).[13]

Though this beverage has been described as an emetic or purgative, it does not cause gagging. Instead vomiting is now a deliberate religious exercise to prove the purity of the body's insides due to fasting (Hudson 1975). Sometimes therapeutic scratching also takes place during this drinking, with herb water rubbed over the skin before wet scratching, which was ~ is less painful than dry scoring without lubricants. The needles of the comb-like scratcher were either a garfish jaw or a fixed row of bone splinters from various potent animals, who transfer or inject, via their sharpened bone point, some of their abilities into the punctures that draw out blood to further purify an individual. Today a single machine-made steel sewing needle is used, though some purists use thorns. Again the aim is increased vitality by releasing impurities.

This economic and psychological support of fellow plants and animals was celebrated at a series of rituals held throughout the year. While crops were maturing in the field, these were largely agricultural rites. Their culmination is called the Busk, from the Creek word *poskita* "to fast," held to thank and honor maize while it was waiting in the fields for harvesting.[14] In the fall, hunting and animals became the symbolic focus, when men wore carved and painted masks in dances to embody the full range of other beings, spirits, and species, from fierce to helpful.[15]

The cult of war reinforced elite might. Relying on images of raptorial birds (falcon, hawk), pouncing felines (panther), and poisonous snakes (rattler) to convey the terror of a sudden fatal blow, as well as an assortment of weapons, warriors fought in raids and as massed troops. As amalgamated composites, armed birdmen, horned catmen, and feathered serpents fused these powerful images into even more fearsome beings. Throughout the Southeast the constant tensions between the old men of peace and the younger men of war appear in the paired use of white and red colors for institutional halves (moieties).

With the collapse of the ancient chiefdoms and their depopulation, the war cult faded, though its former importance is well represented in many martial artifacts from Mississippian sites. Ironically its ideology and imagery may have been transferred to the militaristic slaving societies of the 1600s, which captured and sold off other Natives to be shipped to their doom at hard labor on Caribbean plantations. Today a glimpse of its former fervor can be seen in the two-stick ball games fought between goal posts by teams of men and boys (with medical aid cars or ambulances parked at the ready).

Over thousands of years this dense population benefited from all of the natural and farmed crops. They hunted and fished, using poisons or drugs that worked well in large impounds. They also traded far and wide for specialties, luxuries, and necessities like salt. Elites intermarried and led rituals that drew together many of the faithful. The land was extensively occupied and thoroughly used in sensible ways. Full-scale maize farming relocated towns to fertile waterways, and, in late prehistory, communities clustered (clumped) at strategic locales for defense rather than dispersed over their territory. Mounds were one aspect of this ecological management of the landscape, raising soil above the flood plain, bringing leaders closer to their mythic origins in the sky, and bulging with harnessed vitality.

REEMERGING TO REMOVAL

The earliest known European contacts were with Spanish *entrada* (forays) in the 1500s, sailing out of the Caribbean. Death preceded them as indirect (faceless) epidemics took a massive toll on southeast populations because they were so concentrated. All contacts introduced diseases, some, such as smallpox, repeatedly infecting each new generation. Waves of epidemics decimated populations, which were then brutalized by the Soto (1539–43) *entrada*'s murders (some fed to mastiffs), mayhem, enslavement, and disease (below). Soto was followed by Juan Pardo and others, who witnessed the subsequent devastation.[16]

Throughout the region late in the 1500s, resilient survivors of decimated chiefdoms merged into historic tribes, depending on trade goods earned in the deerskin trade as well as slave raids. Across the Atlantic these skins became items of horse tack or fashion, especially English breeches and gloves, while Native slaves perished at hard labor on Caribbean plantations growing cane for sweets and indigo for military uniforms when all of Europe was at war.

The French-Spanish rivalry (with massacres) for Atlantic Florida established St. Augustine in 1565, expanding by Catholic missions. Jesuits abandoned theirs among the south Florida Calusa in 1569, then Franciscans began in 1574 among the Guale of the outer coast, who periodically revolted (Orista 1576, 1597) before they were scattered by British hostilities. In 1704 a few Anglicans and a thousand Creek allies demolished Florida Catholic missions, selling hundreds of Apalachees into plantation slavery.

The harshest Native slave traders (1670–1715) founded Charleston, South Carolina, sending victims to die on Barbados and other islands. Small predatory tribes that had been briefly successful in the slave trade were each crushed in turn, as British agents assumed their profits. These included war with Oconeechi (1676, Bacon's), Westos (1680), Tuscaroras (1711–13), and Yamasees (1715–28). French forces crushed Natchez nobility (1716, 1729), but two royal army assaults (1736, 1740) on the Chickasaw stronghold were utter routs.

Land cessions increased after the American Revolution. Federal agents, such as Benjamin Hawkins (1754–1816) among the Creeks (1796–1816) and Return Meigs (1740–1823) among Cherokees (1801–23), fostered plow farming by men and loom weaving by women as cottage industries. Livestock, especially cattle, sustained a ranching industry. The ill will and greed of regional leaders, such as Governor William Blout in the 1790s, nicknamed by Natives the "dirt king" for his extravagant land speculations, pressed the removal issue. The Red Stick civil war among Creeks in 1812, especially the battle at Horseshoe Bend, where Cherokees won the attack, became the excuse for a single-handed treaty by Andrew Jackson to deprive Creeks, including his own loyal allies, of two-thirds of their lands. As president he was emphatic that Removal was humane and forced these painful dislocations.

Placing Natives out of harm's way by moving them to the west was first suggested when the Louisiana Purchase provided such lands. The federal Removal Act of 1830 was said to be voluntary but deviously included the proviso that the national government would not interfere with state laws sanctioning brutalities, such as suppression of tribal newspapers, any gatherings, and personal liberties, including imprisonment of devoted missionaries. Such avoidance also denied any protection for the many solemn treaties the United States had signed with these nations.

Georgia proposed a lottery for vacated lands, which increased popular support. The Cherokees mounted a public relations campaign and took their case to the U.S. Supreme Court, where Chief Justice John Marshal used these "Cherokee cases" to define federal legalities by terming tribes "domestic dependent nations." Resident tribes resisted severe pressures until, usually, murders of their members drove their decision to move. All tribes east of the Mississippi were implicated, not just in Mississippi, Alabama, and Georgia, but also prosperous tribes in Ohio. Wyandots in particular fled with the resources to found Kansas City. Chickasaws excelled as militaristic slavers and benefited from the fertility of the Black Belt prairie, which became the prime realm of King Cotton after their removal.

Throughout the South trader fathers educated their Métis children, especially sons, for business and diplomacy, establishing a class of successful Native leaders who were literate and savvy. Among these was Alexander M'Gillivray, a double agent for the British and the Spanish, who described a full Busk (see chapter 4). But they could not withstand clamoring settlers. Led away by "conductors" of varying honor, suffering exposure and poor planning, separate companies trekked to new homelands in Kansas and Oklahoma, in order, by Choctaws (1830), Creeks (1836), Cherokees ("Drive Away") ~ Trail of Tears 1834, after Old Settlers 1819), Seminoles (1833, with heavy resistance), and Chickasaws (1837), who paid their own way but still suffered from bad planning, spoiled food, and random hostilities.

Heading west, they marched in an honored line, often single file. Special men carried bundles containing a token of their ancient town (ashes, fire embers, stone, copper plate) along with soil from their town mound to reseed another one in Oklahoma. It is such continuity, displaced a thousand miles, that provides insight and understanding from today's modest mounds to the mighty ones of the past seen in use by the earliest explorers and settlers.

A FATAL GLIMPSE: HERNANDO DE SOTO ACCORDING TO EL INKA

The surviving reports of early Spanish explorers set the baseline for understanding the subsequent conditions of the Southeast, devastated by epidemics and then by human slaving that carried off thousands. Garcilaso de la Vega, in addition to writing a distinguished account of his mother's Inka Empire before and after the Spanish conquest of Peru, also interviewed survivors of the six-year bullying (1540s) by Hernando de Soto through the modern southeastern United States (Vega 1980: 38) to create a (Spanish) literary masterpiece, published decades after the actual event.[17] Only during the early years of the Spanish colonies could a son of mixed ancestry rise to esteem and success among the governing imperial elite.

Soto's share of riches gained in the slaughter of Peru—from the murder of the Lord Inka, plunder of his gold, and devastation of the Inka Empire—was used to finance his expedition through La Florida. He requested this region as a personal possession from the king of Spain, and received it only for the duration of his own life. If riches were found, then the terms would be renegotiated by the royal court. While he reported no mound-building activity in process, he saw ample temples in use as well as abused in a rival's revenge (below).

Others had previously tried to colonize the region, but they had failed. Juan Ponce de Leon had come to the Florida peninsula with eighty men in 1521, Judge Lucas Vazquez de Ayllon tried with 220 in 1526,[18] and Panfilo de Narvaez lost a force of four hundred in 1528. The handful that survived included the famous author Cabeza de Vaca and three others, who wandered for years before reaching Mexico, as well as a boy named Juan Ortiz, who remained a La Florida captive until he was freed to translate for Soto.

Each invasion spread havoc because, long before they arrived at a place, European germs rushed ahead, wiping out many local people. Diseases, introduced by Native traders with and without direct contact with Europeans, advanced everywhere as a decimating vanguard before actual face-to-face (foul breath to breath) meetings or confrontations. Soto inflicted many cruelties during his own four years (1539–43) of wandering before he himself died of disease, and the expedition wandered on for another two years. Natives slow to answer were tortured, and defended villages were burned. Horses and huge "war dogs" were used to menace, threaten, maim, or kill (and eat) condemned Natives.

Beginning at Tampa Bay, Soto's forces went north and west through the Florida panhandle, northeast through Georgia and South Carolina, west into Tennessee, southwest through Alabama, northwest through Mississippi, and north then west through Arkansas. After Soto succumbed, the force meandered southwest through Arkansas, a tip of Louisiana, and western Texas before retracing their route back to the Mississippi River, building ships and fighting their way downriver and along the coast to reach New Spain (Mexico).

By the end almost three-quarters of the thousand-member expedition were dead, leaving behind several hundred pigs, which spread their own lethal germs. As a precaution against hunger, in case there were no village granaries to pillage, the expedition had started with a herd of a dozen swine. These soon bred into thousands to provide fresh and familiar pork. Turned feral, over time they rooted out many of the foods preferred by local Natives, who slaughtered them whenever possible. A few escaped into the wild to produce today's feral razorback hogs, the Arkansas mascot.

Native communities, felled by unseen and unknown germs, reached the brink of their last glory. Men and women of distinguished families, powerful hereditary leaders carried around on litters, had coordinated the lives of thousands. Intricate rituals accompanied all events, whether personal, civil, military, solar, or religious. This orderly world had been damaged by earlier coastal contacts with the Spanish (and others), but these chiefdoms remained largely in control of their own fates. Away from the mangrove swamps, the forests were park-like because every year thickets were selectively burned and tended by caretakers under chiefly direction, relying on accumulated wisdom and experience of the ecology, so that animal and plant life thrived. Mound centers served as warehouses for food surpluses, allowing families to trek into remote areas to hunt and harvest. Soto's demands on these stored foods, however, depleted supplies and probably left famine in their wake to further destroy Native life and polities.

The great diversity of languages throughout the Southeast, as with the rest of the Americas, made multilingualism a requirement for effective leadership. After Juan Ortiz was able to remember his lapsed Spanish, he stood at the end of a long row of speakers that started with the most recent dialect to be encountered. Unoccupied, game-rich buffer zones separated these clumped political and linguistic communities. Given this Babel, Soto received from Ortiz a decidedly garbled message in less than fluent Spanish, so errors, blunders, and misunderstandings were rife. They became more so after Ortiz died in 1542 at the winter camp near present-day Little Rock, Arkansas.

At Acuera in central Florida, their leader, also called Acuera, announced that he knew the Spanish only too well from previous expeditions: they were professional vagabonds who lived by robbing, sacking, and murdering inoffensive people. To urge them along, his warriors decapitated fourteen members of the expedition, then dug up their fresh graves, dismembered the bodies, and hung the pieces from trees.[19]

Lessons were learned during several novel situations. The first winter (at Tallahassee), Soto's men were shown the penetrating force of Native arrows, which easily pierced chain mail armor.[20] For their own safety soldiers adopted quilted tunics, sewn by women captives, more impervious to arrows and spears.

At Cofitachiqui in present-day South Carolina the ruler was a woman, providing a glimpse of some of the rich complexity of Native rankings. The expedition first heard of this province from a boy who had been raised by professional traders and so had a vast knowledge of places, people, and goods. He thought that yellow metal could be found there. The expedition assumed this was gold, but he probably meant shiny copper, which was much more valuable in terms of Native prestige throughout the Americas.[21]

Garcilaso cast his narrative about this "lady" to evoke the meeting of Marc Anthony with Cleopatra to underscore Roman imperial images favored in Colonial Spain. A younger woman served as the representative of this "queen," explaining that food was scarce because a great pestilence had killed many people during the past year. In all likelihood its causes included the disease vanguard of Soto and his men. Unable to feed the troops, the woman nevertheless earned their goodwill by allowing them to loot thousands of freshwater pearls from her local temple so Soto could send over fifty pounds of them back to Havana as early hopeful news of his expected gains.

The temple of Cofitachiqui was rectangular, a hundred feet by forty, with benches set along interior walls. On these bunks were wooden chests holding the remains of individuals of the royal family. Above each was a carved portrait statue of that man, woman, or child. Smaller boxes and baskets nearby were filled with pearls or animal skins. Six pairs of standing interior posts were carved to look like giant warriors, each pair holding another type of weapon. Along the upper walls were two rows of carved women and men, holding weapons, decorated with inlay, pearls, and tinted fringes. The roof of canes and reeds was decorated, both inside and out, with many hanging shells and long pearl strands. Interior walls were also made of woven cane mats. Behind these walls were eight side rooms, each storing a different type of weapon.

Though Garcilaso heightened his description of the temple with comparisons to Roman and Greek buildings, it was impressive in its own right.[22] As in previous towns, such temples were repositories of tribute and offerings, cult centers for the worship of ancestors, armories for stockpiled weapons, and sepulchers for the bodies and bones of leading families. (Of note, intertown enmity, as mentioned, aimed deliberately at these temples atop mounds. While allied with Soto, Cofaqui of north Georgia secretly sacked the temple and killed many of the Hymahi in South Carolina.)[23]

Regional Native resentment against the invaders continued to build as new local alliances were forged to face this sudden Spanish menace. A physically huge war leader named Tuscalusa lured the Spanish into a trap at Mobila, near modern Selma, where a pitched battle resulted in many casualties. To hold together his weakened force, Soto decided to move north, away from the coast and its rescue ships, into the interior. At least one Spaniard had already deserted to live with the Indiens; others were tempted. Moving into hostile territory would deter further desertions.

When the Soto marauders reached the Mississippi, they joined in the political intrigues among local chiefdoms. These rivals included Casqui and Pacaha, now respectively known as the Parkin site and the Bradley site, the latter in an archaeological cluster called the Nodena phase (Hudson 1997: 294–300).[24] At Parkin, the Casqui leader asked Soto to bring rain because their crops were suffering from a long drought.[25] Saying that only God could decide to bring rain, Soto had a cross set up on the mound of the community. With full Catholic pomp, priests and others marched to the mound, blessed the cross, and prayed. That night it did indeed rain, adding new blessings to the mound.

Within days, guiding the Spaniards toward Pacaha, Casqui saw his chance to triumph. He went into the Pacaha temple, where he tumbled those ancestors out of their containers and stomped on the bones. Chests were smashed and the temple desecrated, though Soto forbade its burning. During combat outside many Pacahas were killed, though the Spanish forbade total slaughter. After a new pact the grieving Pacaha leader restored all the bones of his ancestors within their own temple, then ordered that it be purified and resanctified with a new holy fire. In such disasters, while the actual temple was lost or damaged, reserves of vitality seem to have been drawn upward from within the mound itself to renew town potency.

The next day Soto marched away, and he died soon after. His first grave in the earth seemed too vulnerable, so, for his second burial, he was weighted down into the depths of the Mississippi River (named by him the Espiritu Sancto ~ Holy Spirit). Luis de Moscoso de Alvarado then led the survivors into bleak Texas for a time before returning to the Mississippi. They presumed this hinterland was inhabited by herdsmen because so much meat was left behind after Natives fled from their camps. Yet they never saw a live buffalo (bison) or learned about the enormous herds, some of which were soon to move into the emptied Southeast. For part of the way they were deliberately misguided by a boy for eight days until Moscoso became suspicious and fed this valiant saboteur to the war dogs.

Along the Mississippi, as they prepared to occupy a Native town from which the inhabitants had fled, an old woman who had stayed behind warned Moscoso that the river would greatly overflow as it did every fourteen years. Indeed when their new brigantine ships were nearly built, a huge flood hampered final construction but made launching them much easier.

While Moscoso's force was departing, a local confederacy of ten tribes attacked the Spanish. As survivors floated down the Mississippi, they battled large canoes, each filled with ninety warriors. Every fleet was painted a different color. Eventually some of the Moscoso party reached Mexico, where they fought among themselves about their legacy of success or failure.

Garcilaso mused that these men thought only of precious, portable wealth, not of rich farmland or abundant harvests. The many long-term benefits of the Southeast went unrecognized by Spain for another century, and then were only half-heartedly celebrated. Subsequent disease had taken such a terrible toll that later writers seriously doubted the existence of complex chiefdoms described by Garcilaso and other, more accurate eyewitness chronicles.

The large number and size of mounds stood sentinel to this past greatness. Aspects of it can also be glimpsed in the ethnography of living communities in Oklahoma, where smaller mounds survive. Though more modest in size than those of their ancestors and unpopulated during most of the year, at today's annual Busk members regroup and mounds are rebuilt using ashes removed from the town fireplace and new soil specially taken from an appropriate direction.

Diseases and societal decay destroyed these chiefdoms, then the massive slaving industry of 1620–1700 further devastated the Southeast, selling whole tribes into oblivion, except for a few hapless *mustees*. Others were forced to merge into sizable nations for their own safety and survival. These nations eventually became the Cherokees, Creeks, Choctaws, Chickasaws, Koasati, Catawbas, Yuchi, and others less well known.

In the early 1800s, driven from their homelands in the Southeast, enforced by treaties and a law for "voluntary" Removal embraced by Jackson and his cronies, most of these tribes took land and refuge in Oklahoma. Special bearers, carrying tribal sacra on their backs, often preceded the members of a town on the long walk to the west. There many of the ceremonial grounds that were the last distillation of ancient chiefdoms were able to renew their fires, cache their holy objects, and again build mounds, often on leased or borrowed land that they have never owned. In consequence of this legal and social uncertainly, the mounds remain innocuous, and lesser targets for zealous Christian kin.

CHEROKEES

I now look closely at confederacies, especially the Cherokees and Choctaws, that merged in the aftermath of such damaged chiefdoms. (The next chapter is concerned with the pivotal Mvskoke Creek.) The Chickasaws, close kin of the Choctaws, became predatory militaristic slavers in their own defense.[26] Glimpses of former Sun worship, mound variability, and ranking will be highlighted.

In the southern Appalachians, sheltered in the Great Smoky peaks, Cherokees, during historic times, occupied four regions: Overhill (Upper Tennessee River), expanding into former Creek lands and contending with Chickasaws and Choctaws toward the southwest; Valley (Hiawasee River system), moving southward toward Creeks; Middle (Little Tennessee), noted for famous townhouse mounds, hunting northward in lands drained by the Ohio River, and fighting Yuchis and Iroquoians; and Lower (Upper Savannah), facing eastward and contending with Catawbas of the Carolinas (Fogelson 2004a; Schroedl 2000). The few Out Towns displaced from the eastern frontier provided the Native homesteaders whose property became the core of today's reservation in North Carolina. Despite massive forced removals, these Cherokees have remained in the East, maintaining a continuous presence among their ancestral towns and mounds.

Spoken Cherokee, the surviving southern Iroquoian language, has six pitches.[27] Known dialects (with their distinctive sounds) and their fates include Otali (speaking l, m, tl) of the Overhills, now spoken in Oklahoma; Kituwha (speaking l, m, ts) of the Middle Towns, still spoken at Qualla (Polly); Valley (close to Otali), spoken at Snowbird; and the extinct Elati (speaking r, w, ts) of the Lower Towns. Ironically Elati was the source for the tribal name CheRokee, where others have CheLvki. The genius of Sequoia (George Guess), a silversmith and merchant, produced a syllabary (consonant-vowel pairs) that made it a written and printed language in 1821.

With regard to mound linguistics, the Cherokee word for "earth ~ world" is *ela, eloni, elohi*, in contrast to the Creek *i:kana* (*ekvnv*; Timberlake 2007: 17). James Mooney cited *detsanvli* for "an inclosure or piece of level ground cleared for ceremonial purposes," especially Green Corn Rites, and *gati'yi* for "townhouse," which apparently derives from *gada* 'soil, dirt, earth' and *-yi* a locative for 'place(d).' It has become the term for modern stomp grounds as *gatiyo'i*. The word for mound is *ugwelvtvi* "it's bubbling up."[28] Townhouses were often built atop much more ancient mounds, attributed by some not to their own ancestors but to an ancient people who occupied the region before another group moved in and then were themselves displaced by the Cherokees (Mooney [1900] 1982: 515, 542; King 1975: 183; Feeling 1975: 91, 93, 116, 221).[29] While this denial of continuity was the usual response to impolite questioning, a priestly tradition concerning mound building, expressed by the masterful Swimmer (see introduction), remained specialized, private knowledge (Fogelson 1984; Conley 1993).

In 1762 Lt. Henry Timberlake (2007: 17) reported that the townhouse at Chota (*Itsodiyi* = 'fire place(d)'), where "are transacted all public business and diversions, is raised with wood, and covered over with earth, and has all the appearance of a small mountain at a little distance." Inside five hundred could be seated at this "metropolis" (capitol, sacred fire) of the Overhills. When the Cherokee national government, inspired by Euro-American types, formed in north Georgia, its capital became New Echota, where they fought legally and morally against their eventual deportation ("drive away") to Oklahoma.

Both redeemed and avenged by the U.S. Army execution of Tsali (Charlie) and his sons, some Cherokees remained in the Carolina Great Smokys at Qualla and Snowbird. With recent casino funds they have repurchased, at a cost of millions of dollars, their mother mound of Kituhwa, followed by that of Cowee ("deer"). Nikwasi, as noted, was purchased by local schoolchildren and saved as a public park at the industrial edge of Franklin, North Carolina.

While massive mound building was not a public aspect of Cherokee historical consciousness, a tradition of fire altars continues to this day. Major towns had two of these constantly renewed altars, periodically remantled with another layer of soil before meetings until entirely removed and rebuilt annually. One altar was public in the town council and the other was private within the sanctuary ("house of sacrifice") next door to it that was reserved for the chief priest (*uku* ~ *ukə*) and his aide. Each was composed of dirt piled a foot high, with a flat circular top where the fire burned, fueled by bark from seven kinds of trees (Anderson et al. 2010: 1: 47, 69, 238, 284; 2: 99, 521). Today in northeast Oklahoma, at ceremonial stomp grounds named for Redbird or Stokes Smith (father or son), central fires burn on the flat tops of a yard-high conical concrete base. Again, in miniature, mounding continues among Cherokees today.

CHOCTAWS

According to the earliest missionary among Choctaws, Alfred Wright, the Earth, before any other beings were made, was a "quagmire" with the (quivering!) consistency of clotted blood or jelly:

> At a remote period, the earth was a vast plain... and a mere quagmire. The word, which they use to express this primitive state, is applied to clotted blood, jelly, etc.
>
> While the world was in this situation, a superior being, who is represented to have been in appearance as a red man, came down from above, and alighted near the centre of the Choctaw nation, threw up a large mound, or hill, called in their language *Nunih waiya*, "stooping or sloping hill." When this was done, he caused the red people to come out of it, and when he supposed that a sufficient number had come out, he stamped on the ground with his foot.... The red people being thus formed from the earth, and seated on the area of the hill, their Creator told them that they should live forever. But not understanding him, they inquired what he said, upon which he took away the grant he had given them of immortality, and told them they would become subject to death. (Swanton 1931: 201)[30]

Thus, from the anchoring *Nanih Waiya*, the Creator initially promises immortality, but these emergents instead die because of their ingratitude (and dull wits). This death, however, is only transitional, an uncovering, "as the snake sheds his skin." In this way Choctaws received vitality instead of immortality. Each body had an inner *shilup* and an outer shadow (*shilomish*), but only the *shilup* went to the afterworld. The other became a kind of owl or fox whose terrifying night cries went unanswered by real, flesh-and-blood members of these species.[31]

The Choctaws were the subject of the last tribal compendium published by John Swanton, providing significant data and insights into issues of the southeast tradition.[32] With it he wrote his last massive work on four of the five "Civilized" Tribes. He left to his colleague James Mooney the presentation of Cherokee materials, largely provided by those who remained behind in the Carolinas. Similarly, while most of the Choctaws were forced to move to Oklahoma, some remained in their homeland in Mississippi and eventually prospered. Some resettled in Louisiana and have stayed on as Catholics.

Mounds were well integrated within Choctaw traditions. Some

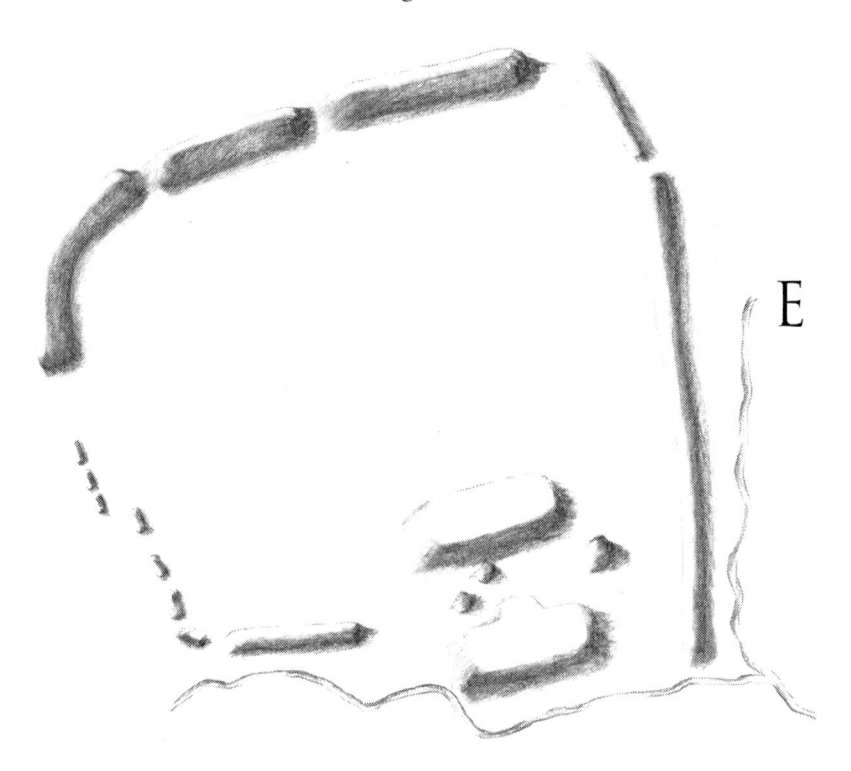

Nanih Waiya overview. Courtesy of the author.

communities traced their origins to a migration from the West, following a pole that began each day leaning toward their next destination. Others believed that their ancestors had come out of the famous "sloping" mound called *Nanih Waiya*.[33] Regardless of what came before, once they were in their homeland this notable mound became their symbolic heart and *tysic* at the confluence of the branches forming the Pearl River. It was also called *chåshki yakni* = 'my mother earth' and *inholitopa iski* = 'mother mound' (Carleton 1996, 1999).

In sum, this mound united people of different origins and regions. There those who had come out of the moist dark interior lay like locusts on its slopes to dry out and firm up to assume human careers. Later in their mythic past they lured up to the surface the Red Crawfish people (*shakchi humma okla* = Chakchiuma), also from an underground existence, and then had them dry out and humanize. There too those who had come from afar carefully piled and covered over the bone bundles of their dead after the guiding pole had disappeared by jabbing its way downward through the top of the mound, forming a long tube.

For those who continued to wander, mound building provided a devotional duty, so "it became an honorable thing to carry and deposit earth on the mound at any time they were not engaged at work in their domestic vocations." As the famous Choctaw leader Peter Perkins Pitchlynn noted, "So pleased were they with all that they saw that they built mounds in all the more beautiful valleys they passed through, so that the Master of Life might know that they were not an ungrateful people" (Swanton 1931: 19, 31; cf. Baird 1972).[34]

Choctaws did not have clans in recent times, though they use the term *iksa* for any special grouping, such as a church congregation of today.[35] They did and do divide into halves or moieties inherited through the mother, respectively called *Inholahta* = 'esteemed people' and *Kashapa okla* (*Imoklasha*) = 'divided people,' equivalent to the regional peace/war, elder/younger, and White/Red divisions.

Farming required a commitment to place, fostering the rise of kinship-based leadership for most communities. Ranking seems to have emerged along riverways, where what had formerly been an exchange along the entire river (upstream, downstream) became concentrated at the mouth as tribute, kickbacks, and favors. Chiefdoms rose and fell, depending on their resources, strategies, defenses, and luck. The major local chiefdom had been Moundville, though it became a necropolis (occupied only by the honored dead, visited for funerals, mourning, and special events) during its last stages.[36] Its descendants shifted to urn burial and moved south eventually to become the eastern Choctaws, associated with the moiety half known as honored *Inholahta*.

The largest continuous occupation near the present homeland was in the northern prairies, around the *Nanih Waiya* mound. These became the western Choctaws of the *Imoklasha* moiety, and the language of the Long People to the north, close to neighboring Chickasaws, became the standard speech shared by all. Their reverence for that mother mound also provided a shared national icon, where the bones of other groups may well have been deposited as an expression of unity. Some other ancestral Choctaw groups had ties to the Mississippi River, such as the Six Towns, who were related to the Natchez.

In their Mississippi homeland Choctaws constitute five bands, each once using an identifying marker. Those of Six Towns put blue tattoos at the corners of their mouth. Some wore a pouch made from a particular animal skin; for example, those of Bok Chito and Turkey Creek used otter skins. After population loss and early dislocations, survivors drew together as eastern and western Choctaws, joining into a populous tribe with dozens of towns. Today Mississippi Choctaws identify with eight rural communities.[37]

Thus Choctaws arose from the destruction of Mississippians between AD 1500 and 1700 in the aftermath of European diseases, slaving, and disruptions (Galloway 1995: 33, 40, 267, 303, 313, 354). The area that became their present homeland was vacant until then, as people had moved into better farming areas after the wholesale adoption of maize as a staple crop. The importance of farming grew as populations increased to overstress local crops and resources. Squash was grown four thousand years ago, but the combination of corn and beans, necessary to buffer the soil that maize alone would deplete, became established 1,200 years ago (AD 700 at Cahokia). Burned shell temper distinguished Mississippian pottery, made in larger forms for more crop storage.[38]

Customs shifted over time. Along the upper Tombigbee, the Miller Complex had grog-tempered pottery and mound burials until, about 1110 BCE, "blessed by an exploding population, Miller III peoples apparently ceased construction of burial mounds in favor of cremation and charnel houses" (Galloway 1995: 55).[39] Dense crowds of the living became reduced in death to ashes by fire rather than overwhelming the mounded earth. Thus cremation lessened the human impact on their territory, equally shared with species and spirits.

While coalescing, Choctaws adopted what had previously been the most honored form of burial, exposure, used for the elite among most tribes. A variety of other forms was applied to the bodies of lesser members. This defleshing by Buzzard Men, secondary burial in bone houses, and then placement into mounds served them until 1800, when it was replaced by the pole pulling, a disguised continuity reacting to Euro-Christian pressures (below).

Men were ranked as chiefs (*mingo*), as beloveds (*hatak holitopa*), as warriors (*tashka*), and as others without honors who had slain a "mere" woman or child. Inspired by fierce animals, warriors disguised their own trail by wearing the feet of panthers, bears, and buffalos and mimicking animal calls. Like others of the Southeast, Choctaws relied on blowguns for hunting small game. Later they learned to make new arrow points from the steel stays of women's corsets, until bows went out of fashion. Guns were acquired in trade and soon became obligatory gear.

Prisoners not sold into slavery were brought home alive, to be either adopted or killed, when all of the hairy parts of their bodies could be turned into scalps ~ trophies carried by women in victory dances. Afterward these are placed atop the community hothouse to decompose (Adair 2005: 199, 390). This direct placement of hair on the top of this domed building, equating it with a head, is notable. The skull was a special concern since Choctaws reshaped their infants' head, molding it under pressure from a weighted bag filled with sand and soil.

As elsewhere great enthusiasm surrounded the ball game (*toli ~ ishtaboli*). In a rare glimpse into the Mississippian era, Henry Halbert noted a shining act by a religious specialist or "prophet" to provide magical protection and vitality for his team: "Each carries a small looking-glass. He turns to the sun, holds his glass towards it with a gyratory motion then turns and throws the rays upon the bodies of the players of his side. This action of the prophet is a survival of the sun worship of the olden time. As all life and power comes from the sun, the prophet flatters himself that he can infuse a portion into his own party; and if he can utilize more of it than the prophet of the opposite side, his side will win the day" (Swanton 1931: 149, citing Halbert).

The game of chunkey (*ålchåpi*), its popularity spread with the rise of Cahokia, had its own special runway in each town, before it lapsed in the historic period. During the territorial shifts after epidemic depopulation, Choctaws and Creeks used two-stick ball games to try to settle the ownership of "a beaver pond on Noxubee River" and of land "between the Tombigbee and Black Warrior Rivers" (Swanton 1931: 148; cf. Ethridge 2003: 212). Both games, though, ended in pitched battles instead.

The most famous aspect of Choctaw culture was their manner of disposal of the dead until about 1800.[40] After someone died, the body was placed away from the house on a high scaffold to decompose. When the flesh was sufficiently loose, special officials (only one source mentions a woman) known as Bone or Buzzard Men—who grew very long nails on their thumb, fore, and middle fingers—prepared the bones into a bundle, which was added to those already in an appropriate bone house. A ladder leaning against this temple was draped with linked hoops made of grapevine. The flesh was either burned or buried, according to moiety.

When a temple was full, the bones were removed, arranged in an orderly pile, and heaped over with dirt that was planted over with grass to form a mound. The bone house itself was probably burned down. Each assemblage of bone bundles belonged to people who were related by kinship and locale, so every large "family" kept its own dead together.[41] At least one source mentions a separate temple holding only the bones of renowned warriors, which suggests that there may also have been some burial mounds based on career specialties or public esteem.

After 1800 Christian Choctaws gave up such exposure burial and left the body in an open grave with long poles, usually seven, placed along the sides as the grave was filled. Later the men who had been the former bone pickers returned in their new role as pole pullers, yanked up the side poles, ate a feast, and then left. Linked (daisy-chain) loops continued to hang from the tallest pole, clearly intended to provide some kind of ladder into the afterworld. Famous ballplayers had ball sticks hanging from their grave poles, suggesting there were special markers for some of the remains.

At their dances Choctaws gave thanks to other beings, often represented by the masks they wore. Like others of the Southeast, they believed that animals caused certain diseases that particular plants had pledged themselves to cure. Only at night did they perform the Snake Dance, making a gradual spiral like that of a coiling and uncoiling rattlesnake. In so doing they asked to be reborn into later lives. This dance was once the preferred way to end all Choctaw dances. Today they begin and end with the Walk Dance, entering and leaving at the east.

Mounds always played a crucial role in tribal identity and security, either by their ongoing construction during prehistory or by their conceptual anchoring of people to the land, as today among Choctaws living in Mississippi and elsewhere who continue to revere *Nanih Waiya*, their vital ancestral wellspring.

SUMMARY

Through tragedy and triumphs, losses and gains, the known tribal composition of the Southeast took shape between the Spanish incursions, led off by Hernando de Soto, and the struggles between English-speaking powers vying in disease, trade, war, and slaving. Comprehension of the enormity of trauma and despair in the Southeast slowly dawned among scholars, along with a grasp of the horrific environmental destruction, particularly of the alluring long-leaf pine forests. Originally this region was bountiful and densely occupied by farmers organized into ranked towns and tribes living along waterways. Many spoke Muskogean languages, though Iroquoians, Siouans, and Caddoans also participated.

Chroniclers of the Soto (then Moscoso) expedition described flourishing chiefdoms, but these soon succumbed to the germs spread by such invading foreign forces. While warfare and brutality took an immediate toll, epidemics were more deadly during the century between invasions. More recently grasped, though deliberately frustrated by obscured paper trails, was the massive scale of slaving (human trafficking) within the southeast shatter zone to sell and ship Natives into the Caribbean. In its aftermath many tribals managed to survive by merging into huge confederacies that coalesced around remnant chiefdoms, often in remote swampy areas where they were more likely to escape attack. The devastating depopulation caused by this destructive inter-Indien slaving soon led to the substitution of African slavery.

For immediate income surviving Natives hunted commercially to sell to the fur trade, especially deerskins. In return they purchased trade goods, which were desired because they were ready-made, without the time-consuming labor required for Native crafts. To supply steady foods women worked diligently in the corn fields. A series of seasonal rites marked the growth stages of the crop, culminating in the Busk to thank the plants before their final harvesting. In addition periodic revitalizations led by prophets served to morph ancestral beliefs and select those to be emphasized in the communal future.

A key example of nation growth is the Choctaws, whose spiritual focus became their mother mound in Mississippi. Nearby, ball games honed warrior skills and abilities while fostering fun and excitement. Farming and festivals unified communities, welcoming visitors. Tracking the motions of sun, moon, and stars served to schedule rituals at special locales, often mounds, temples, or the two combined, as among Chitamachas. Like today's Busk, yearly scheduling of the date depended on the phases of the moon (and sometimes the Big Dipper), while the timing during ritual events mirrored the daily movements of the sun during the actual rite.

Reciprocating, alternating roles as hosts and guests helped determine the annual sequencing of each rite among participating regional towns, so every Busk could be well attended without duplicating rites on the same date and forcing choices among conflicting loyalties. Of particular note, moreover, the songs and dances, though having the same names, were uniquely focused on each town and locale so that it could effectively revitalize itself every year.

Core beliefs and customs concentrated on the treatment of the dead, often during a long series of rites. Specialists oversaw the appropriate observances, depending on former rank and pedigree, for the deceased. While commoners were placed in the ground for once and all, nobles were treated to a laborious sequence of memorials, often involving a burial, exhumation, defleshing (excarnation), bone bundling, charnel house caching, and final mound entombment. Chiefs and their close nobles contributed to tribal unity after death by merging with the mortuary mound of their town, region, or tribe, contributing their life force to that safe weighty beacon on behalf of their descendants and community.

Sustaining these communities was a multilayered world—whose microcosm was the temple on its bulging mound—comprising heavens, sky, earth, waters, and abyss, the underworld of dangerous and terrifying beings.

Constant conflict pitted birds of the air against serpents of the (under) earth, divided by the thin skin of the tight or tensioned Earth's surface with a will of its own. In microcosm the layers of the mound, added at intervals of twenty-five (or so) years, evoked both the stratigraphy of the Earth and the spheres of the heavens. Each was also pierced by a hollow column (tube, duct, trachea) to facilitate the flux and flow of vitality.

IBOFUNGA
OHFVKV / HIGH ABOVE

✺

SUN *hasi* (*hvse*)
birds, winds, blood

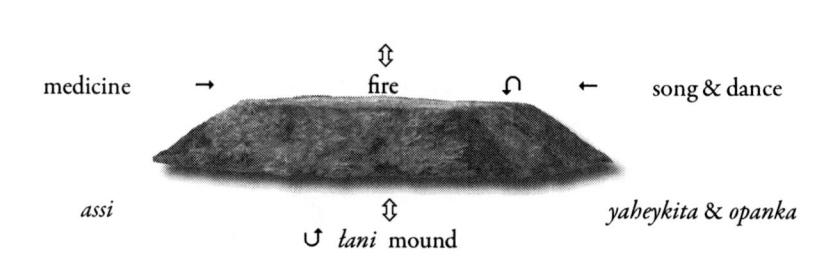

↕

⇕
medicine → fire ⏝ ← song & dance

assi ⇕ yaheykita & opanka
⏜ *łani* mound

↕

EARTH *i:kana* (*ēkvnv*)
honanwa ~ honan-ta:ki = ♂　　♀ = *hokti: ~ hokt-aki*
⇕
snake ~ water ~ turtle
citto ~ oywa ~ loca
ξ ❀

Mound dynamics. Designed by the author with Vic Kucera.

4

Modern Mounding

Since today's most active context for the ongoing construction of mounds is the Busk of the Creeks, the annual Green Corn Ceremony held in Oklahoma at a dozen surviving ceremonial towns (*italwa ~ etalwv*), a series of representative descriptions, over time and locales, compose this chapter.[1] Its major features were ~ are the addition of earth to an existing mound, the lighting of a new fire, the taking of "herb water" (holy *assi*) for purification, and a series of dances. Gender significantly contrasted the Ribbon Dance by women with the Feather Dance by men, mediated by the Buffalo and Stomp dances involving both men and women in alternate rows. For the mother town of Tukabatchee, their rite was described both in the Alabama homeland and then, after Removal, in Oklahoma. This town has since lapsed, and its members now attend Busks in other towns. That they can do so speaks to the overall vitality of the tradition.

MVSKOKE CREEKS

Ibofvnga ('High Above'), at the very start of this world, moved Thought into action, creating all. There had been only sea and sky, where its inhabitants counseled together to make the Earth upon the vast sea below. Eagle, selected to lead and deciding for solid land, sent beings to look for a speck to begin the process. Dove looked for four days but found nothing. Crawfish dove into the water, was gone four days, and returned with a bit in one claw. Eagle took darts, made a ball of the dirt speck, and formed an island, perhaps by throwing at the rolling orb (chunky game?). As waters receded from this land, animals moved in. Based on the actions of these beings at specific places, over twenty matriclans were inspired and named.[2] Divided between Red and White halves, each is traced through the mother; its members once had to marry into the other half. Finally, before humans arrived, these beings met together, each animal admitting which disease it caused and then a plant offering to remedy that malady as a medicine enhanced by dicta (secret ritual formulae) infusing its brewing ~ bubbling.

Migrating from the West, some or all of the Creek people followed a pole toward the sunrise. Each night the pole leaned in the direction of the next day's travel. When it stood upright, often on a mound, it marked the final destination of Creeks and their towns. These Mvskoke peoples, sometimes comparing themselves to swarms of bees (Waselkov and Braund 1995: 143), settled along rivers draining into the Gulf of Mexico and continued traditions extending from Mississippians and other mound builders of prehistory.[3] Each *italwa* ~ *etalwv* was a distinct community, composed of an array of clans and phratries, though identified with only one of the halves as either a White peace town or a Red war town. The outside walls of its palisade, houses, and temples were painted the appropriate color.

These moieties are called by words that mean 'Those alike' (= *Hathagalgi* ~ *hvthakvlke* ~ *hatha:k-alki*) for White and 'Those of different speech' (= *Tcilokogalgi* ~ *celokhohvlke* ~ *cilo:kho:k-alki*) for Red. White towns were devoted to peace and Red ones to war; to domestic tranquility or to foreign relations. White towns, especially the mother towns, provided asylum to all as a sacred trust. When the grand White town of Apalachicola failed to protect English traders who fled there for sanctuary, the town dissolved forever (Swanton 1928e: 250). (Descendants, however, still live in southwest Georgia as well as Oklahoma.)

In time the Red and White halves permeated the large confederacy led by four mother towns. For the Upper Creeks along the Coosa and Tallapoosa branches of the Alabama River, these were Tukabatchee (Red) and Arbihka (White). Along the Flint and Chattahoochee rivers, branching from the Apalachicola of Georgia and Florida, were Kashita (White) and Koweta

(Red ~ Coweta) for the Lower Creeks.[4] Each town had an emblem atop its temple or its ball pole. That of Koweta was an eagle with a blood-spotted mouth. During the 1500s the ancestors of Arbihka belonged to a paramount chiefdom known as Coosa, impacted by the Soto invaders. Tukabatchee may have originally been composed of migrant Shawnees, though links to Coosa also seem likely.[5]

Women and men were ~ are regarded as virtually separate peoples. Women sustained family efforts, doing the cooking, cleaning, and other housework, making pottery and baskets, and spinning and weaving for clothing and coverings. Men hunted and made the tools, weapons, and buildings, working in spurts of intense effort for the hunt, war, ritual, and crafts in wood and stone. Both worked in the fields growing huge crops of corn, beans, squash, and other vegetables. Everyone helped during communal fishing for large quantities, using weirs and fish poisons to stun all those within an impounded area. Nuts, as food and oil, had a prominent role in the southeastern diet and economy, starting thousands of years ago in the Dalton Archaic.

Regular burning over of the landscape, fish impounds, wetlands bounty, and nut harvests and the constant need for firewood helped leaders to manage the entire local ecology systematically. As safeguards intertown buffer zones and transitional ecotones protected animal and plant populations from overkill (Williams and Shapiro 1990: 15, 87, 135, 146).

Competitive activity focused, as noted, on the two-stick ball game, in pole or goal forms. For fun, men played against women around a center pole. When deadly serious, opposing towns fielded men's teams for match games vying between goal posts, with many injuries, casualties, and occasional deaths. In some instances games were played against enemies in lieu of battle, though hostilities often erupted, as noted for the Choctaws and Creeks. The ball game was known as the "younger brother" of war. If teams belonged to either half, the defeat of one by the other four times in a row meant that the losing town had to extinguish its fire, whether Red or White, and rekindle a new one from the fire of the winning town, thereby shifting to the other moiety.

Into the 1700s each *talwa* had a central square where its fire burned, surrounded by open cabins (often called a 'bed') at the sides.[6] That of the Mikko or chief was on the west, facing the east of the rising Sun.[7] Historically, to supply the fur trade, wealthy families similarly lived in compounds with four buildings set around an open courtyard. Each building was put to a different use, such as cooking, storage, warehouse (to hold furs for the best price), guest rooms, summer cool spaces, or winter warm ones. Prehistorically each family had open summer and closed winter houses.

Nearby was the town rotunda ~ hothouse for wintertime use, hosting secluded and sheltered meetings. The front part, nearest its inclined and covered entryway, was used for public meetings. The middle section had seats where leaders quietly conferred together. The back was dark and used by priests to meet in seclusion and to store sacred objects (sacra) out of the way (and sight).

Outside, a long runway was used for the competitive game of chunkey, played, as noted, by throwing long poles after a rolling stone disk. Nearby was a tall stickball pole topped with the emblem of the town, such as a swiveling fish, skull, or wooden ball. In earlier times important towns also had a temple set high on an earthen mound near the middle of the community and poles set up for the torture and sacrifice of captives. Later severe population loss due to European diseases and trauma made impossible such enormous construction projects. Smaller mounds did ~ do survive, however. These piles are added to each year either by using dirt removed by cleaning and scraping off the overgrown surface of the town square or by adding the ashes from the previous year's fires.[8]

Men were ranked on the basis of seniority and of war titles earned by bravery or cleverness. Hereditary grades included those of leaders (*mikkagi*), managers (*henihalgi*), "honored men" (*isti atcagagi*), and warriors (*tastanagali*).[9] Each war party was once entrusted with a special ark, often featuring a stuffed owl, that it was pledged to protect at all cost. The four war titles were ~ are *hardjo* for 'crazy, mad,' *fiksigo* (*fixico*) for 'heartless,' *imathla* for 'leader,' and *yahola* for 'yell, whoop.'[10] The famous patriot, born in an Alabama Creek town before he fled to safety in Florida among the Creek fugitives who became known as Seminoles, was named *Assi Yahola*

= 'herb water whoop' (Osceola). This sound has complex meanings as both a challenge in war and a prayer in ritual. In formal settings a person drank *assi* for the length of time that the cup server sustained *yaahoolaa*.[11]

Creeks have always been famous for the complex skills of their Native doctors (*aliikča* = fasters, with curing specialties; Swanton 1928d: 615, 617). These included knowers (*kiiłła*), who diagnosed from details of the patient's clothing; weather workers, so vital among farmers concerned about the loss of crops; and medicine makers (*hilis haya*), who prepared the herb water (*assi*).

The fasters went through a series of medical workshops known as "bush schools" (seminars) where a skilled healer was hired by a group of novices to teach them his skill.[12] As the students fasted for a fixed number of days (beginning with four, moving on to eight, and then twelve), the healer spoke to them at noon and sunset, when the sun was particularly strong—to add to the quality of that medicine. After these four days the boys and men rested and thought about what they had learned. About a week later they began another session of fixed days, gaining more details about a treatment. After the full twelve-day session the novice was buried underground, breathing through a cane tube. Dry leaves were scattered over this "grave" and set afire. Then the novice was dug out and considered reborn, having experienced his own burial and cremation to graduate as reborn ("cooked") in curing arts.

Certain emblems indicated specialties. These included a buzzard feather for treating gunshot wounds, a horned owl feather for healing skill, and a fox skin for snake bite. Those more skilled used cupping and scratching, as well as sweat baths, to cure patients. Women too were doctors, often midwives and dispensers of home remedies.

The danger of all this knowledge and skill, of course, was that it could be used selfishly and for sorcery. Witches, associated with harmful nighttime activities in the guise of owls and invisibly shooting harm into victims, were despised. In Creek belief a witch had a body full of lizards that had to be fed bewitched victims or else they began to eat up the witch from the inside. Only a more powerful doctor could exorcise, overcome, or kill such a harmful force aimed against the good of the community.

LAMAR

The Creek Confederacy was a historic amalgamation of the survivors of some of the mighty chiefdoms (*talwa*) ravaged by Soto (Smith 1987: 29, 77, 89, 139). Archaeologists refer to this period between 950–1800 CE as Lamar.[13] The Lamar-type site (AD 1400–1600) near Macon (Georgia) had a palisade around two platform mounds, one rectangular and one round with a spiraling outer ramp (like a coiled snake).

At Toqua (site 40MR6), the capital of the Dallas Phase (ancestral to Koasati) of Lamar in the eastern Tennessee Valley, the largest mound aligns the site to the winter solstice.[14] Most burials also share this alignment. Moreover, while other sky alignments also occur, there is a distinct void around the summer solstice orientation, showing that it was distinctly avoided. Within Dallas there are five levels of sociopolitical complexity, extending from farmstead to multimound capital.

Just before and after 1600 in the Georgia pine barrens, the Creek heartland drained by the Okmulgee, Oconee, and Satilla rivers, a distinctive pottery design featured four crossed lines (+) extending from a central encircled dot ⊙. It was named for its obvious evocation as Square Ground Lamar and forcefully symbolized the integrative power that this public plaza exerted on the emerging unity of the Creeks (Williams and Shapiro 1990: 15, 87, 135, 146), who had ceased to build mounds.

To trace the subsequent enormity of epidemic devastation, Marvin Smith has plotted European impact on Interior Southeast sites into five periods, each the length of a long generation. For the famous Coosa River drainage, these periods (with their dated type site) are 1540–70 CE (King site), 1570–1600 (1Ce308, Terrapin Creek after 1590), 1600–1630 (Bradford Ferry), 1630–70 (Cooper Farm), and 1570–1700 (Woods Island). The great divide was 1600, after which no massive mound was ever built again. From 1550 onward the sites shrink and keep moving downriver into the areas of concentration occupied by historic Creek towns whose names can often be traced to chiefdoms ravaged by Soto. Population losses are seen in the lapsing of labor-intensive efforts such as mounds, palisades, moats, fine grave goods, and specialized crafts.

For example, the chiefdom of Oconee (Ocute of Soto) had five town sites, evenly spaced apart, with mounds. The largest (Shoulderbone) had five mounds. Before 1600 European trade goods were hoarded by the elite, but afterward they seem to have been widely available to everyone. During the early trade era individual effort to secure hides, furs, and foods to barter was rewarded by greater access to an increasing number of European traders, who offered glass, iron, brass, and china goods in return.

In the aftermath of killing epidemics, European rivalries, slaving raids, and other life challenges, survivors of destabilized communities migrated to new places and amalgamated with others to assure necessary strength in numbers. Some took up the role of predators for the slave trade. Foremost among these were the Erie, displaced from the eastern Great Lakes in 1654–56. Once they acquired guns they moved to menace western Virginia, and then became known as the Westo around Augusta, Georgia, before 1670. Strongly allied with the South Carolina colony, they raided Spanish Florida for slaves and booty. Once the Carolinians grew in strength, all too typically they hammered and dispersed these former allies in the Westo War of 1680. Survivors fled into the interior to join the emerging Lower Creek confederacy or drifted back to Ohio to merge with the Mingo (Bowne 2005).

The symbolic centering of Creeks on the town and region known as Okmulgee began during the 1680s and lasted until 1716, to avoid attacks by Spanish soldiers and to be nearer traders (Hahn 2004: 49–50).[15] For a thousand years this Macon Plateau had been a province noted for its mounds and a series of huge earth lodges (winter hothouse).[16] After their exile to Oklahoma, the Creek Nation revived Okmulgee as the name of their new capital.

Over time and traumas Ocute became Oconee, Tama (Altamaha) became Yamassee, and mighty Coosa fragmented into closely allied towns such as Arbihka and Tulsa. Tuskegee left eastern Tennessee and slowly moved south into modern Alabama, where black airmen training for combat in World War II made the name famous. Cofitachiqui, noted for its queen kidnapped by Soto, faded in the Carolinas as the Catawbas emerged (see Beck 2009; Fitts and Heath 2009). Of the four Creek mother towns, only

Coosa had extensive contacts with Europeans and became fragmented in consequence, though Arbika survives as its heir. Relying on more remote locations and much less interference, those of the Lower Creek (Kasihta, Kowita) and Upper (Arbika, Tukabatchee) maintained an integrity that provided a model and inspiration for their coalescing confederacy.

Under pressure from land-hungry and unscrupulous settlers, mixed Lower Creek families with Scots trader fathers assumed prominence and began a national government camouflaged as a European model, led by Alexander McGillivray and later by William McIntosh, who was executed by Creek national decree for selling tribal lands in 1825, in violation of an official ban voted by the Creek Nation government.

Of particular note, McGillivray provided our only description of a Busk written by a Creek national. It was the four-day rite typical of the smaller towns, in this case Hickory Ground (*Talisi*; Swan 1855: 251–83, Busk 267–68). For the longer eight-day version in the mother towns, we have (below) an informed (though partial) account for Tukabatchee in 1835, just before the forced move to Oklahoma, as well as a summary for the rite afterward in Oklahoma. Benjamin Hawkins described the eight-day rite at Cussetuh, his spelling for the mother town of Kashita (White). After each account is presented separately, they will be compared to fill in gaps and find consistencies.

During the Red Stick Rebellion (1813–14), a Creek civil war turned to American advantage by Andrew Jackson and others, the confederacy weakened. Their lands were increasingly alienated until, in 1836, 2,500 Creeks were forced to Oklahoma. Another fifteen thousand, suffering high mortality, were driven west in 1837. Once in Oklahoma they reestablished their own bicameral government at the new Okmulgee, and there built at the town center the Creek Council House in stone. It was divided into a House of Kings, composed of the town *mikkos*, and a House of Warriors, with each *talwa* sending two delegates. In 1906, when Oklahoma became a state, Congress arrogantly abolished the governments of the Creek Nation, as well as the other Five ("Civilized") Tribes—Cherokee, Choctaw, Chickasaw, and Seminole. Today, though this land base was taken away, tribal governments still rule at their national headquarters, staffed by elected officials and hired employees. Their sovereignty and jurisdictions cover their past lands that are now listed in terms of state counties. The hub of the Creek National Council and its officers, aptly, is the building called The Mound, an architect's re-creation of an earthen dome with the offices inside and underground surrounding the central meeting space of the National Council.

LITTLE TALISI BY ALEXANDER MCGILLIVRAY

Beginning "the ceremony of the busk is the most important and serious of any observed by the Creek Indians," this Native chronicler describes a four-day rite held when the corn is ripe for harvest (Swan 1855). At dawn a "priest, dressed in white leather moccasins and stockings, with a white dressed deer-skin over his shoulders," kindles a new fire by friction. Once he has a steady flame, he continues his prayers as three sets of four young men (3 x 4 = 12), each entering from a corner, carry in offerings. The first group has four small logs as firewood arranged to form the cross + pointing in the four directions. The second line has ears of corn to place beside each log. The third has new cassina (yapon holly leaves ~ *assi*), which are parched to brew into *herb water* as a few are also fed to the fire.

> [The] warriors and others being assembled, they proceed to drink black drink [as glowing coals] of the new fire [are] left on the outside of the square, for public use. [Women take these coals to restart their fires at home,] which have the day before been cleaned [out], and decorated with green boughs for its reception.... During this day, the women are suffered [*sic*] to dance with the children on the outside of the square, but by no means suffered to come into it. The men keep entirely to themselves, and sleep in the square.
>
> The second day is devoted by the men to taking their war-physic [brewed of] button snake-root, or senneca [sometimes to the excess of producing spasms or worse].
>
> The third day is spent by the young men in hunting or fishing, while the elder ones remain in the square and sleep, or continue their black drink, war-physic, etc., as they choose. During the first three days of busking, while the men are physicking, the women are constantly bathing.[17] It

is unlawful for any man to touch one of them, even with the tip of his finger; and both sexes abstain rigidly from all kinds of food or sustenance, and more particularly from salt.

On the fourth day, the whole town are assembled in the square, men, women and children promiscuously, and devoted to conviviality. All the game, killed the day before by the young hunters, is given to the public; large quantities of new corn, and other provisions, are collected and cooked by the women over the new fire. The whole body of the square is occupied with pots and pans of cooked provisions, and they all partake in general festivity. The evening is spent in dancing, or other trifling amusements, and the ceremony is concluded.

KASHITA, GEORGIA, BY HAWKINS

Benjamin Hawkins, federal agent, described a full eight-day "Boos-ke-tau" at Kashita, the White mother town of the Lower Creeks. Here is his summary (Foster 2003: 75s–77s):

> [1st day] "Warriors clean the yard of the square, and sprinkle white sand, when the a-cee [*assi* = decoction of cassine yupon leaf] is made." [The Fire maker kindles the new flame as early as he can, while warriors cut and bring in four logs, each as long as a span of both extended arms.[18] Shaped into a cross by these logs, the new fire at the center of the square will burn with these logs for four days.]
>
> "They collect old corn cobs and pine burrs, put them into a pot, and burn them to ashes. Four virgins who have never had their menses, bring ashes from their houses, put them in the pot and stir all together [before dividing them into two pots].[19] The men take white clay and mix it with water in two pans. One pan of the clay and one of the ashes are carried to the cabin of the Mic-co, and the other two to that of the warriors. They then rub themselves with the clay and ashes. Two men appointed to that office, bring some flowers of tobacco of a small kind, (Itch-au-chu-le-puc-pug-gee,) or, as the name imports, the old man's tobacco, which was prepared on the first day, and put in a pan on the cabin of the Mic-co, and they give a little of it to every one present.

"The Micco and counselors then go four times round the fire, and every time they face the east, they throw some of the flowers into the fire. They then go and stand to the west. The warriors then repeat the same ceremony. . . .

"The pin-e-bun-gau, (turkey dance,) is danced by the women of the turkey tribe [clan]; and while they are dancing, the possau is brewed. This is a powerful emetic. The possau is drank from twelve o'clock to the middle of the afternoon. After this, the Toc-co-yule-gau, (tadpole,) is danced by four men and four women. (In the evening, the men dance E-ne-hou-bun-gau, the dance of the people second in command.) This they dance till daylight."

[2nd day] "About ten o'clock, the women dance Its-ho-bun-gau, (gun dance.) After twelve, the men go to the new fire, take some of the ashes, rub them on the chin, neck, and belly, and jump head foremost into the river, and they return to the square. The women having prepared the new corn for the feast, the men take some of it and rub it between their hands, then on their faces and breasts, and then they feast."

[3rd day] "The men sit in the square."

[4th day, Women, early in day, get (glowing) coals from the new fire, clean out their own hearths, sprinkle them with sand, and remake their home fires. The initial four logs burn out at the central fire. Men put ashes on their chin, neck, and belly, then go to water.] "This day they eat salt, and they dance Obungauchapco, (the long dance.)"

[5th day, Four new logs were set at the fire. Men drink a-cee.]

[6th day] "They remain in the square."

[7th day] "Is spent in like manner as the sixth."

[8th day] "Two large pots filled with water and fourteen of 'their physic plants' are beaten by chemists (E-lic-chul-gee), who 'blow in it through a small reed, and then it is drank by the men, and rubbed over their joints until the afternoon.'"[20]

"A cane is stuck up at the cabin of the Mic-co with two white feathers in the end of it. One of the Fish [Foster 2003: 78s] tribe, (Thlot-lo-ul-gee,) takes it just as the sun goes down, and goes off towards the river, all following him. When he gets half way to the river, he gives the death whoop; this whoop [*yahola*] he repeats four times, between the square and the water's edge. Here they all place themselves as thick as they can stand, near the edge of the water. He sticks up the cane at the water's edge, and they all put a grain of the old man's tobacco on their heads, and in each ear. Then, at a signal given, four different times, they throw some into the river, and every man at a like signal plunges into the river, and picks up four stones from the bottom. With these they cross themselves on their breasts four times, each time throwing a stone into the river, and giving the death whoop; they then wash themselves, take up the cane and feathers, return and stick it up in the squares, and visit through the town.[21] At night they dance O-bun-gau Haujo, (mad dance,) and this finishes the ceremony.

"This happy institution of the *Boos-ke-tuh*, restores man to himself, to his family and to his nation. It is a general amnesty, which not only absolves the Indians from all crimes, murder only excepted, but seems to bury guilt itself in oblivion."

TUKABATCHEE, ALABAMA, 1835 BY PAYNE

John Howard Payne attended much of the Busk at Tukabahtchee in 1835 (Swanton 1932: 170–95), the year before that town was deported to Oklahoma under federal and state threats during the era of Jackson's brutality and the misnamed "voluntary" Indian Removal Act.[22]

Tukabatchee (Red) mother town was itself distinguished by the ownership of special copper panels displayed at special occasions. Because of its vital position, its Busk lasted eight days instead of the four days celebrated by the many daughter towns like Talisi. Though Payne did not see the entire ceremony, he did note the distinguishing features of each day in the series. These were (1) arrival, (2) women's first Ribbon Dance, (3) New Fire and fasting, (4) Gun Dance, (5) Hunt, (6) women's second Ribbon Dance,

(7) fasting, and (8) finale.²³ In a sense the first four days were devoted to plants and the second four to animals.

Each year three prior dances, spaced about a month apart while the corn was growing in the fields, led toward the Busk. At the first, new pottery vessels to brew *assi* were commissioned from a skilled woman potter. At the second, new mats were planned for the seats inside the four men's cabins. At the third, identical bundles of "broken sticks" were sent out to all of the satellite communities.²⁴ Each discarded one stick per day in order to time their simultaneous arrivals at this Busk; in other words they came together when the last stick had been snapped and counted. Since pottery and mat making were women's specialties, it is likely that particular women of ranking matrilines were being honored by these special requests. Today such honor pertains to the selection of the two women who lead the Ribbon Dance.

This Busk was held at a square ground set apart from the family houses. It had a substantial cabin ('bed') built on each side. Upright log posts were interwoven with wickerwork, plastered over with clay, and often painted either red or white, depending on the moiety affiliation of the town. Each cabin front, facing the central fire, was open, while the sides and back had only low walls to allow for air circulation and viewing below the peaked roofline. Inside was a platform and benches where only men sat. Elders at the front set their feet on the ground, while youngsters on the back benches sat with crossed legs. During the time the men occupied these cabins at the Busk, they went without sleep or food, fasting to give thanks and sacrifice to the crops still ripening in the fields.

Behind the square was a large conical building with a sloped entry, the hothouse, where councils met in winter and bad weather. Two earthen mounds were nearby. One consisted of the ashes scraped up from previous central fires to be "carefully and religiously preserved." The other was composed of soil that was removed from the surface of the open square every year prior to the Green Corn. New soil was then brought in and scattered over the square so that each Busk began with a fresh, untrodden earth surface. Their constituents therefore distinguish these two mounds, one of earth and the other of fireplace ashes.

Before the Busk began, all of the houses were swept out and cleaned. Then every home fire was extinguished. In the center of the square a new fire was started by five chiefs taking turns to whirl a shaft against a wooden base to ignite powdery kindling. Once this sacred fire was blazing, torches were ignited from it to restart all of the family fires. The newly made pots were put on the central fire and, with great solemnity, the "herb water" was brewed, its froth indicating vitality.

After giving three low, deep "wails" (*yahola* = yells, shouts, whoops), men formed double lines to approach the pots, where each drank a gourdful, paused, and then "ejected." Since they had been fasting, they proved their dedication by emitting only the frothy liquid they had just consumed. When all the men had tasted the drink, a seated chief made a speech, presumably of welcome. Everyone responded with "a long sound, seemingly of two syllables, but uttered by all in the same breath." Today that word would be *maa-doe*, meaning 'thank you.'

Accompanied by gourd rattles, the men rose and danced around the fire, using the distinctive stomp style that firmly set the sole of each foot against the ground. Many held fans of feathers that they waved in time with the song. At the end all of the men rushed down a ravine and plunged into the river. Visitors threw coins as offerings into the current, which boys dove to retrieve. Then all the men returned to the square for a series of dances in which their double lines made complicated patterns over the open ground. Sometimes meandering like a snake, the dancers also made spirals at the corners of the square as well as combinations of lines, curves, and rings around the fire.

Bundles of river canes, each with a (white) feather or two tied at the top, were removed from the front posts of each cabin and handed out to the men. Each dancer held one while dancing the Feather Dance, which Payne was told was "meant to immortalize triumphs won at ball-plays." In addition bird and sky images indicate that this dance was intended to evoke the celestial. At the end of the day children were scratched with "sail-needles, awls, and flints" on the legs. As the blood flowed, a stick or bit of bark was used to scrape it off and dash it against the back of the cabin. Of note, boys sat with their uncles (MB) because they belonged to the same clan, while their fathers sat with their own nephews (ZS).

The next day featured the Gun Dance, with women briefly occupying one of the cabins during a song. Four stuffed dummies were set up in the corners of the square. Two painted old men, holding a tomahawk or scalping knife, danced toward each other from halfway around the fire, emitting a low growling that ended in a war whoop as they met. Led by two men with gourd rattles, women filed out of the cabin and onto the larger mound, where they renewed their chant. From surrounding cornfields armed men rushed into the square to dispatch the dummies, variously capturing, knifing, shooting, or tomahawking them. After all this tumult the warriors formed a line and danced around the mound where women stood safely, then danced back into the square. At a final yell they all rushed out to scatter among the crowd, sometimes striking people along the way (to fortify them), before plunging into the river. Then they were entitled to feast on corn.

The next dawn, men went into the forests to hunt, providing meat for feasts. Some fishing was also done, probably using poisons to stun large quantities swimming in impounded waters. Hospitality required an abundance of foods.

During the day, at the Ribbon Dance, the women danced in long dresses, decorated with streaming wide ribbons of many colors. Their lower legs were wrapped with turtle shell rattles set in rows affixed to leather backing. During a shuffle step these shells produced a train-like chugging sound. The line of women circled three and a half times around the fire, led by two senior women, each holding a wooden blade (the *atassa*) with two feathers tied at the tip. After an hour's pause this dance was repeated. (Today this public event has many features of the ancient scalp dance.)

Last, everyone entered the square for the Ancient (Mother) Dance of men and women alternating in the row. Men yelped throughout, until a final whoop marked the very end of the Green Corn, "beginning the year with fasting, with humility, with purification, with prayer, with gratitude," as it is still done today.

Modern Mounding

TUKABATCHEE, OKLAHOMA, 1842 BY HITCHCOCK

In his diary entry for 2 February 1842, Maj. Gen. Ethan Allen Hitchcock (1996: 132–37), the formidable federal inspector, wrote of Tukabatchee and its Busk after the town had been forced to relocate in Oklahoma. He did not witness it but heard it described, so I have added some clarifications. His report fills gaps in Payne, especially for the end of the rite.

Beginning in July four planning meetings were held, spaced apart at intervals of seven (between councils one and two), four (between two and three), and two days (between and four). At the first, pots and utensils were "ordered" (from honored women). At the fourth, seven sticks called "broken days" were sent out, one snapped off each day of the count. On the fifth day the campers arrived at the square ground. The women danced, well decorated (with ribbons?), on the sixth day while fasting. After the dance they bathed in the branch (creek) to wash off 'medicine,' and then they could eat. That night men and women joined in a "friendly familiar dance," probably a stomp. Ball games, men against women, were held throughout the days that people were encamped.

On the sixth day (first of the Busk), after "the sacred fire is made in a small house within a corner of the square," fasting men took medicine. The famous copper and brass plates of this town were scoured shiny clean and then marched into the square about 1 p.m., preceded by two men shaking coconut rattles and followed by all the men singing, and, at the back, holding up river canes (tubes) decorated with white feathers.[25] They danced around the square four times, then danced inside and outside in four sets. Still fasting, they danced all night.

The next morning (the seventh), before dawn, two men appointed to be head warriors began the War (Gun) Dance. Each wore only a loincloth, their body painted and covered in ornaments, and held a pouch containing pipe and tobacco. Women sang the accompanying song, sometimes standing atop a freshly resurfaced (remantled) mound. Men, divided into two teams, scouted the ground from the outside. Three effigies, made to look like two men and a woman, were set up at corners. Once these enemies were spied out, messengers reported to the two dancing men, each of whom was then joined by a deputy.

To the rapid beat of a lone drum, each of these four men stalked a victim, ending up poised on one knee, weapon in hand, before an effigy. A very solemn song was sung, with the warrior teams providing the chorus. Once the women were safe atop the mound, the head warriors led an attack on the effigies and took the scalps, with much shooting and whooping. The men danced around the women on the mound four times, then ended for the day by "going to water" about 9 a.m. All feasted on fresh green corn and other vegetables, but avoided meat and salt.

No one should have eaten fresh corn before this, or even used a fire where new corn had been cooked. All of the home fireplaces were cleaned out, in preparation for starting a new fire from coals brought from the new fire of the square. Those who took medicine had to sleep chaste and alone within the ground for the next four nights.

The eighth day (third one of the Busk), men danced again with the plates, which were then put away for another year. Next they went hunting until about 2 p.m. People still ate only plant crops. On the fourth day of the Busk, fresh meat was served, garnished with salt, at breakfast. Women danced in the square during the day. The paired Buffalo Dance was held that evening. The next day everyone dispersed homeward except those few who remained because of final responsibilities at the mound and diminishing fire (Hitchcock 1996: 137–38).[26]

A SEMINOLE BUSK TODAY

Much of this prior Busk complexity is now gone. One man fills roles that several performed in the past. Fewer numbers are involved, and periodic gatherings to camp at the ground and mound now limit and simplify any involvement since the town is no longer a place of full-time residence. Three studies, two dissertations and a book, provide information on recent practices.[27] By combining their insights and details, a more comprehensive understanding emerges on present practices.[28]

In the best treatment of a modern-day Busk,[29] in one of the Seminole

Creek towns, James Howard and Willie Lena (1984: 123–56) note that it occurs over a long weekend to accommodate the constraints of wage labor during a work week. Families live in nearby villages and cities or come from far away, leaving houses with all the modern conveniences. For their Busk, therefore, members return to a rural place where the women manage camps (*hvpo*) that are roofs held up by support posts, with wood fires for cooking. Since the temperature during the day is often over 100 degrees, the heat is intense around these fires, adding to the sacrifice made by women. Propane-run refrigerators and ovens help to feed the crowds who attend as guests.[30]

The scheduling of dances must take into account events at other square grounds, especially those of ancient allies ("tied up together"), either descended from the same ancestral mother town, such as Coosa, or sharing the same fire by moiety affiliation (Robbins 1976: 67, 111, 121). Over the years towns tend to follow the same order, especially for their Busk, so everyone can plan ahead. The actual date is announced at the Spring Stomp Dance held a few months before the harvest season.

Thursday is the camp-in day, with women readying their outdoor kitchens. A stickball game may be played in the afternoon by men against women around a tall pole. An evening meal is served to all, and another pole game may occupy the twilight. Messengers called (night) deacons are sent by the Mikko (town chief) four times to the camps to announce a Stomp Dance that night. Those attending give money and tobacco (as cigarettes, cigars, and plugs) to the Mikko for the fasting men to smoke during the coming days and nights.[31] At midnight a Long Dance ends the stomp and all go to sleep, the men apart from the women.[32]

At about 5:30 a.m. on Friday the town crier awakens the men and they assemble in their arbors (*api:ti: ~ topv ~* 'bed') at the sides of the square.[33] They have fasted from food and water since midnight. Grabbing garden tools, men rake the entire inner surface of the ground (*pasko:fa* = 'swept within,' *tvceofv*) bare and clean. Any weeds are pulled out, and uneven places are filled in to level the ground for easy dancing. A low circular ridge (*tvce ~ paska tikin* = 'swept to the edge') marks the edge of the ground, made up of all the refuse that was raked out to there. The poles holding up the arbors are inspected and replaced if needed, using young trees cut nearby.

These saplings are always kept upright, never laid on the ground, since they hold up the arbors and thence the sky. Benches are examined for rot or damage to their stump supports and plank seats, and any weakened ones are replaced. Stringers, with some replaced, are evenly spaced out across the roof. Brown, dried willows from past dances are removed from the roofs and taken away to a remote area to decompose. At marshes, pickup trucks are filled with fresh-cut willows that are then driven around the outer square, pausing at each arbor. Some of these moist branches are tossed on each of the four roofs to provide sunshade and cooling by evaporation. Work moves counterclockwise from the Mikko's arbor in the west, to south, east, north, and back to west.

When everything is clean and tidy, all of the men stand outside the ring. Twelve special plants (= wormseed) are used to brush off each of the arbors, posts, and benches. Then one plant is placed in the crook of each of the three front posts. Called "killing the greenwood," it propitiates the freshly cut trees, protects the fresh arbors, and vivifies the square. If it is too hot and dry, water is sprinkled over the bare ground to keep dust down.

Meanwhile the Mikko has instructed men to clean off two oversized wooden knives (*atassi*), then coat them with white clay. The same clay is applied to two coconut-shell rattles. Small white crane feathers are tied at the tip of each knife and top of each rattle. At intervals the deacons are sent (four times in all) to the camps to tell the women to get ready for the Ribbon Dance.

At noon, when the sun is high, at some grounds the women begin the Ribbon Dance (*hoktaki o:panka* = 'women's dance'), wearing long colorful silk strands hanging from their dresses. Theirs is the first public use of the newly cleaned central plaza, and they finish its spiritual preparation. Their long patchwork dresses, beribboned blouses, and rattles secured on their leg calves are seen, while their diligent work remains unseen. Those leg rattles worn toward the front of the line are made of whole turtle shells, and those behind are perforated condensed-milk cans. They are shaken in a distinctive style, as noted, that sounds like a chugging railroad train. To honor the women men also dress up, often in new cowboy-style clothes, to sit in the arbors, urge on the dancing, and watch.

Modern Mounding

A red blanket is spread over a pair of folding chairs in the south arbor to be used by the two singers, who are given the coconut rattles. Each now places a long crane feather in his hat band. The Mikko gives to each of the two deacons a cane staff topped by a white feather. They then lead the women into the inner square ground, drawing a line in the dirt midway between the empty fireplace and the arbors, etching small circles to the side in front of the north and south arbors. The two women in front carry the wooden knives, with the handles wrapped in cloth so there is no direct contact with the skin. All of them wear or carry wet towels to wipe off their dripping faces in the heat of the day.

For the first song the women tread in place, heel-toe left, heel-toe right. At the second dance the lead woman, a respected matron, dances out in front, halfway around the circuit, to stand inside the north scratched circle. Thereafter she keeps a quarter pace ahead of the line, pausing at each arbor. As the women approach the starting point, they hop, pounding the pellets in their leg rattles. Men cry out an encouraging *lodja lodja* = 'turtle turtle.' Small girls at the end of the line are called "the tail" and also thanked loudly.

A second set follows before the drained women are allowed to rest and drink from a bucket and ladle carried among them by the deacons. They are also offered sticks of gum. The final two sets are then danced, and dressed-up men file onto the ground to form a regular Stomp Dance, as a line of alternating men and women, which ends this event. Everyone is invited to eat in the camps. A stick ball game may be held in the afternoon, before supper. Another Stomp Dance is held at 9–12 that night.

The next morning, Saturday, the men, again fasting, gather inside the ring before dawn and use shovels to remove the ashes and mounded earth of the central fireplace (*tvco* ~ *tvcopaskv*). These are added to a nearby mound, at human height, in the southeast.[34] The fire spot is leveled and inspected. Men stand behind each of the middle back posts of the arbors and help to sight on a peg that is pushed into the exact center of the square. New dark soil, often taken from a specific direction, is then brought by wheelbarrow to rebuild and bless this low fire mound.

A new fire is laid with fresh logs in a cross (+ ~ plus sign) shape. A tree has been cut into four lengths, and each is placed to align to a cardinal direction.

Each growing tip is pointed away from the fire, as though nourished by it. The medicine man blows (mouthing dicta) along each length to bless and pray before setting it down. The logs are positioned at the north, south, west, and east. The same procedure is done with four ears of corn, which are placed beside each log.

Tinder is placed in the center and a pure flame is lit to start the fire. Meanwhile women have put out the flames in their own camps and cleaned out their fireplaces. The deacons are told to announce when enough glowing coals have been produced so boys can carry new fire to the family camps, usually on long-handled shovels.

This fire is the earthly parallel of the Sun, buffered from the earth's surface itself by being set atop a small raised and flattened mound disk. It and all the fires in the camps must be extinguished yearly in order that it sink into the ground and "forget" (in short-term memory) any anger of the past year that could have adverse effects (Bell 1984: 100). This forgetting explains why murderers and other offenders gain amnesty if they can safely enter a square during the Busk that is held a year after their crime.[35]

In the square, watched by the new fire, preparations begin for making the medicine. Button snakeroot and red willow have been gathered before dawn.[36] These are pounded soft and placed in a tub or crock of fresh water.[37] The medicine man then blows into them through his cane tube (*spofkita*), bubbling, blessing, and praying while everyone on and near the ground is absolutely silent so only these sounds can enter the medicine. After steeping, one frothy ladleful is sprinkled by a man spiraling around the open plaza, and another measure is poured slowly onto the fire. This offering of medicine serves to "cool" these places. Everyone cries *ma-do* = 'thanks.'

Women and children gather outside the ring. They carry containers to hold medicine, which they drink and wash with. Some is taken back to the camps for immediate use. Women and girls come forward to be scratched with a needle or thorn that marks four parallel lines along the arms and legs. The scratcher should be a man of the same clan, to keep the wounds light and "friendly."

Then the men file up, paired by arbor, to drink and wash with the medicine. Both plants are used only the first time; just willow roots are used for the other three sessions. Each male is given a dipperful, or more by request. Using two fingers, the man first splashes the medicine to the four directions before drinking and washing with it.[38] The crooked left ring finger flicks the medicine because it has "no name" and forgets easily, especially any ill will. Some officials are expected to step off into the field and vomit up a frothy discharge to show that they have indeed fasted. Some are scratched.[39] Each arbor's members proceed in the order of west to south to north.

After the second taking, new members are named, each receiving a plug of tobacco while standing before the west arbor and then running counterclockwise around the fire and whooping. The plug is kept or given to a respected man in hope of a return blessing. The name is recorded in the town ledger kept by the Mikko as that newly named person takes his place in the arbor of his own mother's clan.

The men then prepare for the Feather Dance (= *ta:fv o:panka*), their complement to the Ribbon Dance. A man of the Bird clan takes a staff topped with a white feather and stands on a tiny mound in the northeast that was rebuilt at the same time as the fireplace that morning. It is just wide enough for his two feet. Using a low, drawn-out cry, he "calls the birds." Other men of the Bird clan have tied white feathers atop many cut river canes. These are passed out among the men, each holding one.

The men file around the ground, led by two men shaking the coconut rattles and another beating a water drum formed by a wet skin fastened over a ceramic crock partially filled with water. Four circuits are made during each dance, pausing at each arbor. Overall there are four sets. If the afternoon is very hot, only two sets may be danced, and the last two are done during the cooler evening or next morning. Because they are in the midst of taking and drenching in medicine, the men do not dress up, and young men often wear cutoff jeans. The wands are carried upright during the march but clacked together over the heads of the musicians at the end. The four songs refer in turn to blue crane, snake, buzzard, and circling birds preparing to fly south.

After two dance sets, men take medicine a third time. Then the last two Feather sets are often danced. From the moment they began taking medicine, men pair up for the rest of the night. They are never to be alone so as

Modern Mounding

not to be tempted to sleep, eat, womanize, or drink until the proper time. A collection is taken up for the *hilis haya* and given to him with shouts of *ma-doe*. Transferred out of the town along with the money is any anger or resentment among members because the medicine man is technically an outsider (Bell 1984: 209).

After the Feather Dance and "touching medicine" are finished, a beef (or deer) tongue is placed on the fire "to feed it and give it voice" (Bell 1984: 172, 300). In some cases it is first placed on the swept-up rim around the ground until the medicine "touching" is done, then it is picked up between ball sticks and placed on the fire. Usually, however, it is stuck on a carefully peeled forked stick beside the fire to cook before it is finally put deep into the flames. Its consumption marks the end of the formal fasting.

After the fourth medicine taking, the men "go to water," retiring to a nearby stream or metal tubs to wash off, sometimes counting off so all can hear the exact number of participants. As they march to this location, men whoop back and forth along the line. They return to their arbors for a final prayer and instructions. Then they go to the camps to eat, but they are forbidden to sleep. A stick ball game may occupy the afternoon.

At twilight people, nicely dressed, gather in the square for the Buffalo Dance (= *yanasa panka*), alternating pairs of men and women along the line. The men hold staffs or ball sticks to represent front legs. This dance begins at the tiny mound where the bird caller stood before the Feather Dance and the drummer now stands. The step is a double pat of left foot followed by two rights. At the end the deacons gather up the staffs and the dancers form a single file for the twisting, spiraling Long Dance and a final Stomp Dance. The camps again feed everyone.

At dusk the men of the ground gather for a special evocation of their ancestors in the Mothers ~ Ancient Dance. Then only members of the ground dance the first four Stomps, each led by a member of one of the arbors. Thereafter visitors are selected by the deacons to lead stomps all through the night. No medicine taker can sleep, but they can eat and drink tea, coffee, soda (pop), and water.

On Sunday, after the sun appears in the sky, the last dance is held, and the men take a final round of medicine before they go to water and are dismissed after a final speech. During the morning a stick ball game is held while everyone waits for the seen fire to burn itself out for another year.

Members of a square ground will gather four times during the year to take medicine, but the Busk is the most elaborate and intense of these. The Stomp Dance season is active from the first budding of trees to first frost. Two of these dances are held in the spring, the Busk in late summer, and the fourth in the fall, according to the Gregorian calendar. For Creeks, however, the sequence begins with the Busk and continues through the fall and spring to bracket the winter and assure vital regrowth.

Towns move periodically, so even they are not constant. Over time dancing feet will wear down a central depression that can threaten the fire in heavy rains. Disputes among members themselves or concerns about continuing on leased land can also move a fire. Few tribal towns have not had occasional gaps in their continuity, though their fires are believed to continue burning underground, endangering unprotected members. Presumably, in ancient times this vitality resided within the big mound chamber.

A town that relocates takes along ashes from its ancestral fire, establishing direct continuity with its ancestral past. After holding stomps for four years at the new site, a pole is set up in the center to cast a shadow at sunrise on the solstice to mark the location for the center front post of the Mikko's (west) arbor. As the sun moves through that day, the locations and separating spacing for the central front posts of each arbor are marked to the north and south. Once all the arbors are in place, the pole is pulled up to leave a hole, ashes from the prior fireplace are buried (cached) by the medicine man (*hilis haya*) at arm's length into the bottom of that hole, and the new fire is built atop a small mound placed over the top as the town's *axis mundi tysic* (see Bell 1984: 98, 219). At every subsequent Busk the placing of the central peg repeats this founding of the town and arbors from shadows cast by this pole.

In sum, Creek rituals and culture regard an entity as moving among fixed contexts rather than blending them together (Bell 1984: 54, 77, 136, 218). All are engendered as male (variously grandfather ~ light ~ sun ~ defended) or female (variously grandmother ~ dark ~ water ~ nurtured). Acting in partnership, men sustain the old, while women create the new.

More dynamic and dangerous, further equations are hot/cold, growth/stasis, and conflict/peace. Repeated rituals and well-lived, clean lives serve to check the extreme growth of superheated tumult because "weeds grow at night" as a sign of danger and chaos.

BUSKING

Glimpses of their Mississippian past survive among modern Creeks, despite their great traumas and dislocations. Though they differ in their scale of kinship systems and rituals, those of today provide comparative and coherent insights into ancient complexities.

The Busk is clearly a world-renewal rite, as well as a thanksgiving to the ripe corn yet growing in the fields (Gilbert 1947). It was once much more complex, especially in terms of personnel, with a greater range of past officials and workers. It is preceded by a series of dances, now weekend stomps but probably also variously named social dances in ancient times. At these earlier events preparations included commissioning new pots for brewing the herb water and new mats for the arbor beds, honoring special women and their families. The spacing between these events must have been timed according to the conditions of the crop, the movements of celestial bodies in the sky, and the routines of a town and its affiliated neighbors. Throughout the harvest each town took its turn as host, and then more frequently as guest among all the others.

The square and beds were cleaned and renewed before a new fire, forgetting hostilities of the past year, was rekindled to represent the vivifying Sun and serve as the central focus. Throughout, invoking this fire and many other spiritual witnesses, everyone prayed and propitiated the cosmos. This respect is most obvious in "killing the greenwood" to atone for cutting the fresh trees and to protect the refurbished arbors from outside harm. Adding a new outer mantle to the mounds offered the same hope of new beginning and vitality.

At Tukabatchi the eight days were evenly divided between plant and meat foods. Today the Feather Dance by men has subsumed the Gun Dance, the women dance Ribbon only once, and the Buffalo Dance involves the entire town and loyal visitors, paired by gender and age.

Of note, in the past, during the War Dance, when armed men protected the town, women took refuge atop a mound. After defeating the enemies in effigy, men danced four times around the base of the mound with the women above. At the end of events men "went to water" to purify. Though they could not sleep, they could eat. At first they feasted on fresh green corn and other vegetables, but avoided meat and salt. Later they again ate meat and fish.

During the eight days at Kashita new fires were kindled on the first and fifth days. Women took coals to their camp fires on the fourth day, in contrast to the four virgins who brought ashes from home into the ground on the first day. Everyone feasted on corn on the second day rather than waiting until the end. Men, divided into Chiefs and Warriors, bathed in ashes and white paint before they "went to water," where they offered tobacco flowers, as they also did to the new fire. They anointed their ears, the better to hear what others say. Several dances were hosted by specific clans, such as the Turkey Dance by its clanswomen because these birds were fierce warriors.[40] On the last day an elaborate drink of fourteen herbs was brewed in two basins for drinking and washing by men.

The town's unity was symbolized by a single cane, a reed with two white feathers tied to the top, set before the Mikko's arbor, then taken to water in the grip of a Fish clansman who led a procession from the arbors. There all the men bathed and used four immortal stones to absorb and expel any harm. Following the feathered cane, they returned to their arbors to be released from their fast to visit, thank, and feast. The last night was devoted to the Crazy (Exhausted, Drunk) Dance, which ended the rite. No mounds are mentioned by Hawkins, though they clearly already were a feature of the town.

During any Busk, in the same way that the herb water brought together plant life to benefit the world, so the remounding made this manifest. Men and women, plant and animal, old and new, hot and cold, and night and day were brought together as a whole, ready to continue for another year. At the center of all was the fire, rekindled anew to forget the transgressions of the past year at the same time as its ashes in the mound assured its perpetual link to ancestors of the town. As a very pivotal location, it had links to both the heart and the Sun. During the cleaning in preparation for the Busk, old men in charge sat on front seats as 'arbor weights ~ press-downers' (*topv 'mvwetenv ~ topa 'mawitiina*; Hill n.d.-a: text 18, line 5) to evoke the importance of the mound and square as safe microcosmic banked, blessed, and ballast bulge.

IBOFVNGA

Set in sharp contrast to these external "outsider" views of Creek culture and prehistory is the lifelong work of Jean Hill, a member of an important family of religious leaders. Her book, published after her death, provides a much better understanding of the philosophical underpinnings of their universe.[41] She builds on the basic observation: "The [Creek] world and all that it contained were the products of mind and bore everywhere the marks of mind . . . visibly manifested in the so-called 'living things'" (Swanton 1922: 142).

Creeks had and have profound respect for the orderly motions of their world, which they believe was pervaded by an all-embracing energy (*boea fikcha ~ puyvfekca* literally 'inner heart,' also meaning soul, spirit, ghost). Because pulsing, quivering movement is a fundamental manifestation of this active energy, the link between right living and world order means that "when people lose their moral path, the earth will tremble" (Chaudhuri and Chaudhuri 2001: 106). Increasing tensions, resistance, and uncertainties—often between culture and nature, humans and others—are its cause. Hence while a slow, steady pulsing was the steady state of this world, any disruption resulted in its intensification toward violent trembling. At fault were humans disrupting the world and, like geologic faults, causing earthly distress.

Ibofvnga, deified mental energy (cosmic Mind), willed the conjoining of four elements at creation. Two were male (fire, wind) and two were female (earth, water). Within each pair one is definite and specific (fire, earth) while the other is indefinite and diffuse (wind, water). As breath, wind animates all life. Winds individuate by direction, indicated by the crossed logs at the sacred fire. From the sky Grandfather Sun and Grandmother Moon provide moderating heat and light and communicate with the Earth through the fire. Today the Christian God is known to Creeks as Breath

Holder (*Hesagedamese*), addressed in prayers and hymns at local churches in both Mvskoki and English.

Turtle, an amphibian whose shell has the shape of the Earth, was a primal mediator among all these elements, the specific icon contrasting with the diffuse *Ibofvnga*. Representing both the Earth and turtle is piled-up soil in the form of mounds. These provide locales for studying the movements of the sky as well as "placating nature ritually." Mounds (*gun halwa ~ iganhalwv*[*-ji*] = 'high place ~ mountain,' or with *ji* = the smaller 'little high place') served as observatories aligned with standing poles to study the passage of the planets and stars across the sky (Chaudhuri and Chaudhuri 2001: 7).[42] In addition the sinuous as well as striking motions of energy was ~ is embodied in beliefs about snakes, which both slither along or strike outward. Their bodies also duplicate the hollow tube that holds life.

Every being, human and other, is like a tube for the flow of breath and life, with the heart (*fi:ki*), a pump, at its center. Similarly each *talwa* (town) once had a central sacred fire, open square, men's cabins (*topv*, bed, arbor) along each of the four sides, a tall pole (tube-like) for scoring in two-stick ball, other game yards, earthen mounds composed of special soils, and a winter chamber (*chogo biloxi* = hothouse, roundhouse).[43] Hamlets, farmsteads, camps, and other satellite dwellings lacked these features and therefore linked with the greater *talwa* that served as their ritual center (Chaudhuri and Chaudhuri 2001: 83, 97).

An all-pervading duality of White/Red (reflective/active) characterized life, especially as communities. White towns often had only three instead of four cabins (beds, arbors), leaving the east side open for direct access to the vivifying sunrise and solar potency. These moieties influenced personal attitudes as well as national polices. The entire Creek confederacy had mother towns with several mounds, providing ancient blessed bulge in an unpredictable world nonetheless potent with vitality and human-made safe havens.

5

Mounds in Full

Print endures, teaching by both mistake and true report. We still read and consult the earliest mound publications, though without any accurate time line and ignorant of the enormity of the historical traumas that took place. Scholarship improves, but it moves slowly to eclipse prior misunderstandings or sidesteps entirely to better reflect an external reality. Mound building is a particularly choice example because while archaeologists and political theorists debate the reasons and roles of mound building in the abstract, they ignore the dozens of mounds still rebuilt every summer in Oklahoma by devoted humans who maintain them.[1] This hostile tradition began long before Andrew Jackson and his cronies by "voluntary" law forced tribes descended from Mississippians to move there in the early 1800s. Five hundred years after Soto, and despite another 150 years of relentless Southern Baptist pressure (Methodists are kinder), a dozen Creek *talwa* and other towns still gather at their squares ~ ceremonial grounds. There they celebrate the ripening of corn by all-night fasting, thirsting, and dancing centered around a sacred fire, arbors, ball pole, and at least one modest earthen mound, slowly and surely increasing each year.[2] In doing so they honor the most obvious fact that mounds compress the ground underneath them; they sit poised and attentive.

Today, moreover, the present smaller size of mounds and town squares probably has more to do with lack of legal ownership of that plot of land than the degree of religious fervor. These grounds are often located on pastures owned by rancher families but used seasonally for ball games and rituals on the basis of long-term leases. The Creek Nation has recently begun buying back these lands, and each secured *talwa* has now made more substantial investments in its locale. Similarly when the Cherokee Nation bought the Loyal Shawnee ground, what had been an open pasture suddenly became a fenced enclave with showers, toilets, and paved camp sites. Archaeologists should be aware that such legal considerations make for what seem to be slight occupations, when people are actually hoping for much more intensive use once secured by legal guarantees of ownership.

Before and during such Green Corn ceremonials, especially a Creek Busk, careful and prolonged attention is paid to the surface of the earth within the confines of each square ground. The inner circle is plucked of plants, cleaned, hoed, and raked outward to leave a low perimeter ridge of debris. The previous year's raised fireplace disc is carefully removed by the shovelful and added as the next covering layer (mantle) to a six-foot mound dominating the landscape of the ground. The surface tension of the added earth forms a peak that will be beaten down by the weather over the coming year. Fasting men depart from the ground to dig up fresh soil, of a contrasting color from an appropriate direction, and fill a wheelbarrow (the modern form of a pack basket) to then rebuild the fireplace and another small mound, associated with Moon and sky, used for the Feather, Buffalo, and Mothers dances. These dances—accompanied by song, drum, and rattles—provide order and pace to pray for a calm world of men and women.

When all is ready, the Mikko, sitting ("pressing down") in the west arbor, faces the east at the tip of an imagined pie-slice-shaped triangle whose middle is the fire. Its southeast angle is the large earthen mound, and its northeast angle the small sky mound. This geometry is obvious to any viewer, though the symbolism is known only to insiders. Because they are so massively and physically positional, it seems best to consider such mound dimensionality throughout the United States in terms of prepositions (across, into, inside, above, and most especially under, on, and for) instead of the more usual interrogatives (who, what, where, when) in my preface. Underlying all of these other aspects, moreover, is the vital action of safe mounds as honored earth, blessed bubble, holy ballast, and secured bank deposit also providing a protective weight and haven for members living in a sometimes tumultuous world.

ACROSS

Across the Americas this rebuilding or renewal of mounds took place at or during preparations for world-renewal rites, particularly well illustrated by the cooperating but highly diverse nations during their ten-day Earth Fixing rite along the Klamath River of northern California. The priestly leader (*Lo'*) is accompanied by archers, who literally pin the earth in places by shooting arrows into it. On the last night the leader stands beside what is called locally a half-yard-high sand pile (*yuxpit*), but that elsewhere would be called a mound. The sand itself is carried by two women, in two basket-loads each, from a nearby boat landing, a place of obvious safe haven. They shape the deposited mass into a miniature copy of the looming sacred mountain ("God's Mountain" ~ Mt. Offield) on the horizon that is the focus of the leader's vigil throughout that night. The next day the famous White Deerskin Dance, or another dance displaying treasured family heirlooms, is held, before the leaders go into seclusion for a week (Kroeber and Gifford 1949).

Around Seattle the Shamanic Odyssey took a team of shamans to the Afterworld to retrieve lost vitalities of souls, minds, or spirits in order to cure community members who were then patients withering away during long, wet, dark winters. The spirit guides, called Little Earths, who actually make the journey mimed by the doctors, live inside hollow earth mounds near springs, which they share with other creatures. Foremost among these were ~ are snakes, who also lend their powers to particular shamans in times of need, such as difficult childbirths when lithe Snake and Lizard spirits are particularly effective in easing out the baby (Miller 1988, 1999b).

In the Midwest the Hochungaras (Winnebagos) made miniature mounds during the elaborate initiation rites that accompanied their Medicine Dance, their version of the Midewiwin. In their origin epic, *Ma'una* (Earthmaker) had trouble steadying the Earth until huge snakes were anchored, tail first, at the four corners. Looking east, these island weights (and heights) watch, guard, fixate, and ballast the world.

In the Northeast, before the Hurons abandoned a town they removed the remains of loved ones from their graves or scaffolds, celebrated their memory at a fe(a)stivity called The Kettle, and then buried them together in a common ossuary. Separate treatment, however, was accorded those who had drowned or frozen to death because these people had offended powerful sky and water spirits. Instead their flesh was cremated, and their bones were buried. Those who died violently were buried apart, with a hut atop a mound over the grave to hold them down and provide safe shelter.

In the Plains, during the Pawnee Big Doctoring, large effigies were built inside an earth lodge. These included a turtle-shaped basin as the hearth, an encircling sixty-foot snake, and a seated female. In the spring the Pawnee year began with a ceremony in honor of their original creation by Moon, Sun, and Venus (divided into engendered Morning and Evening Stars). Their farming year ended with three rites: a Green Corn, a Ripe Corn, and a harvest Four Pole Rite that featured a small mound piled at the gap in an encircling embankment, made from dirt excavated from a yard-wide hole used as the fireplace (Weltfish 1977: 308, 313, 332).

INTO

But what goes into a mound? Certainly more than just the obviously selective dirt. At every Green Corn men members of the ground carry their individual shovelfuls as offerings to the common pile. For yet another year people and mound blend together and increase vitality. Surface tension provides its conical shape, balancing forces of gravity and aspiration. These many separate loads fuse through laborious effort and subsequent forces of nature into a common whole. Prayers, sweat, and good thoughts further consolidate these distinct parts into a shared, honored, and blessed whole. In the past, burials of offerings and human remains fueled ~ fed ~ seeded some mounds.

As air sustains life, so song sustains the land. Singing sets the rhythms of the Feather, Ribbon, and Buffalo dances, while the distinctive stomp step pumps these into the ground, where some bubble up into mounds. Song is a vehicle for *powha*, strengthened in these instances by their sacred, communal expression. Special songs breathe life into specific plots of land and bolster mounds, which are periodically resealed by new layers of colored earths and capping clays to contain these beneficial infusions of vitality.

In other words, what goes into a mound is cosmic harmony ~ unity blessed by human song, as "Communion" (Creek = *anogechka ~ vnokeckv*), by outreach as well as ingestion; feasting does support solidarity. Vast farming benefited by people working together, and mounds especially encouraged another aspect of this public effort. Working the land resulted in building it up, allowing the reuse of a hallowed, special spot for eons.

Cremations (cremains) occupy many mounds, along with intact and bundle burials. The use of fire to incinerate most of the body provides an ironic contrast with the permanence of the mound itself. In all, mound cremations probably evoked the full range of elementals: earth, fire, water, and air. Individual bodies quickly transformed back into such basic component elements. Only the earth harbors a lasting trace, composed of these other residues. As closed, hollow, heated spaces (from inner fires), mounds also served as ovens, cooking on many symbolic levels.

INSIDE

While mounds are still built up incrementally, there is also the belief that they are not solid inside, likened to a whole torso or a component such as heart, navel, or womb. In the reconstructed mound-shaped council house of the Apalachee at San Luis (in Tallahassee, Florida), the hollow, open inside is filled with platforms and other furnishings to make it livable by the resident men. Like the mound homes of the northwestern Little Earths, the insides of mounds across the Americas (and Europe, for that matter) were the indwelling places of community beings and spirits. The posts supporting these bunks and domestic furniture also serve to stake, stretch, and pin the skin of the vital Earth at that place. As noted, in recent centuries, with the abandonment of mounds and mound building, community leaders moved inside into rotunda ~ council houses to insulate their community during horrific times.

Pawnee animal homes, human earth lodges, and Creek and Choctaw origin epics also underscore that mounds are the abodes of many beings. Snakes, locusts, ants, bees, spiders, toads, bears, alligators, foxes, owls, birds, and other creatures with dens or mounded nests are specifically linked with mound symbolism. These slitherings live close to the earth, personifying it by contact, context, and attributes, depending on the times and situations.

Because they are hollow but not empty, mounds are also equated with hearts, pulsing with life blood, and with tubes ~ ducts, reverberating with breath, fluids, and dicta. They are containers as well as wombs, cooking up nourishment and birthing new life. Indeed mounds often supported a tall pole serving as an energy conductor, such as the one that led the Choctaws before it pneumatically subsumed into *Nanih Waiya*. Hollowness is an essential characteristic of the Earth, concentrating energy along webbings through thin and thick.

ABOVE

Mounds also serve as high platforms, providing panoramas of earth and sky and shelter in floods. Modern Creeks and others say they are observatories.[3] And they were more. They represent the higher authority of earthly leaders that came ~ comes from the sky, from kinship with stars, planets, and especially the Sun. Their azimuths and alignments bespeak celestial precision and cosmic unity. Yet the top of a mound was like a two-way mirror, the reflective surface of a bubble. One side brought people upward, toward the sky, but the other led them into the depths, earthward, recursively represented by the dark, unlit room inside the tribal temple set on these heights. Standing in the temple doorway to greet the sunrise, a chief ~ priest could therefore move in all directions (orbits) simultaneously.

UNDER

Especially important for understanding mounds, moreover, is what is under them, an opening of some kind. Each has a deep cache (real or symbolic) of offerings to dedicate that site, and at least one supposedly covers a ring of crystals.[4] At each Green Corn the cleaning and recovering of ground surfaces, though widely known and reported, has more wide-ranging consequences since these surfaces are actually the changing skins of the mound (old) and plaza (new). In Mvskoke the word for skin *hałpi* ~ *hvrpe* refers to one's skin, hide, casing, chaff, hull, shell, and outer bark (Martin and Mauldin 2000: 59). Recognizing all these skins (for what they indeed are) thereby immediately invokes all of the associated Mississippian symbolism of snakes, which routinely change skins of their own accord. Such shedding is a function of health and size, since snakes continue to grow as long as they live. Thus while they do shed after resuming feeding in the spring, that does not preclude them from shedding again during a well-fed summer before they return to winter hibernation. As Ho-Chunk esoteric language makes clear, such shedding is a sign of immortality, conferred through initiated membership into their Mystic Rite.

Mounds, in sum, *compress* vitality into ballast, bulk, and bulge and (in) still the earth by weighing it down on behalf of a worshipful human community of males and females, while they also lift it up toward the sky. During aptly named Stomp Dances, the light but forceful downward step also helps to press the fresh earth into an easy smoothness as it is inflated or infused with regular, rhythmic song.

There are additional ramifications, moreover, that are consequences of this perception of the Earth's thin skin as loose, sloughing, writhing, convulsing, and thus sometimes dangerous. The danger comes from both the thrashing around and from poisonous toxins, such as toad skins. The staking of the posts forming arbors (beds) on the sides of the square thus serves to anchor, stretch, and hold firm the skin under this cleansed ceremonial ground, as well as under the surrounding camps where wives and children host visitors.

By refurbishing the grounds, humans shed, reskin, and reseal their own carefully prepared piece of earth, selecting the time and place for such renewal and thus hopefully averting any natural cataclysm that would randomly if not chaotically harm their portion of the Earth's surface. Doing so is a sign of health, growth, and vital well-being; as well as a deterrent to keep the Earth from shaking itself free from its own mantle, as during an earthquake. By envisioning the Earth as snake-like with loose and (re)movable skin, mounds and stakes provide banked ballast for holding steady one spot of it. Posts both hold up and pin down a surface within a balanced tension that is capable of storing and transmitting *powha*.

Evidence that this is not ideal ~ idle speculation is sculpted into the action of the Birger Figurine from a Cahokia suburb. A woman kneels down so that her hoe and hand directly touch the body of an enormous Earth-size snake with a forked tail. Similarly the largest figure in the Pawnee earth lodge for a Big Doctoring was another forked-tail snake. Representing immortality, snakes serve as representatives of the larger class of reptiles, such as turtles, lizards, alligators, and crocodiles. The Delaware, Iroquois, and Creek worlds rest on the back of a Turtle whose domed shell repeats the mound form.

Far to the south the Maya creator is a crocodile-like being called *Itzamna*. This link is evident because female crocodiles and alligators, whose genders look virtually identical, build elevated mounds in swamps to serve as nests for a hundred or so eggs that hatch in three months. Over time these nests sprout trees and plants to look like miniatures of the Earth itself. "The female estuarine crocodile builds a mound of mud and decaying plant material, in the center of which are the eggs. With her tail the female splashes water onto the nest. This promotes the heat-generating process of vegetative decay" (Wermuth 1978: 288) with specific temperature ranges determining the gender of the hatch. Just before emerging, the young begin squeaking from inside to alert their mother to uncover the eggs for easier hatching.

For the first four years the young grow a foot a year, reaching sexual maturity after ten years. The forefeet have five toes, but the hind feet have only four webbed toes. Gators also retreat in cold weather into burrows at or below the water line, hibernating inside a river bank. Adult gators emit a range of sounds that include a hiss and grunt, while the males roar spectacularly, tensing "the musculatures of its body so that the head and tail rise high out of the water [and] its flanks may vibrate so violently that water is sprayed high into the air from each side" (Wermuth 1978: 89).

In all, then—in terms of across, into, inside, above, and under—mounds are honored, hollow homes with banked and balanced surface tension for binding together (in communion) human builders, sky beings, and spirit residents whose combined weight—built of dirt, prayers, sweat, offerings, blessings, songs, and substance (or consubstantiation)—manages to sustain a vitalized safe haven on a precarious Earth, always verging on the turbulent, unsteady, and uncertain, especially due to human faults. Its thin surface is loose, particularly like the skin of snakes, other reptiles, and mammals like bears who constantly challenge the human ability to survive by "the skin of our teeth (and hands)." An insistent regular order is provided by song and dance working in conjunction, the song lifting up and the stomp step packing down to achieve poise, beauty, and balance.

While harmony, balance, and respect were ~ are the hopeful rule across the Americas, they are reinforced by continuous threat, terror, and dread of retribution for human faults from the mindful universe itself. This terror served ~ serves to motivate whole communities, as everyone, not just responsible members, joins together in enforced consensus. By this means, along with acknowledged personal and family benefits, communities were able to build a huge mound, to concentrate weight and height at a selected location. Blending song, sweat, blood, tears, and dirt, they reached a blessed communion that combines devotion for most and threat for the rest. The greatest threat, beyond reach of police or armed forces, was and is the geophysical violence inherent within the planet, subject both to universal laws known to adepts and to its own response to moral outrage due to human faults and breaches that ripple through a community and locale.[5] While there are many reasons and ways of building mounds, the basic one involves banking protective ballooning ballast in the hope of assuring cosmic vitality. Community well-being, atonement, public works, and havens also play roles, but as complements rather than the underlying core principle of compression.

Mounds, then, apply holy height and weight to hold, steady, stabilize, atone, calm, and (in)still a very active Earth skin. Much more a place for a physicist's model reeling through chaos than for archaeologists sifting through debris that seems piecemeal and inert, this world of flux and flow has mounded zones of safety so people, place, and *powha* can usefully link up with vitality. Mounds instill, with their shape, size, and effort proportional to their guarantee of safe refuge. The biggest mound is most likely to be the best haven, as Cayugas claimed (Speck [1949] 1995), regardless of the forces directed against it.

This is a world with spin, speed, spread, motion, shake, rumble, and roll. Mounds are its steadying heights and weights, covering the restless dead, sheltering immortals in holy homes, and holding up temples and icons for engendered humans and other residents. Indeed this very need to still or rhythmically steady such motion was represented in the aptly named Stomp Dance, using a step that the ill-fated John Lawson ([1709] 1967: 45) described as "nothing but a sort of stamping Motion, much like the treading upon Founders Bellows."

Twenty years ago Robert Hall (1979: 260) noted that mound rituals, using colored marsh muds in Wisconsin and hides staked over Illinois Hopewell graves, probably re-created aspects of the Earth Diver epic in which the first land was formed from a speck brought up from the bottom of the primordial sea by an aquatic hero. A mound therefore was a frozen monument to such dynamic creation. Once this earth grew outward and stabilized, it supported a varied population of living, thinking denizens, who well knew its origins, took none of its features for granted, and assumed constant flux.

In confirmation of such insecurity, the most solid of shapes was believed to be hollow tubes ~ ducts inside bodies, caverns inside mountains, chambers inside mounds, and a chasm inside the Earth. In Celtic folklore, best known from Ireland, similar hallowed hills (Shidhe) remain the dwelling places of fairies (Tuatha De Danann; Rees and Rees 1978; Scherman 1981). Once a human got inside, he or she became thoroughly enchanted by what seemed to be ornate palaces. Like American mounds, the Shidhe were the focus of periodic rituals, particularly during the four times each year when "magic mounds open[ed] up" because the barrier between mortals and immortals became very thin. Saints Patrick and Bridget resanctified these hills and lands with churches and shrines to accord with the Irish Catholic Church, keeping them hallowed and hollow to this day.

For Ireland, as for Native America, this constant pressure applied by mounds as bulky weight and bulging height explains why Watson Brake was built and then left to anchor an oval space, why the Karuk mound made of soil from a boat landing assured continuity for another year, why the Lushootseed expanding universe was dotted with mounded hills occupied by Little Earths, why Cayugas were known for a giant refuge mound, why Hurons once anchored their unquiet dead at grave mounds, why the Hochungara creative Earthmaker pierced the spinning Earth with huge serpents, why Osages rush through great bundle tribal priest initiations to make sure the halves of the universe remain secure and vitalized.

Mounds in Full

Karuk provide the reminder that mounds may not be so much built and added to as sculpted and shaped to conform to particular models, such as the local high mountain or, in the case of the hundreds of mounds at Cahokia, geometric indicators ranging from boundary markers to functional use as burials, temples, solar observations, and engineered urban spaces (Fowler 1997: 189–97).

Indeed the use of mounds as obvious high ground, with all that implies, is pan-human, since the famous Dobu, keeping a member's skull and name in the "milk" matriline, believe "at death one attains a permanent haven in the village mound where one is at last free from untrustworthy outsiders" (Bloch and Perry 1982: 29). Everywhere, it seems, mounds were more than landmarks; they were obviously sanctified steadying weights in a morass of uncertainty, shape-shifting species, and treacherous lands. Out of this real concern that mounds had been raised by the "quaking noise," Mississippians kept adding to mounds, Catholic monks took vows of stability, and others now buy disaster insurance.

ON

Mounds weigh on and compress the ground on which they sit, and, unlike the analogy of a safe, activity once took place atop front plazas and in temples. Resting on "new earth," churned up to access the underworld, they provide a conduit for *powha*.

FOR

Mounds do all of these vital things and many, many more because their banked hollow mass, special holy precautions, and bulging height and ballasting weight serve to provide singing humans with a *safe* means for atoning for their own transgressions on the Earth and for seeing the unseen in all of its ramifications and multidimensions. By periodic human effort of men and women, especially via dance, prayer, and song, they correct for their own faults and, for a time, hold steady in sanctuary a thin skin suspended in time and anchored in a specific safe place.[6] They do all this and more because, first and foremost, they touch earth upon earth to compress the ground on which they sit.

NOTES

PREFACE

1. Claude Lévi-Strauss, discussing his three academic "mistresses," cited geology, where strata, vastly eroded over eons, must be traced across far distances to piece together their original full extent and significance.
2. Attention, brief and direct, is drawn to my "best case" use of archaeological analogy in an ethnolinguistic context despite past hostilities. The problem, of course, is not with the data or comparisons but with those archaeologists fighting for wrong-headed turf while oblivious that "this too, too solid soil would melt."
3. For Vi Hilbert, a fluent Lushootseed teacher, the purifying aspects of brushing off with fresh cedar boughs combines with the image of a mother bird protectively spreading her wings over her brood to more fully translate *-ti-* as "take care of, hope for, indicate regard or concern" (Miller and Hilbert 1993: 238). These morphemes can be traced in Bates et al. 1994: 245, which provides *-ti-* "spreading" and *-tǝd* "implement," with the implication that the earth is constantly expanding, or getting away (see also xvii for *s-*, 240 for *t'ixw* "brush, shake off," 226 for *tixw* "bail out a boat," *-ti-* "spread," 220 for *-tǝd* implement suffix, and 246 for *-waw'-* "take full advantage of"). Altogether they provide the translation given in the text.
4. At an elders' lunch near Seattle I was stunned when an old friend mentioned that she knew from her family that they had ancestors buried in one of these mounds. It is also noteworthy that northwest earthen forts and mounds (see n2, this chapter) were referenced by George Gibbs (1855), the Harvard-trained lawyer whose notes and publications from the mid-1800s had a large part in winning treaty rights to salmon and other resources in federal court in the late 1900s.
5. Late in this process I realized the overlap of mounds and totem poles as land-based monuments of and to vitality, installed and maintained by song and dance. The standing totem pole, decorated with matriclan and family crests, represents the spinal column of the ranking hereditary name channeling revitalizing *powha* energy into the hereditary lands, as the tubular spinal column formed by the

vertebrae of the named house head does for its members. See Miller 1997: 52. The sections in this book titled "Why Masks?" and "Why Hats?" are aspects of the same internal dialogue that led me to "Why Mounds?" Similarly tubes emphasized throughout this mound study do the same thing, channeling energy ~ power into persons, events, places, and especially mounds.

Before his suicide Wilson Duff made much of the Haida proverb about their own sense of precariousness as island people who truly lived on the edge on all fronts (cf. Abbott 1981). John Swanton switched his early career from Lakota to Haida and Tlingit, before turning exclusively to the Southeast, without a look back. I hope to rectify this oversight.

6. A key difference is long-range influences since much of North America felt diffusions from the Valley of Mexico, while those to the northwest originated in China. The Southeast also had contacts with the Caribbean, without adopting Taino mound fields (*conuco*, each mound three feet high and nine feet across) for growing and storing root crops. See Rouse 1992: 12.

7. The Keres study is now posted online: Jay Miller, "Keresan Pueblos and Chaco Canyon," 2007, Ohio State Library, Knowledge Bank, http://kb.osu.edu/dspace/handle/1811/29276. *Delaware Integrity* is now available from Amazon.

8. Because today's Woodland rites coincide with those of the Plains during summer in Oklahoma, one is unlikely to attend both a Green Corn and a Sun Dance without advance planning and dispensation from either of these separately interlocked ritual communities.

9. Most academics are astoundingly callous about scholarship without affiliation, as though a common lot of endless meetings, esteemed titles, numbing grading, and derivative teaching is the ideal. While I could use libraries, I could not check out any books because I had no official standing. Asking to have an adjunct appointment only added more professional entanglements to drain my efforts. The personal libraries of scholars such as Ray Fogelson, Blue Clark, Janet Ford, and Bob Hall became all the more important. A year at Ole Miss and two at Ohio State with their venerable libraries of untouched classics did much to supply gaps in my references, both past and present.

10. Caddo shares with Muskogean languages meaningful particles such as *-kid-*, indicating "something done on a raised surface like an altar," and *-haat-*, meaning "something done in water," as when Busk worshipers "go to water"; see Chafe 1976.

11. By convention Mvskoke words are written both in technical, universal IPA (International Phonetic Alphabet of linguists) fonts as well as in the venerable missionary alphabet still used in their churches and hymnals.

12. See chapter 2, n37, for the Mvskoke dictionary entries.
13. In far northeastern California this heart-mound link saves the Earth. At the conflagration intended to destroy the world, the heart of Lizard pops out of his burning chest and flies to the top of Mt. Shasta to form a mound and to sing until Bluejay digs it up and gives it to his wife. She puts it into a water-filled basket near the warming fire until it forms a tiny boy that grows into Lizard, who creates a twin from his bulging forehead (brimming with vitality!). Together they kill the Loons who are destroying the world and make it safe, though Lizard perpetually mourns the loss of all his children, See Angulo 1990: 91.
14. The best known Clovis caches (with known blade count, state name, and date of discovery) are Simon (29 artifacts, Idaho, 1961), Anzick (100+, Montana, 1968), Drake (13, Colorado, 1978), Rickey/East Wenatchee (60, Washington, 1987), and Fenn (56, ?, 1902?), the last of which was purchased from a family that was vague about how and where it was found, but a dry cave seems likely because it is so intact. See Frison and Bradley 1999.
15. The most succinct illustration of mound as microcosm occurs in Cherokee preventative medicine, where a tiny mounded cone of smoldering ashes serves as a device for locating witches intent on harming a patient. Dried tobacco flakes are crumbled over it so that wherever there is a tiny flare-up it shows that a witch is approaching or working harm from that direction of the wider world. See Mooney 1932: 74.

The outstanding prehistoric example of anchoring a mound by pinning it to the earth is the founding dome and raised ring beneath Twin mound at Pinson, looking like a patterned pin cushion because of the array of stakes pounded into the slopes of its white clay cap. See Mainfort 2013: 112, fig. 4.30.
16. While supporting data for this analysis have been drawn from excavations, summaries, and reports of archaeology, their use here, after much discussion at the Native "summer seminar," can best be understood as moving analysis from the dark side to the bright side of cultural context, ethnography, and ongoing religious tradition. Though implicit Eurobias is undergoing self-evaluation (Thomas 2000), it involves fundable capitalist views on individualism, prosperity, consumerism, monopoly, and scholarly fads. Native America, by contrast, appreciates thriving tribal diversity, in the fullest sense: respected differences, not cattle-car sameness, cookie-cutter unity, or lockstep uniformity. Culturally therefore some archaeologists ain't got rhythm, nor song or dance, but do have a strong turf defensiveness. Similarly fasting pervades these rituals, easing concerns with camp sanitation, yet it is feasting that fills the academic record, since it leaves traces that fasting does not. See Pauketat 2007.

In Canada historians have forced archaeologists to understand the direct link between major sites, such as Marpole at Vancouver, and descendants, such as Musqueam Salish on a reserve on the edge of the University of British Columbia, the major university whose pioneer archaeologist, tenured to teach German, directed most of the salvage excavations. See Roy 2010.

For comparison, England's "national disgrace" resulted in breaking archaeology's monopoly on Stonehenge in favor of an overdue summary (Cleal et al. 1995) and more diverse scholarship for a more complex understanding of the site, its builders, and its place in the universe. "History, notoriously, is written by the winners and the overall winners in the academic struggle for the stones have been the archaeologists.... But Stonehenge does not belong to archaeology, or not to archaeology alone" (Hill 2008: 2, 3).

17. Thanks to Barbara Duncan of the Museum of the Cherokee for conferring with Wiggins Black Fox of Qualla, Roger Smoker of Snowbird, and others to provide this usage. Text message of 4 April 2008 at 1:48 p.m.
18. See also Schilling 2010.

1. MOUNDING UP

1. While *Native American* is the popular term for the indigenous inhabitants of the Americas, the spelling *Indien*, for someone from the Indies instead of India, provides a better term since many elders prefer this self-designation. It will occasionally appear here, among other optional ethnonyms.
2. *Ballast* comes from the Danish, meaning "bare load" as a noun, including the underbed of a road, track, or moral character; it is used here in its verbal sense of conferring weight, balance, security, and stability in an uncertain world. As mounds and other geoforms, it is made blessed by the care, prayer, and rites associated with its transport from a certain direction or place, such as a barrow pit, as well as by the ongoing communal activities of men and women for the mound's upkeep to provide security and sanctuary.
3. In her Creek-language lessons, Linda Alexander tells the story of a smashed Turtle who is given a song that he sings four times to heal himself. The song is specific to him, and its effectiveness depends on repeating it four times. Such is the vitalizing power of localized song. See Innes et al. 2004, audio CD, tracks 32, 33. Earnest Gouge (2004: 33, 113) provided bilingual texts that specify the lewdness that got turtle mashed.
4. My own coinage, combining two Native terms from eastern and western language stocks, *powha* is all-pervading cosmic energy ~ vitality ~ charge ~ force ~ power at the heart of Native American cosmologies, as explained in "Conventions."

5. Seeking a more respectful term, the builders of this site have now been called Tamaroha, from Tunican words for 'mound' (*tama*) and 'cave' (*roha*) by analogy with the phrase "water mountain" that in Mesoamerica means "city." The intent is to be "more appealing to tourists and more uplifting of the state's image" (Clark et al. 2010: 244).
6. In a spiritual, comparative sense; archaeologists certainly have camp songs such as (made politically correct) "Those Athabaskan Guys from the North" and "What a Friend We Have in Quezalcoatl."
7. The great value of scientific predictability cannot be denied, along with rational reasons in plate tectonics, orbits, and gravity, but these have shifted blame away from humans, with obvious consequences. Native rituals, probity, and interspecies morphing restore that balance and assign direct responsibility. In addition recognition of such natural predictability was well known from the ceaseless observations of Native astronomers and morphologists.
8. A favorite overlook is atop Turtle Mound overlooking the expanse of Mosquito Lagoon on the Atlantic Florida coast, viewing that semitropical ecology while blocking any view of the nearby Kennedy Space Center.
9. The only other known argument that deals with this placement of the Serpent is that of a Baptist minister, all too typical of Ohio, who announced it marked the location of the biblical Garden of Eden and the Fall (Shetrone 1930: 233). Of particular note, Robert Rankin (1996, 2006, 2007), a comparative Siouanist, has found that the distinct language subset of Ohio Valley Siouan (Biloxi, Ofo, Monyton, Occaneechi, Tutelo, Saponi) collapsed standard Siouan words for *God* and *medicine* to mean "snake."
10. Romain (2000: 233–53) argues for earlier Hopewell construction; see also Kennedy 1994: 64. Regardless of its date, its location in violently altered terrain makes the snake image very appropriate. Though I never confirmed it, Brad Lepper told me a snake-like stone nose protrudes from the bank under the head of this snake, suggesting the mound is the upper surface of a truly subterranean body.
11. Starting from the neck, left bend 1 is moon maximum south set, right bend 1 is moon minimum north rise, left bend 2 is moon midpoint set, right bend 2 is moon midpoint rise, left bend 3 is moon minimum north set, and right bend 3 is moon maximum south rise, Cf. Romain 2000.
12. Mooney ([1900] 1982: 337–41, 419) notes that Haywood confounds the Georgia traprock petroglyphs, five miles east of Blairsville above Brasstown Creek, with others in North Carolina, which are indeed linked with *Tsul'kălû*, the "slant-eyed giant." Brasstown Bald is the highest mountain in Georgia, in the

northwest corner near Tennessee, and a frequent locus for thunder and lightning, perpetuating such images of turmoil.

13. As one reviewer summarized, archaeological interpretations today range from raw economic (as a calendar for determining planting and harvests), to mortuary (an alternative form of burial to indicate status), to political (monuments commemorating a socioreligious leader's conquest).

14. In addition to European diseases, those from Africa, such as malaria, took a heavy toll, as did germs from (misnamed) livestock like pigs. Cf. Boyd 1999: 17; Ethridge 2010.

15. Ethridge (2001, 2002) dates such slaving to 1620–1700. Cf. Dincauze and Hasenstab 1989: 67–87; Brose et al. 2001; Gallay 2002. Such Native slavery is told with the intensity of a novel in Hudson 2000.

16. Gibson (2004: 254–69), much to his credit, has tried to turn the academic discussion toward "beneficent obligation" (debt of gratitude) as a way of providing a better understanding of Native motivation, as indeed it does, based in present-day tribal activities and beliefs.

17. Margaret Mauldin reflected, "When you hear these songs . . . it kind of takes you back to a memory of security. We were very, very secure" (Maynor 2000: 97). Creek hymns, and all rituals, emphasize persevering endurance "to go on together." Compilations of Creek hymns are Berryhill 2007; Bunny et al. (1936) 1998. The significance of Christian hymns for Lumbees is considered by tribal member Malinda Maynor (2000).

18. Use of these whistles of different lengths was confirmed by a son of the next generation to James Howard (Howard and Levine 1990: 30). As a negative instance, David Lewis, a modern Creek medicine man, refused to talk about song because it was too sacred, though he noted the importance of "pushing song" into medicine to make it effective. His term for the blowtube used to do this is "medicine stick" and that for powerful dicta is "chant." A reed used for such a blowtube must be living in running water when it is cut. Similarly "all the words that we use are alive. . . . We always put them in a capped container so that the words will never get away. They will stay within the medicine itself. All the medicines that are made are done that way. We always cap these things" (Lewis and Jordan 2002: 53, 95, 111). In contrast, Bear Heart (Marcellus Williams), who studied with Lewis's father, gives specific examples of song's effectiveness (Bear Heart and Larkin 1996: 42, 78).

19. Global implications of the tube include, in Japan, an initializing "reed shoot . . . conceived of as divinity" emerging from the primordial chaos (Levy 1998: 157).

20. Such central well shafts of stacked fires were indeed found during the Bureau of American Ethnology excavations of mounds along rivers in the Tennessee basin occupied by Cherokee ancestors. See Thomas (1894) 1985: 381, 400.
21. They are particularly well known, thanks to the 1908–13 research, followed by lifelong publications (see all) by Paul Radin (1883–1959).
22. Henry Roe Cloud (1929: 564) ~ Wa-na-xi-lay Hunkah (1884–1950)—Ho-Chunk, Presbyterian minister, and Yale anthropology MA—told Ohioans that the Creator "stretched out his arm and that became the moon. But the earth shook and fell apart. To make it cohere he set into it trees, and, not succeeding, he set into it grasses and roots of every sort. Then he weighs it down with innumerable rocks and stones until rest and equilibrium were attained."
23. Marino (1968: 388, 422) names these snake stabilizers *widjirasewe* = island-weights; *widjirawasewe* = weights, island-weights (in ritual). Cf. *cewe, xewe*; *witc* island in Radin (1950: 1, 9 line 23, 19 line 37, 63, 64 line 16).
24. Displaying their inherent capabilities, light moves straight along the rays of this web, and water curves along the rings, through tubular circuitry.

2. BREAKING GROUND

1. Gibson 1986: 201–38; Gibson 2006; Gibson and Carr 2004; Hall 1997; Howard 1968; Mainfort and Sullivan 1998; Mainfort and Walling 1996; Kennedy 1994; Korp 1990; Morgan 1999; O'Shea 1981; Shaffer 1992; Thomas (1894) 1985; Squier and Davis (1848) 1998; Brown 1996.
2. After a lifetime devoted to Georgia and British Colonial history, John Juricek sagely remarked to me, "The English were blind to mounds," which were, of course, obvious evidence of Natives "improving the land," like the barrows built by their own British ancestors.
3. See Gatschet (1883: 158) for *ŏ'sh hätchina* = 'buzzards picking up.'
4. The reference here is clearly to what is familiarly known as an "outie" or bulging umbilicus scar, the vital contact point of babe with placental womb, and of human with Mother Earth. Despite my repeated inquiries among speakers and officials, a Chickasaw word for *mound* was not forthcoming, but the new *Chickasaw Coloring Book* (2012: 14), with art work by Dustin Mater, confirms *ittialbish* = "mound" and *Chickasaw: An Analytical Dictionary* defines it as "navel" (Munro and Willmond 1994: 187).
5. Only "high" *chaaha* is confirmed in a Chickasaw dictionary (Munro and Willmond 1994: 73).

The accuracy of Adair (2005: 35, 277, 497n121) has been questioned because, as he himself notes, he was excluded from ceremonies, had an escort on occasion, and had to sleep apart while traveling. Such separation has to be put into context since these same stipulations apply today during rituals. The concern is not racial but religious since everyone involved has to be "of good mind + heart" and above reproach. Each participant has a buddy to help avoid temptation (during fast, thirst, and continence) and bear witness to good conduct. Data provided to Adair were therefore reliable, though his mental lack of consensus (empathy) with the community was clearly in question.

6. This solution is much like that by the Nishga, Tsimshianics of the Nass River, after their conversion to Anglicanism. By reducing the system to its building blocks in named totemic matri-Houses, they always have the potential of restoring the whole system in short order. Fifty Chickasaw House names have been recorded, an estimated half of those formerly in use.

7. Also intriguing is the translation of the word for raccoon = *inukwal* as 'singer,' given its frequency in Mississippian art (Van Tuyl 1979: 103). See also Sam 1976.

8. Though listed as dormant for more than a century, the last Tutelo speakers lived unrecorded into the later 1900s. This Tutelo rite, which switched to spoken Cayuga Iroquoian except for a few original sentences, is a curious blend of the ritual feeding of the dead, Midewiwin (re)member reincarnation prevalent among tribes of the Great Lakes, and the revivification of hereditary names among towns of the Pacific Northwest.

9. Carver (1998: 57, 141, 172) tries to correlate each mound with an East Anglia king named by Venerable Bede, prove chemically that their bodies were placed inside (since nothing remains), and document the "sand body" stains of criminals hanged nearby at the *cwealmstow* (killing place) where Anglo-Saxon Christian kings enforced their laws by executions. In drawing comparisons Carver notes a religious continuity with mounds at Jelling, Denmark, where Harold Bluetooth built mounds for each of his parents but, after he converted to Christianity, moved his father's skeleton (King Gorm) from its mound into his new church. His mother remains in her mound, in keeping with the universally female associations of the Earth.

10. Incidentally, tracing references to such mounding proved particularly convoluted since Cyrus Thomas initially reported only that ongoing mound use had been seen by James Mooney at a Cherokee Green Corn and by Alice Fletcher among Hochungara (Winnebago) (cf. Miller 2001b: 162n7). Only in his entry on mounds and mound builders in the first *Handbook of North American Indians* does Thomas explicitly say, "According to Miss Fletcher, the Winnebago build miniature mounds in the lodge during certain ceremonies" (Hodge 1907: 951).

11. At Blood Run hundreds of mounds dating around AD 1700 demonstrate that the as-yet-unseparated Omaha-Ponka tribe had indeed revived their mound-building tradition inspired by Ioway. See Betts, 2003, 2010 (also n51 below).
12. Some may have been usual words put to unusual usage; for example, ancient Maya used the word 'trees' for the elaborately carved stone stelae standing in their plazas.
13. Trained by both Charles Hudson and John Juricek, Hahn provides a skilled overview of early Creek history but does not explore the fascinating bonds of ancient memory that brought Lower Creeks back (1690–1715) to the Macon Plateau, where massive earth lodges and mounds at Ocmulgee, Ochese, and Lamar mark a polity that was centuries older. Similarly, when the Yamacraws led by Tomochichi were banished, they renewed an ancestral claim to Irene Mound near Savannah in time to welcome James Oglethorpe and his Georgia settlers.
14. Much southeastern archaeology was done under federal auspices during the Depression, with a chilling episode during the excavation of Irene Mound near Savannah, Georgia, by a crew of African American women who were forbidden to use wheelbarrows because it was unladylike. See White et al. 1999: 92–114, chapter 5 (Cheryl Claassen). Cf. Caldwell and McCann 1941. Photos of the women at work (1937–40) are in *The Waring Papers* (Williams 1968: 299 fig. 96).

    Equally bizarre are the mound excavations by the southern Plains warriors jailed at St. Augustine in the mid-1870s to reform them and expose them to "civilized ways." At the request of Spencer Baird, later second secretary of the Smithsonian, three mounds were sketched, cleared off, and excavated and the contents shipped in barrels to add to the early growth of the Smithsonian's collections. Put on display in cases, these were erroneously attributed to John Wesley Powell, head of the Bureau of American Ethnology, who merely had accessioned them. See Pratt 1964: 130–31.
15. Lawson was tortured to death by Tuscaroras after he helped to plant a colony of Swiss in North Carolina. The means of his execution is accurately described in his own ethnography of the Native Carolinas.
16. My visits to the Mississippi Delta and reading of Faulkner (below) made this "mound as flood haven" argument all the more plausible, but only in secondary terms of height and size, not in terms of motivating purposes. This seems more of a dividend than a cause, though there are many, many obvious mounds in the flood zone. See Phillips et al. 1951; Phillips 1970.
17. Until this publication Bartram's assessment, written in 1788, was known only through an overly edited 1853 work.

18. Tara incorporates a Neolithic tomb called the Mound of the Hostages, adding its venerable age to this seat of the Irish high kings (James 1993: 157).
19. The *Notes* were drafted at the end of the American Revolution (1781) in response to questions raised by French allies nervous about future U.S. prospects. Jefferson was then the thirty-seven-year-old governor of Virginia.
20. Its twenty-three chapters took "notice" of Virginia's boundaries, rivers, mountains, cascades and caverns, mines, vegetation, population, militia, navy, Natives (Indiens), counties and townships, charters and constitution, law and justice, colleges and roads, Tory assets, religions, local customs, commerce, European imports, measures and currency, public income, histories, and memorials. Appendices considered a draft constitution, an act for establishing religious freedom, and, in later editions, an examination of the 1774 murder of the "entire" family of Logan, a Mingo (Ohio Iroquois) leader who, with great eloquence and pathos, lamented that he alone was left to mourn for all of his murdered kin.

    Jefferson quoted Logan's speech in his chapter Query 6 while refuting the claim of Count Buffon (Comte Georges Louis Leclerc, 1707–88) and other French scholars that "vapors" in the defective soil of America caused its inhabitants to degenerate. After commenting on the great size and diversity of American animals, he considered the aboriginal peoples, arguing against certain claims made by these Frenchmen about body stature and ardor. As evidence of insight and ability, he quoted Logan's speech and named the murderer, but subsequent evidence has shown the leader of the murderers to be Daniel Greathouse, whose brother and sister-in-law, in revenge, suffered excruciating tortures to the death.
21. By digging into the mound, Lucas "violates the land" and risks punishment. See Volpe 1964: 237.
22. Note the interweaving of fertility, birth, snakes, and vitality.
23. Franz Boas, Edward Sapir, Mary Haas, Carl Voegelin, Joseph Greenberg, and Ives Goddard have continued these efforts.
24. In his masterful summary of Georgia "antiquities," native son Charles Jones ([1873] 1999), though writing from New York, recognized six types: sepulchral tumuli, chieftain mounds (single burial), family or tribal mounds (multiple burials), shell mounds, embankments, and elevations for observation, retreat, and signaling by fire.

    Over a century later Gordon Willey, premier Harvard archeologist, noted in *Archeology of the Florida Gulf Coast* ([1949] 1998: 20–21) the "functional categories of burial mounds, house platform mounds, refuse piles, and the canals, terraces, basins, etc., of the keys [islands] below Tampa." After midcentury, seriation became correlated with dates to provide more time-accurate chronologies.

Akin to the Smithsonian's Western U.S. River Basin Surveys after World War II, southeastern drainages have been the focus of recent researches, such as the "fetid" Mobile-Tensaw Delta. See Fuller and Brown 1998 (featuring a major Pensacola site with at least eighteen mounds); I. Brown 2003.

25. Rembert (AD 1450–1650), east of Athens, was damaged by floods before being covered by a reservoir; though its spiral ramp might have been due to "cattle grazing," the dated context suggests otherwise. Cf. Caldwell 1953; Waselkov and Braund 1995: 73, 252n83, 269n6, 298.

Today only Lamar's spiral and Etowah's partial ramp survive under federal protection, though William Bartram described Rembert and Winslow Walker salvaged a bit of Troyville before they were destroyed. Joe Saunders, by remote sensing, has found significant traces of Troyville mounds still under the ground of modern Jonesville, Louisiana (cf. Saunders et al. n.d.). Unique to Louisiana (and Europe), the Jonesville Catholic Church sits atop one of these, while elsewhere in the South small Baptist churches never come closer than the base of a mound. Family cemeteries, however, frequently cover mound tops, which have incongruously helped preserve them.

26. Thomas ([1894] 1985: 81, 196, 673) described coverings of muck in mounds and burials, which might be evocations of the Earth Diver creation epic, as noted by Hall (1997, 18), or, if the actual cause of the fatality, attributed to drowning by an angered Underwater Panther.

27. Biloxi dried the body of their chief and stood him (like a statue), with a club in one hand and a pipe in the other, in their temple upon an altar, six feet wide by ten feet long by six inches high, covered by a cane mat woven into red and yellow squares. The temple stood a league from the town and the door was always open, since it had no perpetual fire or attendant. The death of a chief displaced the body of the prior chief to join all of the previous chiefs standing in a side room of the temple.

A creeper vine tied the middle of the body to a tall, red-painted pole set up behind it. From its top hung the most famous of the calumet (= pipe stem with fan of eagle feathers) given him during his career. Every day food, such as hominy, was offered to the chief on this altar, as were first fruits of each harvest, which were consumed there by animals or travelers but attributed to consumption by the chief himself. His widow, close kin, and retainers visited him occasionally, discussed recent events, and promised his continued care.

Biloxi, belonging to the Ohio Valley subset of the Siouan Stock, were correctly Ta'neks anya "First People" (shifted through Mobilian Jargon: t > b, n > l = Biloxi), also known to the French as Annochy. Close allies of the Biloxi, the Pascagoula also stood up their deceased chiefs in their own temple. See Swanton 1912: 7.

28. Subsequently his grave was robbed and his body subjected to bizarre twists. See Sherfy 2005.
29. "Oldest Earthen Mounds Heighten Mystery," *Science* 277 (1997): 1761.
30. Joe Saunders, email to author, 5 December 2006.
31. Another Snodgrass site is located in Missouri.
32. The most vivid link between these paired earthworks and the Shawnees, whose homeland in colonial times was this section of Ohio, appears in the field notes of Erminie Wheeler Voegelin (*Shawnee Fieldnotes*, Box 32, Folder 290, p. 96, Newberry Library, Chicago, quoting from Mark Raymond Harrington), where Shawnee William Skye noted that such locales are paired as grandfather and (grand)mother, such as a flint quarry and a corn field. Shawnee elder Jim Clark described mound builders themselves as four feet tall, with vertical eyes and feet set backward, wearing fur (not clothes), and able to whoop like little boys (*Shawnee Fieldnotes*, Box 32, Folder 291, Book 12, p. 27, 1934). For today's Shawnees the Creator herself is addressed as Grandmother in prayer and ceremony.
33. These birds appear on the four bulging sides of special Hopewell pottery, suggesting its rounded square form was intended as a microcosm: globose body and square collar, especially when holding water as per the Earth Diver epic. Cf. Shetrone 1930: 136, 139 fig. 79.
34. Dr. Robert Walls provided a timely copy of this chapter via Notre Dame's "scan~ xerox~ email~ fax~ espresso machine."
35. Reilly and Garber (2007: 3, 40) rename the SECC the MIIS = Mississippian Ideological Interaction Sphere.
36. Closer examination, however, calls for realignment among these cults on the basis of theories of linguistic markedness and structuralism. For humanity, semantic and conceptual relationships are inherently threeway (as a matrix) such that they are nested or embedded within each other. The smallest unit is marked or exclusive, fitting within an unmarked or inclusive one, and these together are contained within an overall mediating or enclosive category. Thus for enclosive 'length,' the component of 'short' is marked and of 'long' is unmarked. This matrix can be represented as an equation: long (length) short. While Knight suggested a matrix of mighties (ministers) mounds, a better one is mighties (mounds) ministers, with the two human components balanced against the human-made earthen one, or, more simply, humans/humus.

37. Cf. Martin and Mauldin (2000: 23, 71): "= *i:kana* n[oun]. 1. ground, land, earth, 2. world + *leyk-ita* v[erb]. 1. to sit, be situated, exist (of a person, God, land, a town, money in the bank [*nota bene: a safe*], or something about evenly tall, wide, and long . . . 2. to settle, live (in a house, a place), reside (of one), [with *ka:k-ita* the dual number (of two)]."
38. According to Loughridge and Hodge ([1890] 1964: 38, 51, 181), 'high' is *homahtv, hv'lwe*, while their actual listing for 'mound' is *Ekvn-hv'lwuce, Rv'ne*, with *rvne* [*łane*] alone meaning 'mount, mound,' and the preferred word used by today's Oklahoma Creek and Seminole traditionalists.
39. Tribal words for 'mound' suggest some varieties are equated with organic life. In addition to the vitality ~ fertility associations of the pubic bulge included in one of the Creek words, Cherokees describe boils as towns built by *tsga'ya* (bug and worm spirits), acting as avenging animals to punish the hurt and harm done by a human to their ubiquitous kin. Its swelling evokes the town mound, while the hard tip was presumably the council house where decisions were made by microbes about the degree of fever, tremor, and pain inflicted on the patient until a shaman could work a cure. See Mooney (1891) 1982: 308, 361.
40. While Caddo ancestors built impressive mounds, their Pawnee linguistic relatives revered a constellation of earth-lodge-like hills on the central plains (Parks and Wedel 1985). Pawnees also mounded graves. Wichita ancestors, also Caddoan speakers, dug out a snake effigy.
41. Today the use of the word 'heart' for town mounds reverberates with their active, pulsing, throbbing, hollow qualities (see introduction).
42. In 1730 Sir Alexander Cuming dramatically convened a council in the town-house atop Nikwasi to appoint Moytoy of Tellico as "emperor" of the nation and delegate seven "chiefs" who visited England to further confirm this "treaty" (see Duncan and Riggs 2003: 153). Today Nikwasi survives as a heavily urbanized Franklin town park, purchased by coins collected by schoolchildren. Traditions of its Nunnehi help against the Creeks and Yankees continue. See Duncan (1998: 99, 201), where Davey Arch mentions it as a refuge for women and children and Freeman Owle tells of its helpful "little soldiers."
43. The Pueblo of Zuni in New Mexico calls itself *Halona*, the anthill at the center or Earth navel of the world, as measured out by a Spider stretching its legs evenly in all directions, according to their origin saga.
44. John Howard Payne (9 June 1791–1852), from an old Massachusetts family, was the sixth of nine children. Taught elocution, diction, and delivery by his own father, he became an actor, the first American to invade the British stage. He wrote "Home Sweet Home" in 1822, but it was first sung in Covent Garden,

England, in 1823 as part of the opera *Clari, the Maid of Milan*. Back in the United States he was hired to do public relations by the Cherokees on the brink of their removal to Oklahoma and toured the Southeast. He died while American consul to Tunis, Africa. See Anderson et al. 2010.

45. Jim Thompson, the narrator, indicated these "charged" sweepings were from the west side of the Big House (Delaware temple), where old ashes were carried out the west door and specially deposited on the outside. Once these had been scattered around the outside edge of the lake, the water boiled and the horned serpent floated up dead, but warned that others remained alive.

46. By analogy based on town plans in Swanton (1928e: 269 Eufaula, 274 Coweta, and especially 258 Hillibi), this mound marks the ancient location of the town's hothouse. Thus while the bird caller seems to stand on a few inches of raised dirt, he symbolically stands on the roof of a high enclosure used for winter, private, and secret meetings. It was just such large communal buildings that incorporated mound functions in recent centuries. Creeks today continue to proudly note the wisdom of their ancestors in building these hothouses for winter use in their southern homelands.

47. Based on present use, the number of mounds derives from their functions, not from sponsoring by corporate kin groups or other considerations, contra Randolph Widmer (2004), who argues that the number of mounds at a site reflected its number of "lineages" or corporate kin groups.

48. The equation here is clearly, based on their sources, chert = land, shell = water, and copper = sky (by shiny reflection of sunrays). See introduction.

49. This dwarf from northwest Alabama was about seventeen years old and forty inches tall. Thousands of years later two achondroplastic dwarves were buried at Moundville, a lone male and a female together with a normal adult male. Both were in their forties and about fifty inches tall. See Bahn 2002: 24–26.

50. Robert Hall (personal communication) called this formulation an "energy sink."

51. Such sealing by clay caps at Mound 72 and Blood Run assured their survival for centuries.

3. SEEING MOUNDS

1. This chapter title is an anagram for SEeing this SE.
2. Fogelson 2004b: 3, based on summaries by Frank Speck and John Swanton. Fogelson in conversation muses that research in the Southeast proceeded as though Swanton were in the church cemetery even as Speck was at the baptismal font, looking to the past or to the present and future.

3. Winds passing through its long needles waving high in the air produce literally singing pines. Canebrakes also make a distinctive clacking noise during breezes. Subsequent ecological casualties include, due to overgrazing, peavine (Ethridge 2003: 43, 164), passenger pigeon, and chestnut.
4. Bushnell (1908) relies on an interview with this twenty-six-year-old Tawasa slave by Robert Beverly, the famous Colonial Virginia historian. Tawasa occupied ten refugee towns near Pensacola until Creek slavers (not Tuscarora, as usually identified due to garbling by a Tuscarora translator) destroyed three in 1706, then another four in 1707, when Lamhatty was taken as others fled to the Alabamas before eventually (and ironically) merging with Creeks. For six weeks Lamhatty's captors took him through several Creek towns, including Arbika, before he was made to tend fields along the Tallapoosa for four months. Six weeks later he worked among the Opponys (Georgia Oconee) and a month later was sold to Shawnees along the Savannah River. After six weeks he escaped down the Mattapony River into the Virginia tidewater, took refuge with Andrew Clark, met Beverly, and was assigned to Lieutenant Colonel Walker, who, after initial fascination, decided to treat him as a slave and so "ill-used" him that melancholy set in. He escaped during the warm 1707 spring and disappeared. Though previously listed as Hitchiti-speaking, the only Tawasa word list indicates affinity with Timucua of north Florida. See Waselkov 1989: 313–20; Ethridge 2010: 152, 220, 284n12.
5. Upheavals of the Southeast are treated in Ethridge and Shuck-Hall 2009; Gallay 2002; Dobyns 1983; Bushnell 1908; Galloway 1982b, 1997; Wood et al. 1989; Ethridge and Hudson 2002; Forbes 1993; Williams and Shapiro 1990; Wright 1981; Kwachka 1994. The overview, though suffering from its long gestation, is Fogelson 2004b; the ethnographically rich, ahistorically static reference is Swanton 1928a. Contemporary Native southern communities are discussed in Bonney and Paredes 2001.
6. A gesture with the hands straight together, called the *gua* (*gwa*) for the word that accompanied it, also survived in this community, as a sign of reverence and respect. Cf. Hann 1988.
7. Beads are another expression of this tube. They are prominent in Cherokee conjuring and medicines. The renamee at a Tutelo spirit adoption wore a bandolier of ancient beads. During each summer's Yuchi Bread Dance white glass beads are thrown over the heads of the dancing men to invite the dead into the square. In the past such beads were also thrown at the Ribbon Dance to invite in the women dead. See Jackson 2003: 254.

Notes to pages 67–71

8. Jason Jackson (2003) is the source for this insight since Frank Speck's 1907 monograph includes matriclans that seem to derive from Creek intermarriages.
9. Swanton (1931: 116, 118–19) includes a quote from Bossu that the molding of infants involved applying to "their foreheads a mass of earth" of increasing weight. Infant molding and therapies were once widespread across the Americas but today are best known among Navaho, where the molding and shaping of the infant Changing Woman set the template for human babies.
10. At the marriage, "in the presence of the wedding guests, he sticks his Reed down, upright in the ground, when soon after his sweet-heart comes forth with another Reed, which she sticks down by the side of his, when they are married; then they exchange Reeds, which are laid by as evidences or certificates of the marriage" (Waselkov and Braund 1995: 128).
11. For these smooth discoids, pecked and polished from beautiful and dense stone, as town property, see Adair 2005: 395.
12. Today only Yuchi boys serving this drink bend down in a position of respect, as was generally done centuries ago. See Adair 2005: 101, 151; Waselkov and Braund 1995: 147, 151, 248n70, both of whom also note that temples tended their own transplanted plots of cussena yaupon holly.
13. Contra the authors in Hudson (2004), modern Creek women do ("touch") take medicine, and a few also fast, a true devotion since they are also cooking for guests.
14. Today the most common Creek term for the Busk is *poskita łako* = 'big fast.'
15. Fragile wooden masks were among the spectacular finds at Key Marco in southwest Florida (Gilliland 1975, 1989). When I ask elder Creeks why masks were once worn in the fall, they suggested that that is the time when the Earth too changes the way it looks. Moreover there is the well-known linkage between matriliny and masking. See Miller 1991.
16. In 1566–68, thirty years after Soto, Capt. Juan Pardo explored the Carolinas and set up a line of forts. Mounds and regalia were still in evidence. Olamico, the capitol of Chiaha chiefdom (Dandridge, Tennessee), was located on Zimmerman Island and featured a thirty-foot earth mound. At Cofitachiqui (Camden, South Carolina), famous for its woman ruler when Soto invaded, the capitol was Talimeco, with allied multimound towns along the Wateree River. There were, however, some exceptions. The Guatari chiefdom (Salisbury, North Carolina), with a woman leader, distinctively lacked any substructure mounds (Hudson 1990b: 37, 70, 93).

Moreover better data from modern Creeks indicate that Hudson, quoting Jim Knight, errs on the Muskoke word *i:kanhalwi* ~ *ekvnhvlwe* 'hill' (land +

high) as meaning 'mound' instead of its more proper archaic form, *i:kanleyki* ~ *ekvnlike* 'land seated, sitting,' or the presently preferred one, *łani* ~ *rvne* 'mound, mons veneris,' cf. *łanissi* ~ *rvnesse* = 'pubic hair,' with a clearly female referent (Martin and Mauldin 2000: 23, 58, 71, 105).

17. El Inka Garcilaso de la Vega was born in April 1539, a month before Soto (as he signed his own name) left Havana. The son of a Spanish officer and an Inka princess, though never legally married, Garcilaso was baptized as Gomez Suarez de Figueroa, but, after leaving Peru and settling in Spain, he created an identity befitting his own literary aspirations, taking the name of a distinguished poet related to his father and preceding it with the self-designation "El Inka" for his royal bloodline. His life as a soldier, writer, and minor cleric took him from the Peru of his foremothers to Spain, where he was buried in a crypt in his own chapel in the converted mosque that is the cathedral of Cordova.

    After centuries when European scholars published reports based on oral interviews with Native authorities, Garcilaso's 1605 Lisbon publication relied on a Soto veteran (Gonzalo Silvestre) who was his neighbor in Spain, bolstered by insights and understandings gained as a child among his own Inka relations, erudition from a classical education, and his own deep concern for literary style. His writings about Soto overlapped with his work on a history of Peru. Each is filled with digressions and observations held together by a strict adherence to chronology. *La Florida* is divided into six books, one for each year of the Soto expedition.

    In addition to evoking the reckless enormity of a thousand brutal invaders marching through the swamps and plains of the Southeast, Garcilaso had a personal reason for honoring Soto. As a young soldier in Peru, Soto helped end the bloody career of Lord Inka Atahualpa. Just before the Spanish arrived, Atahualpa took the throne from his "pure" half-brother Huascar, who had ruled the heartland from the capital at Cuzco. Their father had divided his domain between this rightful heir by his queen ~ sister ~ wife and Atahualpa, his son by a foreign noblewomen from Quito, who received this northern province but wanted the whole empire. His own mixed ethnicity, however, precluded claims to the racial purity required of the Lord Inka, and Atahualpa became ruthless in eliminating other claimants. When his army occupied Cuzco, using the pretense of a victory celebration, he demanded that all royal women and children assemble at a park outside the city. There, over many months, his soldiers raped, tortured, and butchered them all.

    Only a few children escaped. Among these were the mother and the uncle (Francisco Hualla Tupac Inka Yupanqui) of Garcilaso. By extolling the exploits of Soto, who was the first Spaniard to denounce Atahualpa and take part in his subsequent capture, torture, ransom, and murder; El Inka avenged the murder of his many Inkan relatives with his pen. In this violent age of defeat and disease, revenge took many forms, including literary ones.

The other, more accurate sources are either unnamed or by bureaucrats who make dull reading. These were Rodrigo Rangel (Ranjel), Soto's secretary, provided to Gonzalo Fernandez de Oviedo y Valdez, royal historian of the Indies; Luys Hernandez de Biedma, factor to the crown; and Fray Sebastian de Cañete, in a one-page summary. The anonymous gentleman of Elvas in Portugal published his own personal account in 1557.

It is especially ironic that a skilled Native writer had to interview illiterate conquistadors to provide the most colorful (but less accurate) account of the havoc they left among chiefdoms along the Gulf states, both in terms of mangled bodies and wholesale epidemics.

18. Enslaved during this Ayllon fiasco was Francisco Chicora (see chapter 2).
19. For comparison, similar, very European sentiments were expressed by Shakespeare in *Henry VI, Part 3* (Act I, Scene 3, lines 27–31), where Lord Clifford says, just before he kills Edmund, Earl of Rutland, the young son of the Duke of York:

> No, if I digg'd up thy forefathers' graves
> And hung their rotten coffins up in chains,
> I could not slake mine ire, nor ease my heart.
> The sight of any of the house of York
> Is as a fury to torment my soul.

20. A scatter of such chain mail and a dated coin identified the Governor Martin Site in downtown Tallahassee as the location of this 1540 winter camp.
21. Yet the first U.S. Gold Rush (1829) was in Cherokee Georgia and helped precipitate Removal, sprouting the town named Dahlonega, based on the Cherokee word for "yellow," and a U.S. mint after 1838.
22. As impressive as such a temple was, Spanish bigotry prevailed. While great skill was shown in its design and construction, this indicated to the Spanish and their priests what conversion to Catholicism could do to improve Native lives. Ironically such a Native edifice was also called a "mosque," a nasty reminder of Spain's expulsion of the Moors.
23. As noted in the introduction, since vitality resided in the mound, the cleaned and rebuilt temple drew from inside the monument below it to revive and continue its sanctity.

24. Though other locations for these sites have been proposed, I follow Hudson in tribute to his dedication to tracing out the route despite being denied outside funding and grants. Instead, ironically, his students and colleagues received funds for related spinoff studies. While his work is steeped in the documentary record, it is deficient (those "gaping holes" again) in terms of fieldwork with living mound builders. My own experience, though, is that direct questioning leads nowhere, and only proximity to chance remarks over many years yields useful information and insight into Mississippian continuities.
25. Parkin is one of the very few known Soto sites to survive for excavation and protection, located near Memphis and just off Interstate 40, as an Arkansas State Monument.
26. Chickasaw sources include works by Adair (1775) 1930; Nairne 1988; Swanton 1928b; Gibson 1971; Galloway 1982a; Johnson 1997, 2000; Johnson et al. 1994; Morgan 1994. These culminated in Ethridge 2010.
27. These six pitch accents (with their numeric or graphic characterizations) are low fall = 1 \\, low = 2 \, low rise = 23 \/, high = 3 /, high fall = 32 ^, high rise = 4 //.
28. Thanks to Barbara Duncan of the Museum of the Cherokee for conferring with Wiggins Black Fox of Qualla, Roger Smoker of Snowbird, and others to provide this usage. Text message of 4 April 2008 at 1:48.
29. Cf. *gaduhv'i* = town, *gadugi* = mutual aid co-op. Mooney ([1900] 1982: 527) lists the famous mound of *Nikwasi* on the same page as *nakwisi* = star, meadowlark, suggesting that, like landmarks in western Washington State, such as the geological Grand Mound, it may represent a Star being who plunged into the Earth. More annoying for those afflicted, there is also a reference to a boil as a tiny mound topped by a council house for its resident "bugs" and microbes. See chapter 2.
30. Thus, if asking a direct question during a Busk is rude, questioning the Creator kills.
31. Four thousand years in the same region link the Red Owl effigy beads of Poverty Point to the Choctaw belief that the shadow (*shilomish*) becomes a fox or owl, until Protestantism and Removal attenuated this link two centuries ago.
32. This section relies on the following sources: Swanton 1931: 2, 19, 31, 191; Bushnell 1909; Peterson 1985; Faiman-Silva 1997; Howe 2001; Pesantubbee 2005; Mould 2003, 2004; Lambert 2007, who notes her people were barely spared from federal termination just the day before it was to be executed on 25 August 1970.

In terms of accommodating to Euro-American patterns, Swanton thought that, of the Five Tribes, the Choctaws and Cherokees were most "advanced," with the Chickasaws intermediate, the Creeks and Seminoles most conservative and tenacious of ancestral traditions, while Cherokees were later intrusions into the region.

33. *Nanih Waiya* is actually a more ancient mound complex that includes the large named earthen platform, with an axis northwest by southeast. It is 25 feet high, 218 feet long, and 140 feet wide at the base (seven-tenths of an acre), and 152 feet by 56 feet on top (one-sixth of an acre). A low mound about eight feet high was located 250 yards northeast of the platform mound but was removed in the construction of a road and visitors area. A much-damaged rampart, stretching a mile and a half in circumference and up to four feet high, enclosed a larger area that once also included a few small mounds. One Choctaw thought this earthen wall once had eighteen segments with as many openings. See Brown 1926: 24–28.

34. Other such "labor of love" offerings in the Americas included the personal vow to build a wayside (trail, hunter) cabin along paths through Iroquois country (see Gehring and Starna 1988: 25n7; cf. Snow et al. 1996). Offerings of stones, tobacco, or small gifts are still routinely given to special places, often the abode of a petrified person, along waterways and trails.

35. *Iksa* is also the term used for Christians or "church people" and each separate denomination.

36. Studying five death images on Moundville pottery, George Lankford (2007b: 210) discovered a direct link between a Raptor and a variant Alabama-Seminole account of the path of souls on the way to the land of the dead through the sky. Ned Jenkins (personal communication, 2009) has also traced the movement of some Moundville pottery makers (women) to elite Creek sites. Seminoles are Creeks who moved into Florida in the aftermath of epidemics and European devastation of local tribes.

37. These modern Choctaw communities are Pearl River, Bogue Chitto, Red Water, Tucker, Conehatta, Standing Pine, Bogue Homa, and Crystal River.

38. Larger pots marked elite families, a sign of their generous hospitality. See Wesson 1997, 1999.

39. By implication, as noted, compact cremains decreased the human footprint on the land for living and dead.

40. In her deft summary Galloway (2006: 400) explains that Choctaw bodies formerly decomposed on a scaffold next to the house until the bone pickers made up the bone bundle for deposit in the charnel house ossuary and eventual mound; then, at this later time, the family buried the body next to the house, put up a scaffold over the grave, had the bone pickers take it apart at the appropriate time, and thus continued the intent of the same mortuary rites.

41. Knight (1981: 124) suggests three potential reburial rites involving more inclusive Choctaw social units: close kin for the first, clan for the second, and tribe (both moieties) for the third.

4. MODERN MOUNDING

1. Sources for Creeks (Mvskoke) include the classic works of Swanton 1928c, 1928d, 1928e; Speck 1907; as well as more recent efforts by Robbins 1976; Bell 1984, 1990; Wright 1986; Bossu 1962; Green 1979, 1982; Saunt 1999; Ethridge 2003; Grantham 2002; Moore 1994, 2001; Thorne 2003; Piker 2004; Hahn 2004; Foster 2007; Hall 2001; Hurt 2000; Mason 1963; Wesson 1997; Zellar 2007; Clark 1975.
2. As noted, the Creek word for a clan is *em vliketa* ~ *im-a-leyk-ita* from *em* 'they' + *liketa* = 'to sit, be situated, exist; to settle, live (in a house, place), reside (of one).' Cf. chapter 2, n37.
3. "Prehistory" is pejorative because it implies Cheeks had no history without writing, but this is patently false; still, it is a term of art in colonialist history.
4. Hahn (2004) skillfully treats how leaders and councils at Coweta forged a sense of the Creek Nation without ever mentioning that as the Red town it had this right to guide international diplomacy. He also slights the wide applications of kin terms, especially "mother," for providing a broad network of matrikin.
5. Shawnees were ~ are universally acknowledged for their great spiritual powers, well illustrated by a released captive who killed an Uktena and gained its crystal for the Cherokees. Their use of a variant of the name of the Shawnee warrior sept (Kishpoko) therefore may have been a way to harness and redirect their power, much as Nuyaka, an Oakfuskee subtown formerly called Tukpafka (= 'ember punk'), relocated and named itself for New York City, either in 1777 to gain goodwill during the American Revolution or for the 1790 Creek treaty signed in this first U.S. capital. See Swanton (1922) 1998: 248.
6. These arbors are believed to hold up the heavens and to represent the sky on earth (cf. Jackson 2003: 294n1). Therefore abandoning the grounds and the rite would bring on the collapse of the sky and the end of the world.
7. At the back of the Mikko's cabin was the town "sanctorium," which held the "physic pot, rattles, chaplets of deer's hoofs, and other apparatus of conjuration; and likewise the calumet or great pipe of peace, the imperial standard or eagle's wing." At the town of Autossee (Otasse), which claimed kinship to snakes, the front pillars of its council house were adorned with "vast speckled serpents, ascending upwards" (Waselkov and Braund 1995: 105). Its name evokes the *atassa* (*vtvssv*; Martin and Muldin 2000: 145, derived from "cut off"), the wooden "war

knives" held by the two lead women at the Creek Ribbon Dance and used to combat harm, which is appropriate in this historical context because diseases kept devastating the population of this town (Ethridge 2003: 80). Since some towns even had a sharp-edged pillar to split apart any approaching harm, these speckled snakes were doing double duty.

8. The flow is inside ash from the fire and sky mound moved to the tall town mound before outside soil, from specific places of certain color, is brought inside the ring to rebuild the fireplace and sky mound. Ashes and dirt, crossing inside and outside, thereby reinforce the bonds of the town.

9. At Tuskegee town the *mikko* and *heniha* wore red paint on one side of the face and black on the other, while warriors (= *taskaya*) wore under their eyes four stripes of alternating red and yellow (Speck 1907: 114).

10. War titles were confirmed by the father's clan, in contrast to personal names conferred by the mother's clan.

11. In part-for-whole (metonym) logic, *assi* literally means 'dried leaf' and is the proper name for 'herb water.'

12. David Lewis, a medicine maker and Creek national councilor, strongly denies any such "schools," probably in reaction to the bad experiences of Native children in Anglo classrooms, but such training sessions are known from the Southeast and other regions. To qualify their character I have found appropriate academic terms for them here. See Lewis and Jordan 2002.

13. Usually it is phrased as "Lamar culture" or "complex," but these terms ignore much that is lost to archaeology. A better term would be "kit," since it is mostly a lucky assortment of impervious tools that survive.

14. Koasati includes fascinating words for Mississippian features, such as town (= *o:la*), house (= *i:sa*), church (= *iscoba*), bridge (= *palpiya:ka*), foot log (= *filbaca*), continuous walls of house or basket (= *chakpa*; Kimball 1994: 74, 75). During excavations part of a painted wall was found at the Toqua townhouse (Waselkov and Braund 1995: 259n138).

15. Coweta and Cusseta moved in 1680 to Ochese Creek, then Apalachicola joined them, 1691–1716.

16. During the 1930s Depression, work crews excavated at the mounds of Okmulgee and, benefiting from cheap labor, rebuilt the hothouse. Opposite the long entryway, keeping out winter cold, the carefully excavated floor has a raised bird image with square depressions along its base marking three seats for leaders. From its historic trading post, James Moore with a thousand Creek allies left in 1704 to lay waste to the Florida Spanish missions, glutting the Native slave markets.

Nearby, and again threatened by highway construction, is the proto-historic Lamar site that gave its name to that late archaeological period. That the Lamars, a Georgia colonial family, eventually spawned Mirabeau Buonapart Lamar, an Indian-hating governor of Texas after tolerant Sam Houston, only goes to show how sadly ironic history can be.

17. The men inside the ring are purging their insides, while the women on the outside are washing off their skins.
18. The length of the logs determined how long the original fire would burn; it was an art to make sure that even with periodic feeding of firewood, the last bit of the four foundation logs burned up at the end of the two-day rite.
19. Hawkins mentions only one pot of ashes here, but there clearly have to be two to account for the four containers mentioned immediately afterward.
20. The physic plants are specifically numbered and named: (1) mic-co-ho-yon-e-juh, (2) toloh, (3) a-che-nau, (4) cup-pau-pos-cau, (5) chu-lis-sau (the roots), (6) tuck-thlau-lus-te, (7) tote-cul-hil-lis-so-wau, (8) chofeinsuck-cau-fuk-au, (9) cho-fe-mus-see, (10) hil-lis-hut-ke, (11) to-te-cuh choo-his-see, (12) welau-nuh, (13) oak-chon-utch-co, (14) co-hal-le-wau-gee.
21. Stone is emblematic of permanence, if not immortality. Combining pebbles with the war cry asserts long life, represented by the feathered cane tube.
22. See chapter 2, n44. Payne was a sometime actor, author, publicist, and composer, best known for "Home Sweet Home." He arrived at the height of the backcountry fervor by the "scum of humanity" to dispossess the Natives of their homelands by "force or fraud" for a chance at the notorious Georgia state land lottery (Swanton 1932). Soon these Native towns and people were struggling West to rebuild their lives in Oklahoma.
23. Feather Dance is not in this list, though Hitchcock implied it for Oklahoma, as indicated by the river canes tipped with white feathers that accompanied the display of the copper plates.
24. These sticks, snapped apart one per day, are *nittakachka* = *nettv* 'broken' + *kvckv* 'days.'
25. These brass plates of Tukabatchi have now been traced to dismembered French kettles traded south in the early 1600s by Neutrals who were based on the north shore of Lake Erie. Cf. Fox 2004; Warren and Noe 2009: 184.
26. He also noted other customs. The Hilishaya (*heles hayv* = medicine maker) of Tukabatchee diagnosed the angry animals that caused particular diseases. Among these, bowel pain was from a mad dog, bladder stricture was from a mad wolf, and costiveness (constipation) was from two beavers damming the innards, with a bear fighting a beaver when there was accompanying pain.

27. Robbins (1976), based on his own "touching medicine" at Greenleaf (*Asilanibi*); Bell (1984), based on Seminole-Eufaula, with visits to all the other towns; Howard and Lena (1984), based on New Tulsa (Talisi Little River).
28. Bell gained some fluency in Mvskoki and recorded many of the relevant terms, which have been updated according to the new dictionary of Muskogee (Martin and Mauldin 2000).
29. Howard's earlier description of the Busk in this town (1968: 103–19) did not have the insights later provided by Lena. His prior diagram also misplaces the main mound.
30. A duplicate pattern of open buildings periodically or seasonally occupied by families occurs in the church camps of Creek and Seminole Christians.
31. Bell (1984: 234n1) lists tube-like objects closely associated with men as, for instance, cigarettes, ball sticks, feather canes, and long flashlights.
32. Rules and restraints (*siyinfayatka ~ sintackita*) are a defining duty of men, while women have their own obligations, and both together remain well aware that their wrong actions will harm others and the whole town as well as themselves. See Robbins 1976: 153.
33. Only men sit in the arbors, which are called their "home," assigned by matriclan such that those clans named for land animals are often in the north arbor, those for birds and other sky beings in the south, and amphibians with the Mikko in the west—serving as cosmic mediators. This male earth/sky opposition balances against that of the female Red/White moieties.
34. Bell (1984: 100n17, 166) said these ashes were scattered in the woods, but this is preposterous. As a woman, she would not have been involved nor well informed about such men's business.
35. Many sources insist that a murderer did not gain amnesty by entering the square and only wergild or execution resolved this heinous crime.
36. Yaupon holly, a key ingredient in the Southeast, grows only in a tiny spot in Oklahoma.
37. Only ordinary, everyday items (crocks, sauce pans, lawn chairs, buckets) are now used, though they are dedicated to this ritual purpose and are carefully stored away from women. As such, their common availability helps disguise and protect the Busk, in lieu of the attention-getting Mississippian artworks for which the region is so famous. See Townsend 2004.
38. Such liquid flicking was once typical of every meal, such as venison soup, when eaters would "dip their middle finger in the broth, and sprinkle it over the domestic tombs of their dead" under the house floor (Adair 2005: 159).

39. Throughout the Southeast people, especially men, would ritually vomit before hazardous or critical undertakings. Often this was associated with gorging on the caffeinated Black Drink, but this was not an automatic response. Such purging had to be physically or psychologically induced, most often by leaders and officials. Doing so in public proved, by the frothy byproduct, a commitment to fasting, as well as providing a means of divination and a litmus test for any diagnosis of internal conditions. The immediate object was to fill the mouth with saliva and thereby gain the support of the lower world, associated with water and the river as "long man." By contrast the upper world is associated with fire and with blood, which is purged from the body by scratching to remove impurities, gain strength, and win stamina. Cf. Hudson 1975.
40. Mainstream thoughts about turkeys being dumb are erroneous, as my own encounter with turkeys guarding the homestead of an elderly Navajo woman quickly dispelled.
41. The masterful work of Ella Jean Hill Chaudhuri underscores the wisdom of distinguishing the natives of India (Indians) from those of the American Indies (Indiens). Her Creek family is responsible for the ceremonial square ground of *Asalanabi* (Greenleaf). She married an academic from India trained in political science. After she died, he finished the editing of her book. His own Indian background and comparative interests, on occasion, intrude on the Indien philosophy inherent in his wife's work, but her Mvskoke content and insights remain unmatched.
42. Such a pole was a gnomon, casting shadows like a sundial.
43. Such poles stood across the Americas, decorated according to local fashion, such as the totem pole in Northwest Coast villages. Cf. Hall 1997: chapter 13, 102–8. Of note, when a new replacement ball pole is dedicated at a square ground, the first game is played "upside down" by scoring at the base instead of the top of the post.

5. MOUNDS IN FULL

1. At Ole Miss and later in Ohio, these disjuncts became mlm = "martin luther moments" to keep ironic humor foremost as I grappled with meshing a living mound culture with some misguided archaeological opinion.
2. Many of their relatives, however, gather at local Indian Baptist and Methodist churches, where the architectural setup is much the same, but the position of the plaza and the mound is occupied by the church and steeple. See Schultz 1999.

3. In the broadest sense possible, since Navajo say that their deities wrote Laws into the stars so all could see and adhere to them. See Holiday and McPherson 2005: 121, 202–4, 344n15; Levy 1998.
4. As noted, Cherokee mounds can cover a central perpetual fire within a ring of stones having at least one crystal (Mooney [1900] 1982: 297, 396).
5. Chehalis of Washington State warn of the dangerous "wink of the eye of the earth" (Miller 1999a: 16).
6. July 2014 included several downpours when inches of rain fell in a few minutes, making for wet conditions. The ground at *latokalka* was particularly gummy at the start of the night's dancing, but the steady stomp of a multitude of dances around the central fire acted to firm it up until the sun rose at dawn to finish the drying out of the ground. In the original Southeast, therefore, where rain is more common than in Oklahoma and the soil full of clay, the New Year of the Green Corn Busk routinely became a tactile re-creation of the world.

While there are such strong cultural continuities, Wind is no longer a potent force despite its name for a leading matriclan and role in clearing the primordial world. Loess soils no longer form mounds, nor do pennants wave from poles.

BIBLIOGRAPHY

Abbott, Donald. 1981. *The World Is as Sharp as A Knife: An Anthology in Honour of Wilson Duff.* Victoria: British Columbia Provincial Museum.

Abrams, Elliot, and AnnCorinne Freter, eds. 2005. *The Emergence of the Moundbuilders: The Archaeology of Tribal Societies in Southeastern Ohio.* Athens: Ohio University Press.

Adair, James. (1775) 1930. *History of the American Indian.* Edited by Samuel Cole Williams. New York: Promontory Press.

———. 2005. *History of the American Indian.* Edited by Kathryn Holland Braund. Tuscaloosa: University of Alabama Press.

Aftandilian, Dave. 2007a. "Frogs, Snakes, and Agricultural Fertility: Interpreting Illinois Mississippian Representations." In *What Are the Animals to Us? Approaches from Science, Religion, Folklore, Literature, and Art,* edited by Dave Aftandilian. 53–86. Knoxville: University of Tennessee Press.

———, ed. 2007b. *What Are the Animals to Us? Approaches from Science, Religion, Folklore, Literature, and Art.* Knoxville: University of Tennessee Press.

Ahler, Steven, ed. 2000. *Mounds, Modoc, and Mesoamerica: Papers in Honor of Melvin L. Fowler.* Scientific Papers 18. Springfield: Illinois State Museum.

Ames, Kenneth, and Herbert Maschner. 1999. *Peoples of the Northwest Coast: Their Archaeology and Prehistory.* London: Thames and Hudson.

Anderson, William, Jane Brown, and Anne Rogers, eds. 2010. *The Payne-Butrick Papers.* 6 vols. Lincoln: University of Nebraska Press.

Angulo, Jaime de. 1990 *Indians in Overalls.* San Francisco: City Light Books.

Bahn, Paul, ed. 2002. *Written in Bones: How Human Remains Unlock the Secrets of the Dead.* Devon, England: David and Charles.

Bailey, Garrick A, ed. 1995. *The Osage and the Invisible World: From the Works of Francis La Flesche.* Norman: University of Oklahoma Press.

Baird, W. David. 1972. *Peter Pitchlynn: Chief of the Choctaws.* Norman: University of Oklahoma Press.

Bartram, John, and William Bartram. 1957. *Bartram's America: Selections from the Writings of the Philadelphia Naturalists*. Edited by Helen Gere Cruickshank. New York: Devin-Adair.

Bates, Dawn, Thom Hess, and Vi Hilbert. 1994. *Lushootseed Dictionary*. Seattle: University of Washington Press.

Bear Heart and Molly Larkin. 1996. *The Wind Is My Mother: The Life and Teachings of a Native American Shaman*. New York: Clarkson Potter.

Beck, Robin. 2009. "Catawba Coalescence and the Shattering of the Carolina Piedmont, 1540–1675." In *Mapping the Mississippian Shatter Zone: The Colonial Indian Slave Trade and Regional Instability in the American South*, edited by Robbie Ethridge and Sheri Shuck-Hall. 115–41. Lincoln: University of Nebraska Press.

Bell, Amelia Rector. 1984. "Creek Ritual: The Path to Peace." PhD diss., University of Chicago.

——— . 1990. "Separate People: Speaking of Creek Men and Women." *American Anthropologist* 92: 332–42.

Benedict, Ruth Fulton. 1923. "The Concept of the Guardian Spirit in North America." *Memoirs of the American Anthropological Association* 29.

Berryhill, Alfred, ed. 2007. *Este Mvskukvlke Svkvsmkv En Yahiketv: Muscogee People's Praise and Worship Hymns*. Okmulgee OK: Self-published.

Betts, Colin M. 2003. "Protohistoric Oneota Mound Construction: An Early Revitalization Movement." Paper presented at Midwest Archaeological Conference 29, Milwaukee, 18 October.

——— . 2010. "Oneota Mound Construction: An Early Revitalization Movement." *Plains Anthropologist* 55 (214): 97–110.

Birmingham, Robert. 2010. *Spirits of Earth: The Effigy Mound Landscape of Madison and the Four Lakes*. Madison: University of Wisconsin Press.

Birmingham, Robert, and Leslie Eisenberg. 2000. *Indian Mounds of Wisconsin*. Madison: University of Wisconsin Press.

Blitz, John. 2010. "New Perspectives in Mississippian Archaeology." *Journal of Archaeological Research* 18: 1–39.

Bloch, Maurice, and Jonathan Perry, eds. 1982. *Death and the Regeneration of Life*. Cambridge, England: Cambridge University Press.

Bonney, Rachel, and J. Anthony Paredes, eds. 2001. *Anthropologists and Indians in the New South*. Tuscaloosa: University of Alabama Press.

Bossu, Jean-Bernard. 1962. *Travels in the Interior of North American, 1751–1762*. Translated and edited by Seymour Feiler. Norman: University of Oklahoma Press.

Bowers, Alfred. 1965. *Hidatsa Social and Ceremonial Organization*. Bulletin 194. Washington DC: Bureau of American Ethnology.

Bowne, Eric. 2005. *The Westo Indians: Slave Traders of the Early Colonial South.* Tuscaloosa: University of Alabama Press.

Boyd, Robert. 1999. *The Coming of the Spirit of Pestilence: Introduced Infectious Diseases and Population Decline among Northwest Coast Indians, 1774–1874.* Seattle: University of Washington Press.

Bradley, R. B. 1993. *Altering the Earth.* Monograph 8. Edinburgh: Society of Antiquities of Scotland.

Brookes, Sam. 1997. "Aspects of the Middle Archaic: The Atassa." In *Results of Recent Archaeological Investigations in the Greater Mid-South: Proceedings of the 17th Mid-South Archaeological Conference, Memphis, Tennessee, 29–30 June 1996,* edited by Charles McNutt. 55–70. Occasional Paper 18. Memphis TN: University of Memphis, Anthropological Research Center.

Brose, David, James Brown, and David Penney, eds. 1985. *Ancient Art of the American Woodland Indians.* New York: Harry N. Abrams and Detroit Institute of Arts.

Brose, David, C. Wesley Cowan, and Robert C. Mainfort Jr. 2001. *Societies in Eclipse: Archaeology of the Eastern Woodlands Indians ad 1400–1700.* Washington DC: Smithsonian Institution Press.

Brown, Calvin. 1926. *The Archaeology of Mississippi.* University MS: Mississippi Geological Survey.

Brown, Ian, ed. 2003. *Bottle Creek: A Pensacola Culture Site in South Alabama.* Tuscaloosa: University of Alabama Press.

Brown, James A. 1985. *The Mississippian Period.* Section. 3 of *Ancient Art of the American Woodland Indians,* edited by David Brose, James Brown, and David Penny. 93–145. New York: Harry N. Abrams and Detroit Institute of Arts.

———. 1996. *The Spiro Ceremonial Center: An Archaeology of Arkansas Valley Caddoan Culture in Eastern Oklahoma.* Memoirs of the Museum of Anthropology 29. 2 vols. Ann Arbor: University of Michigan

———. 2003. "The Cahokia Mound 72-Sub 1 Burials as Collective Representation." In "A Deep-Time Perspective: Studies in Symbols, Meaning and the Archeological Record. Papers in Honor of Robert L. Hall." Special issue of *Wisconsin Archeologist* 84 (1–2): 81–97.

———. 2006a. "The Shamanic Element in Hopewellian Period Ritual." In *Recreating Hopewell,* edited by Douglas Charles and Jane Buikstra. 475–88. Gainesville: University Press of Florida.

———. 2006b. "Where's the Power in Mound Building: An Eastern Woodlands Perspective." In *Leadership and Polity in Mississippian Society,* edited by Brian M. Butler and Paul D. Welch. Occasional Paper 33. Carbondale IL: Center for Archaeological Investigation.

———. 2007. "On the Identity of the Birdman within Mississippian Period Art and Iconography." In *Ancient Objects and Sacred Realms: Interpretations of Mississippian Iconography*, edited by Kent Reilly and James Garber. 56–106. Austin: University of Texas Press.

Bruce-Mitford, R. L .S. 1964. *The Sutton Hoo Ship Burial*. London: British Museum.

Buffalohead, Eric. 2004. "Dhegihan History: A Personal Journey." *Plains Anthropologist* 49 (192): 327–43.

Buikstra, Jane, and Douglas Charles. 1999. "Centering the Ancestors: Cemeteries, Mounds, and Sacred Landscapes of the Ancient North American Midcontinent." In *Archaeologies of Landscape: Contemporary Perspectives*, edited by Wendy Ashmore and A. Bernard Knapp. 201–28. Oxford: Blackwell.

Bunny, George, Woodrow Haney, James Wesley, and Morina Wildcat. (1936) 1998. *Nakcokv Esyvhiketv: Muckogee Hymns*. New York: United Methodist Church, General Commission on Religion and Race, with the permission of Presbyterian Board of Christian Education.

Bushnell, David I. 1908. "The Account of Lamhatty." *American Anthropologist* 10: 568–74.

———. 1909. *The Choctaw of Bayou Lacomb*. Bulletin 48. Washington DC: Bureau of American Ethnology.

———. 1910. "Myths of the Louisiana Choctaw." *American Anthropologist* 12: 526–35.

———. 1927. *Burials of the Algonquian, Siouan, and Caddoan Tribes West of the Mississippi*. Bulletin 83. Washington DC: Bureau of American Ethnology.

Byers, A. Martin. 1996. "Social Structure and the Pragmatic Meaning of Material Culture: Ohio Hopewell as an Ecclesiastical-Communal Cult." In *A View from the Core: A Synthesis of Ohio Hopewell Archaeology*, edited by Paul J. Pacheco. 174–92. Columbus: Ohio Archaeological Council.

Caldwell, Joseph. 1953. *The Rembert Mounds, Elbert County, Georgia*. Bulletin 154. Washington DC: Bureau of American Ethnology.

Caldwell, Joseph, and Catherine McCann. 1941. *Irene Mound Site, Chatham County, Georgia*. Athens: University of Georgia Press.

Carleton, Kenneth. 1996. "Nanih Waiya: Mother Mound of the Choctaw." *Common Ground* 1 (1): 32–33.

———. 1999. "Nanih Waiya (22W1500): An Historical and Archaeological Overview." *Mississippi Archaeology* 34 (2): 125–55.

Carlson, Keith Thor, ed. 2001. *A Sto:lō and Coast Salish Historical Atlas*. Vancouver: Douglas and McIntyre.

Carver, Martin. 1998. *Sutton Hoo, Burial Ground of Kings?* Philadelphia: University of Pennsylvania Press.

Chafe, Wallace. 1976. *The Caddoan, Iroquoian, and Siouian Languages*. The Hague: Mouton.

Chappell, Sally A. Kitt. 2002. *Cahokia: Mirror of the Cosmos*. Chicago: University of Chicago Press.

Charles, Douglas, and Jane Buikstra. 2006. *Recreating Hopewell*. Gainesville: University Press of Florida.

Chaudhuri, Jean Hill, and Joyotpaul Chaudhuri. 2001. *A Sacred Path: The Way of the Muscogee Creeks*. Los Angeles: UCLA American Indian Studies Center.

Chickasaw Coloring Book. 2012. Ada OK: Chickasaw Nation Division of Arts and Humanities.

Child, Brenda. 2012. *Holding Our World Together: Ojibwe Women and the Survival of Community*. Penguin Library of American Indian History. New York: Viking.

Clark, Blue ~ Holatte Cvpvkke. 1975. "'Drove Off Like Dogs': Creek Removal." In *Indians of the Lower South: Past and Present*, edited by John Mahon. 118–24. Pensacola FL: Gulf Coast History and Humanities Conference.

Clark, J., Jon Gibson, and J. Zeider. 2010. "First Towns in the Americas: Searching for Agriculture, Population Growth, and Other Enabling Conditions." In *Becoming Villagers: Comparing Early Village Societies*, edited by Matthew Bandy and Jake Fox. 205–45. Tucson: University of Arizona Press.

Cleal, Rosamund M. J., K. E. Walker, and R. Montague. 1995. *Stonehenge in Its Landscape: Twentieth-Century Excavations*. English Heritage Archaeological Report 10. London: English Heritage.

Cloud, Henry Roe ~ Wa-na-xi-lay Hunkah. 1929. "Mythologies of Our Aborigines in Relation to Prehistoric Mound Builders in America." *Ohio Archaeological and Historical Society Publications* 38 (4 May): 560–67.

Conley, Robert. 1993. *The Dark Way: A Novel*. Norman: University of Oklahoma Press.

———. 2005. *Cherokee Medicine Man: The Life and Work of a Modern-Day Healer*. Norman: University of Oklahoma Press.

Crawford, Michael. 1978. *The Mobilian Trade Language*. Knoxville: University of Tennessee Press.

Culin, Stewart. (1907) 1975. *Games of the North American Indians*. Mineola NY: Dover.

d'Anghiera, Peter Martyr. (1912) 1970. *De Orbe Novo: The Eight Decades of Pietro d'Anghiera Martire*. Translated by Francis Augustus MacNutt. New York: G. P. Putnam's Sons.

Densmore, Frances. 1943. *Choctaw Music*. Bulletin 136. Washington DC: Bureau of American Ethnology.

———. 1956. *Seminole Music*. Bulletin 156. Washington DC: Bureau of American Ethnology.

Dincauze, Dena, and Robert Hasenstab. 1989. "Explaining the Iroquois: Tribalization on a Prehistoric Periphery. In *Centre and Periphery: Comparative Studies in Archaeology*, edited by T. C. Champion. 67–87. London: Unwin Hyman.

Dobyns, Henry F. 1983. *Their Number Become Thinned: Native American Population Dynamics in Eastern North America*. Knoxville: University of Tennessee Press.

Doran, Glen, ed. 2002. *Windover: Multidisciplinary Investigations of an Early Archaic Florida Cemetery*. Gainesville: University Press of Florida.

Dorsey, James Owen, and John Swanton. 1912. *A Dictionary of the Biloxi and Ofo Languages: Accompanied with Thirty-one Biloxi Texts and Numerous Biloxi Phrases*. Bulletin 47. Washington DC: Bureau of American Ethnology.

Dragoo, Don. 1963. *Mounds for the Dead: An Analysis of Adena Culture*. Pittsburgh PA: Carnegie Museum of Natural History.

Drechsel, Emanuel. 1997. *Mobilian Jargon: Linguistics and Sociohistorical Aspects of a Native American Pidgin*. Oxford Studies in Language Contact. Oxford: Oxford University Press.

———. 2001. "Mobilian Jargon in Southeastern Indian Anthropology." In *Anthropologists and Indians in the New South*, edited by Rachel Bonney and Anthony Paredes. 175–83. Tuscaloosa: University of Alabama Press.

Driver, Harold. 1965. *Indians of North America*. Chicago: University of Chicago Press.

Duncan, Barbara R. 1998. *Living Stories of the Cherokee*. Chapel Hill: University of North Carolina Press.

Duncan, Barbara, and Brett Riggs. 2003. *Cherokee Heritage Trails Guidebook*. Chapel Hill: University of North Carolina Press for the Museum of the Cherokee Indian.

Emerson, Thomas. 1982. *Mississippian Stone Images in Illinois*. Circular 6. Urbana-Champaign: Illinois Archaeological Survey.

Esarey, Duane. 2004. "Mississippian Spider Redux." Paper presented at the Joint Meeting of the 50th Midwestern Archaeological Conference and 61st Southeastern Archaeological Conference, St. Louis MO, 20–23 October.

Ethridge, Robbie. 2001. *Raiding the Remains: The Indian Slave Trade and the Collapse of the Mississippian Chiefdoms*. Paper at the Southeastern Archaeological Conference, Chattanooga TN.

———. 2002. "Shatter Zone: Early Colonial Slave Raiding and Its Consequences for the Natives of the Eastern Woodland." Paper presented at American Society for Ethnohistory, Riverside CA, 7–12 November.

———. 2003. *Creek Country: The Creek Indians and Their World*. Chapel Hill: University of North Carolina Press.

Bibliography

———. 2010. *From Chicaza to Chickasaw: The European Invasion and the Transformation of the Mississippian World, 1540–1715*. Chapel Hill: University of North Carolina Press.

Ethridge, Robbie, and Charles Hudson. 2002. *The Transformation of the Southeastern Indians, 1540–1760*. Jackson: University Press of Mississippi.

Ethridge, Robbie, and Sheri Shuck-Hall, eds. 2009. *Mapping the Mississippian Shatter Zone: The Colonial Indian Slave Trade and Regional Instability in the American South*. Lincoln: University of Nebraska Press.

Faiman-Silva, Sandra. 1997. *Choctaws at the Crossroads: The Political Economy of Class and Culture in the Oklahoma Timber Region*. Lincoln: University of Nebraska Press.

Faulkner, William. 1939. *The Wild Palms*. New York: Vintage.

———. 1940. *Go Down, Moses*. New York: Vintage.

———. 1957. *The Town*. New York: Vintage.

Feeling, Durbin. 1975. *Cherokee-English Dictionary*. Tahlequah: Cherokee Nation of Oklahoma.

Fienup-Riordan, Ann. 1994. *Boundaries and Passages: Rule and Ritual in Yup'ik Eskimo Oral Tradition*. Norman: University of Oklahoma Press.

Fitts, Mary Elizabeth, and Charles Heath. 2009. "'Indians Refusing to Carry Burdens': Understanding the Success of Catawba Political, Military, and Settlement Strategies in Colonial Carolina." In *Mapping the Mississippian Shatter Zone: The Colonial Indian Slave Trade and Regional Instability in the American South*, edited by Robbie Ethridge and Sheri Shuck-Hall. 142–62. Lincoln: University of Nebraska Press.

Fletcher, Alice. (1893) 1994. *A Study of Omaha Indian Music*. Lincoln: University of Nebraska.

Fletcher, Alice, and Francis LaFlesche. (1911) 1992. *The Omaha Tribe*. Lincoln: University of Nebraska Press.

Fogelson, Raymond. 1961. "Change, Persistence, and Accommodation in Cherokee Medico-Magical Beliefs." In *Symposium on Cherokee and Iroquois Culture*, edited by William N. Fenton and John Gulick. 213–25. Bulletin 180. Washington DC: Bureau of American Ethnology.

———. 1984. "Who Were the Ani-Kutani? An Excursion into Cherokee Historical Thought." *Ethnohistory* 31: 255–63.

———. 2004a. "Cherokee in the East." In *Southeast*. Vol. 14 of *Handbook of North American Indians*, edited by Raymond Fogelson. 337–53. Washington DC: Smithsonian Institution Press.

———, ed. 2004b. *Southeast*. Vol. 14 of *Handbook of North American Indians*. Washington DC: Smithsonian Institution Press.

Forbes, Jack D. 1993. *Africans and Native Americans: The Language of Race and the Evolution of Red-Black People*. Urbana: University of Illinois Press.

Ford, James. 1951. *Greenhouse: A Troyville-Coles Creek Period Site in Avoyelles Parish, Louisiana*. Anthropological Papers of the American Museum of Natural History, vol. 44, part 1. New York: American Museum of Natural History.

———. 1969. *A Comparison of Formative Cultures in the Americas: Diffusion or the Psychic Unity of Man*. Washington DC: Smithsonian Institution Press.

Foster, H. Thomas, II, ed. 2003. *The Collected Works of Benjamin Hawkins, 1796–1810*. Tuscaloosa: University of Alabama Press.

———. 2007. *Archaeology of the Lower Muskogee Creek Indians, 1715–1836*. Tuscaloosa: University of Alabama Press.

Fowler, Melvin. 1997. *The Cahokia Atlas: A Historical Atlas of Cahokia Archaeology*. Studies in Illinois Archaeology 2. Springfield: Illinois Historic Preservation Agency.

Fowler, Melvin, Jerome Rose, Barbara Vander Leest, and Steven Ahler. 1999. *The Mound 72 Area: Dedicated and Sacred Space in Early Cahokia*. Reports of Investigations 54. Springfield: Illinois State Museum.

Fox, William. 2004. "The North-South Copper Axis." *Southeastern Archaeology* 2 (1): 85–97.

Frison, George, and Bruce Bradley. 1999. *The Fenn Cache, Clovis Weapons and Tools*. Santa Fe NM: One Horse Land & Cattle.

Fuller, Richard, and Ian Brown. 1998. *The Mound Island Project: An Archaeological Survey in the Mobile-Tensaw Delta*. Bulletin 19. Tuscaloosa: Alabama Museum of Natural History.

Gallay, Alan. 2002. *The Indian Slave Trade: The Rise of the English Empire in the American South, 1670–1717*. New Haven CT: Yale University Press.

Galloway, Patricia. 1982a. "Henri de Tonti du village des Chacta, 1702: The Beginning of the French Alliance." In *La Salle and His Legacy: Frenchmen and Indians in the Lower Mississippi Valley*, edited by Patricia Galloway. 146–75. Jackson: University Press of Mississippi.

———, ed. 1982b. *La Salle and His Legacy: Frenchmen and Indians in the Lower Mississippi Valley*. Jackson: University Press of Mississippi.

———. 1995. *Choctaw Genesis, 1500–1700*. Lincoln: University of Nebraska Press.

———, ed. 1997. *The Hernando de Soto Expedition: History, Historiography, and "Discovery" in the Southeast*. Lincoln: University of Nebraska Press.

———. 2006. *Practicing Ethnohistory: Mining Archives, Hearing Testimony, Constructing Narrative*. Lincoln: University of Nebraska Press.

Gatschet, Albert. 1883. "The Shetimasha Indians of St. Mary's Parish, Southern Louisiana." Washington DC: *Transactions of the Anthropological Society of Washington* 2 (7 February to 15 May): 148–59.

Gatschet, Albert, and John Swanton. 1932. *A Dictionary of the Atakapa Language, Accompanied by Text Material.* Bulletin 108. Washington DC: Bureau of American Ethnology.

Gehring, Charles, and William Starna, eds. 1988. *A Journey into Mohawk and Oneida Country, 1634–1635: The Journal of Herman Meyndertsz van den Bogaert.* Syracuse NY: Syracuse University Press.

Gibbs, George. 1855. *Indian Affairs J. Report on the Indian Tribes of Washington Territory. Report of Explorations for a Route for the Pacific Railroad. Report of Explorations and Surveys . . . 1853–54.* 33rd Congress, 2nd Session, Senate Executive Document 78 (Serial 758). Washington DC: Beverly Tucker, Printer.

Gibson, Arrell. 1971. *The Chickasaws.* Norman: University of Oklahoma Press.

Gibson, Jon. 1986. "Earth Sitting: Architectural Masses at Poverty Point, Northeastern Louisiana." *Louisiana Archaeology* 13: 201–38.

———. 1996. "Religion of the Rings: Poverty Point Iconography and Ceremonialism." In *Mounds, Embankment, and Ceremonialism in the Midsouth*, edited by Robert C. Mainfort and Richard Walling. 1–6. Research Series 46. Fayetteville: Arkansas Archaeological Survey.

———. 2001. *The Ancient Mounds of Poverty Point: Place of Rings.* Gainesville: University Press of Florida.

———. 2004. "The Power of Beneficent Obligation in First Mound-Building Societies." In *Signs of Power: The Rise of Cultural Complexity in the Southeast*, edited by Jon Gibson and Philip Carr. 254–69. Tuscaloosa: University of Alabama Press.

———. 2006. "Navels of the Earth: Sedentism in Early Mound-Building Cultures in the Lower Mississippi Valley." *World Archaeology* 38 (2): 311–29.

Gibson, Jon, and Philip Carr, eds. 2004. *Signs of Power: The Rise of Cultural Complexity in the Southeast.* Tuscaloosa: University of Alabama Press.

Gilbert, William Harlen. 1947. "New Fire Ceremonialism in America." *Revista del Instituto de Anthropologia de la Universidad National de Tucuman* 3 (3): 233–316.

Gilliland, Marion Spjut. 1975. *The Material Culture of Key Marco, Florida.* Gainesville: University Press of Florida.

———. 1989. *Key Marco's Buried Treasure: Archaeology and Adventure in the Nineteenth Century.* Gainesville: University Press of Florida.

Goldstein, Lynne. 2000. "Mississippian Ritual as Viewed through the Practice of Secondary Disposal of the Dead." In *Mounds, Modoc, and Mesoamerica: Papers in Honor of Melvin L. Fowler*, edited by Steven Ahler. 193–205. Scientific Papers 18. Springfield: Illinois State Museum.

Gouge, Earnest. 2004. *Totkv Mocvse / New Fire: Creek Folktales*. Edited by Jack Martin, Margaret McKane Mauldin, and Juanita McGirt. Norman: University of Oklahoma Press.

Granberry, Julian. 1993. *A Grammar and Dictionary of the Timucua Language*. Tuscaloosa: University of Alabama Press.

Grantham, Bill. 2002. *Creation Myths and Legends of the Creek Indians*. Gainesville: University Press of Florida.

Green, Michael. 1979. *The Creeks: A Critical Bibliography*. Newberry Library Bibliography Series. Bloomington: Indiana University Press.

———. 1982. *The Politics of Indian Removal: Creek Government and Society in Crisis*. Lincoln: University of Nebraska Press.

Haas, Mary. 1941. Tunica. In *Handbook of North American Indian Languages*. Vol. 4: 1–143. Edited by Franz Boas. New York: Columbia University Press.

———. 1946. "A Grammatical Sketch of Tunica." In *Linguistic Structures of Native America*, edited by Harry Hoijer. 337–66. Viking Fund Publications in Anthropology 6. New York: Viking.

———. 1953. "Tunica Dictionary." *University of California Publications in Linguistics* 6 (2): 175–332.

———. 1969. *The Prehistory of Languages*. Series Minor 57. The Hague: Janua Linguarum.

Hahn, Steven. 2004. *The Invention of the Creek Nation, 1670–1763*. Lincoln: University of Nebraska Press.

Halbert, Henry S. 1899. "Nanih Waiya, the Sacred Mound of the Choctaw." *Mississippi Historical Society* 2: 223–34.

Hall, Joseph M., Jr. 2001. "Making An Indian People: Creek Formation in the Colonial Southeast, 1590–1735." PhD diss., University Wisconsin, Madison.

Hall, Robert L. 1979. "In Search of the Ideology of the Adena-Hopewell Climax." In *Hopewell Archaeology: The Chillecothe Conference*, edited by David Brose and N'omi Greber. 258–65. Kent OH: Kent State University Press.

———. 1997. *An Archaeology of the Soul: North American Indian Belief and Ritual*. Urbana: University of Illinois Press.

Hann, John. 1988. *Apalachee: The Land between Two Rivers*. Gainesville: University Press of Florida.

Hann, John, and Bonnie McEwan. 1998. *The Apalachee Indians and Mission San Luis*. Gainesville: University Press of Florida.

Hawkins, Benjamin. 1848. "A Sketch of the Creek Country in 1798 and 1799." *Collections of the Georgia Historical Society*, vol. 3, part I, 1–88. Savannah.

———. 1916. "Letters of Benjamin Hawkins, 1796–1806." *Collections of the Georgia Historical Society*, vol. 11. Savannah.

Haywood, John. (1823) 1959. *The Natural and Aboriginal History of Tennessee, Up to the First Settlements there in by the White People in the Year 1768*. Edited by Mary Rothrock. Jackson TN: McCowat-Mercer Press.

Heckewelder, John. (1876) 1971. *History, Manners, and Customs of the Indian Nations Who Once Inhabited Pennsylvania, and Neighboring States*. New York: Arno Press.

Hedges, John. 1984. *Tomb of the Eagles: Death and Life in a Stone Age Tribe*. New York: New Amsterdam Books.

Henning, Dale R., and Thomas D. Theissen, eds. 2004. "Dhegihan and Chiwere Siouans in the Plains: Historical and Archaeological Perspectives. Part Two." *Plains Anthropologist* 49 (192): Memoir 36.

Henri, Florette. 1986. *The Southern Indians and Benjamin Hawkins, 1796–1816*. Norman: University of Oklahoma Press.

Hill, James H. N.d.-a. "Description of Hilabi Round House." Creek Texts by Mary R. Haas and James H. Hill. APS. http://lingspace.wm.edu/lingspace/creek/texts/haas-hill/.

———. N.d.-b. "Origin of the Spokokaki." Creek Texts by Mary R. Haas and James H. Hill. APS. http://lingspace.wm.edu/lingspace/creek/texts/haas-hill/.

Hill, Rosemary. 2008. *Stonehenge*. Wonders of the World. Cambridge MA: Harvard University Press.

Hitchcock, Ethan Allen. 1996. *A Traveler in Indian Territory*. Edited by Grant Foreman. Norman: University of Oklahoma Press.

Hodge, Frederick. 1907. Bulletin 30. Washington DC: Bureau of American Ethnology.

Holiday, John, and Robert McPherson. 2005. *A Navajo Legacy: The Life and Teachings of John Holiday*. Norman: University of Oklahoma Press.

Howard, James. 1968. *The Southeastern Ceremonial Complex and Its Interpretation*. Memoir Series 6. Springfield: Missouri Archaeological Society.

Howard, James, with Willie Lena. 1984. *Oklahoma Seminoles: Medicines, Magic, and Religion*. Norman: University of Oklahoma Press.

Howard, James, and Victoria Lindsay Levine. 1990. *Choctaw Music and Dance*. Norman: University of Oklahoma Press.

Howe, LeAnne. 2001. *Shell Shaker*. San Francisco: Aunt Lute.

Hudson, Charles. 1975. "Vomiting for Purity: Ritual Emesis in the Aboriginal Southeastern United States." In *Symbols and Society. Essays on Belief Systems in Action*, edited by Carole Hill. 93–102. Southern Anthropological Society, Proceedings 9. Athens: University of Georgia Press.

———. 1976. *The Southeastern Indians*. Knoxville: University of Tennessee Press.

———. 1990a. "Conversations with the High Priest of Coosa." In *Lamar Archaeology: Mississippian Chiefdoms in the Deep South*, edited by Mark Williams and Gary Shapiro. 214–30. Tuscaloosa: University of Alabama Press.

———. 1990b. *The Juan Pardo Expeditions: Exploration of the Carolinas and Tennessee, 1566–1568*. Washington DC: Smithsonian Institution Press.

———. 1997. *Knights of Spain, Warriors of the Sun: Hernando de Soto and the South's Ancient Chiefdoms*. Athens: University of Georgia Press.

———. 2003. *Conversations with the High Priest of Coosa*. Chapel Hill: University of North Carolina Press.

———, ed. 2004. *Black Drink: A Native American Tea*. Athens: University of Georgia Press.

Hudson, Joyce Rockwood. 2000. *Apalachee*. Athens: University of Georgia Press.

Hugh-Jones, Stephen. 1979. *The Palm and the Pleiades Initiation and Cosmology in Northwestern Amazonia*. Cambridge Studies in Social Anthropology. Cambridge, England: Cambridge University Press.

Hurley, William. 1975. *An Analysis of Effigy Mound Complexes in Wisconsin*. Anthropological Papers 59. University of Michigan, Museum of Anthropology.

Hurt, Douglas A. 2000. "The Shaping of a Creek (Muscogee) Homeland in Indian Territory, 1828–1907." PhD diss., University of Oklahoma.

Innes, Pamela, Linda Alexander, and Bertha Tilkens. 2004. *Beginning Creek: Mvskoke Emponvkv*. Norman: University of Oklahoma Press.

Jackson, Jason. 2003. *Yuchi Ceremonial Life: Performance, Meaning, and Tradition in a Contemporary American Indian Community*. Studies in the Anthropology of North American Indians. Lincoln: University of Nebraska Press.

James, Simon. 1993. *The World of the Celts*. London: Thames and Hudson.

Jefferson, Thomas. (1785) 1972. *Notes on the State of Virginia*. New York: Norton.

Jenkins, Ned. 2009. "Tracing the Origins of the Early Creeks, 1050–1700 CE." In *Mapping the Mississippian Shatter Zone: The Colonial Indian Slave Trade and Regional Instability in the American South*, edited by Robbie Ethridge and Sheri Shuck-Hall. 188–249. Lincoln: University of Nebraska Press.

Johnson, Jay. 1997. "Stone Tools, Politics, and the Eighteenth-Century Chickasaw in Northeast Mississippi." *American Antiquity* 62 (2): 215–30.

———. 2000. "The Chickasaws." In *Indians of the Greater Southeast: Historical Archaeology and Ethnohistory*, edited by Bonnie McEwan. 85–121. Gainesville: University Press of Florida.

Johnson, Jay, Gena Aleo, Rodney Stuart, and John Sullivan. 2002. *The 1996 Excavations at the Batesville Mounds: A Woodland Period Platform Mound Complex in Northwest Mississippi*. Archaeological Report 32. Jackson: Mississippi Department of Archives and History.

Johnson, Jay, and Samuel Brookes. 1989. "Benton Points, Turkey Tails, and Cache Blades: Middle Archaic Exchange in the Midsouth." *Southeastern Archaeology* 8 (2): 134–45.

Johnson, Jay, Susan Scott, James Atkinson, and Andrea Brewer Shea. 1994. "Late Prehistoric/Protohistoric Settlement and Subsistence on the Black Prairie: Buffalo Hunting in Mississippi." *North American Archaeologist* 15 (2): 167–79.

Jones, Charles. (1873) 1999. *Antiquities of the Southern Indians, Particularly of the Georgia Tribes*. Edited by Frank Schnell. Tuscaloosa: University of Alabama Press.

Kane, Allen. 1989. "Did the Sheep Look Up? Sociopolitical Complexity in Ninth Century Dolores Society." In *The Sociopolitical Structure of Prehistoric Southwestern Societies*, edited by S. Upham, K. G. Lightfoot, and R. A. Jewett. 307–61. Boulder CO: Westview Press.

Kehoe, Alice. 2007. "Osage Texts and Cahokia Data." In *Ancient Objects and Sacred Realms: Interpretations of Mississippian Iconography*, edited by Kent Reilly and James Garber. 246–61. Austin: University of Texas Press.

Kennedy, Roger. 1994. *Hidden Cities: The Discovery and Loss of Ancient North American Civilization*. New York: Free Press.

Kenyon, Walter A. 1986. *Mounds of Sacred Earth: Burial Mounds of Ontario*. Archaeology Monograph 9. Toronto: Royal Ontario Museum.

Kimball, Geoffrey. 1994. "Making the Connection: Is It Possible to Link the Koasati to an Archaeological Culture." In *Perspectives on the SE: Linguistics, Archaeology, and Ethnohistory*, edited by Patricia Kwachka. 71–79. Southern Anthropological Society Proceedings 27. Athens: University of Georgia Press.

King, Duane Harold. 1975. "A Grammar and Dictionary of the Cherokee Language." PhD diss., University of Georgia.

Knight, Vernon James. 1981. "Mississippian Ritual." PhD diss., University of Florida, Gainesville.

———. 1986. "The Institutional Organization of Mississippian Religion." *American Antiquity* 51 (4): 675–87.

———. 1989. "Symbolism of Mississippian Mounds." In *Powhatan's Mantle: Indians in the Colonial Southeast*, edited by Peter Wood, Gregory Waselkov, and M. Thomas Hatley. 279–91. Lincoln: University of Nebraska Press.

———. 1998. "Moundville as a Diagrammatic Ceremonial Center." In *Archaeology of the Moundville Chiefdom*, edited by Vernon James Knight Jr. and Vincas P. Steponaitis. 44–62. Washington DC: Smithsonian Institution Press.

———. 2004. "Ceremonialism until 1500." In *Southeast*, edited by Raymond Fogelson. 14: 734–41. Washington DC: Smithsonian Institution Press.

Knight, Vernon James, Jr., and Vincas P. Steponaitis, eds. 1998. *Archaeology of the Moundville Chiefdom*. Washington DC: Smithsonian Institution Press.

Konrad, C. F. 1994. *Plutarch's Sertorius: A Historical Commentary*. Chapel Hill: University of North Carolina Press.

Korp, Maureen. 1990. *The Sacred Geography of the American Mound Builders*. Lampetere, Wales: Edwin Mellen Press.

Krause, Richard. 1996. "Observations on the Excavation of a Mississippian Mound." In *Mounds, Embankments, and Ceremonialism in the Midsouth*, edited by Robert C. Mainfort Jr. and Richard Walling. 54–63. Research Series 46. Fayetteville: Arkansas Archaeological Survey.

Kroeber, A. L., and E. W. Gifford. 1949. "World Renewal: A Cult System of Native Northwest California." *Anthropological Records* 13 (1): 1–156.

Kwachka, Patricia. 1994. *Perspectives on the Southeast: Linguistics, Archaeology, and Ethnohistory*. Southern Anthropological Society Proceedings 27. Athens: University of George Press.

Lambert, Valerie Long. 2007. *Choctaw Nation: A Story of American Indian Resurgence*. Lincoln: University of Nebraska Press.

Lankford, George, ed. 1987. *Native American Legends. Southeastern Legends: Tales from the Natchez, Caddo, Biloxi, Chickasaw, and Other Nations*. Little Rock AR: August House.

———. 2007a. "The Great Serpent in Eastern North America." In *Ancient Objects and Sacred Realms: Interpretations of Mississippian Iconography*, edited by Kent Reilly and James Garber. 107–35. Austin: University of Texas Press.

———. 2007b. "The 'Path of Souls': Some Death Imagery in the Southeastern Ceremonial Complex." In *Ancient Objects and Sacred Realms: Interpretations of Mississippian Iconography*, edited by Kent Reilly and James Garber. 174–212. Austin: University of Texas Press.

Lawson, John. (1709) 1967. *A New Voyage to Carolina*. Edited by Hugh Talmage Lefler. Chapel Hill: University of North Carolina Press.

Lepper, Bradley. 2005. *Ohio Archaeology, with Feature Articles Contributed by over 20 Archaeologists and Scholars*. Wilmington OH: Voyager Media Group.

Levy, Jerrold. 1998. *In the Beginning: The Navajo Genesis*. Berkeley: University of California Press.

Lewis, David, Jr., and Ann Jordan. 2002. *Creek Indian Medicine Ways: The Enduring Power of Mvskoke Religion*. Albuquerque: University of New Mexico Press.

Lindauer, Owen, and John Blitz. 1997. "Higher Ground." *Journal of Archaeological Research* 5 (2): 169–207.

Long, Fred, and George Scott. (1936) 1998. *Nakcokv Esyvhiketv: Muskokee Hymns*. New York: General Commission on Religion and Race, United Methodist Church.

Loughridge, R. M., and David Hodge. (1890) 1964. *English and Muskokee Dictionary*. Okmulgee OK: Baptist Home Mission Board.

McEwan, Bonnie, ed. 2000. *Indians of the Greater Southeast: Historical Archaeology and Ethnohistory*. Gainesville: University Press of Florida.

Mainfort, Robert, Jr. 2013. *Pinson Mounds: Middle Woodland Ceremonialism in the Midsouth*. Fayetteville: University of Arkansas Press.

Mainfort, Robert, Jr., and Lynne Sullivan. 1998. *Ancient Earthen Enclosures of the Eastern Woodlands*. Gainesville: University Press of Florida.

Mainfort, Robert, Jr., and Richard Walling, eds. 1996. *Mounds, Embankments, and Ceremonialism in the Midsouth*. Research Series 46. Fayetteville: Arkansas Archaeological Survey.

Mallam, Clark. 1976. *The Iowa Effigy Mound Manifestation: An Interpretative Model*. Report 9. Iowa City: Office of the State Archaeologist.

———. 1982. "Ideology from the Earth: Effigy Mounds in the Midwest." *Archaeology* 35 (4): 59–64.

———. 1984. "The Serpent: A Prehistoric Life-Metaphor in South Central Kansas." *Kansas Anthropological Association Journal* 5 (2): 40–83.

Mann, Barbara Alice. 2003. *Native Americans, Archaeologists, and the Mounds*. Vol. 14 of *American Indian Studies*. New York: Peter Lang.

Marino, Mary Carolyn. 1968. "A Dictionary of Winnebago: An Analysis and Reference Grammar of the Radin Lexical File." PhD diss., University of California, Berkeley.

Martin, Jack, and Margaret McKane Mauldin. 2000. *A Dictionary of Creek/Muskogee*. Studies in the Anthropology of North American Indians. Lincoln: University of Nebraska Press.

Mason, Carol Ann Irwin. 1963. "The Archaeology of Ocmulgee Old Fields, Macon, Georgia." PhD diss., University of Michigan.

Maynor, Malinda. 2000. "Indians Got Rhythm: Lumbee and African American Church Song." In "American Indian Issue." Special issue of *North Dakota Quarterly* 67 (3–4): 72–91.

Milanich, Jerald. 1998. *Florida's Indians from Ancient Times to the Present*. Gainesville: University Press of Florida.

———. 1999. *Laboring in the Fields of the Lord: Spanish Missions and Southeastern Indians*. Washington DC: Smithsonian Institution Press.

———. 2000. "The Timucua Indians of Northern Florida and Southern Georgia." In *Indians of the Greater Southeast: Historical Archaeology and Ethnohistory*, edited by Bonnie McEwan. 1–15. Gainesville: University Press of Florida.

Milanich, Jerald T., Ann S. Cordell, Vernon J. Knight Jr., Timothy Kohler, and Brenda J. Sigler-Lavalle. 1984. *The McKeithen Weeden Island Culture: The Culture of Northern Florida AD 200–900*. Orlando: Academic Press.

Milanich, Jerald T., Ann S. Cordell, Vernon J. Knight Jr., Timothy Kohler, and Brenda J. Sigler-Lavalle. 1997. *Archaeology of Northern Florida AD 200–900: The McKeithen Weeden Island Culture*. Gainesville: University Press of Florida.

Miller, Jay. 1974a. "The Delaware as Women: A Symbolic Solution." *American Ethnologist* 1 (3): 507–14.

———. 1974b "Why the World Is on the Back of a Turtle." *Man* 9 (2): 306–8.

———. 1979. "A 'Struckon' Model of Delaware Culture and the Positioning of Mediators." *American Ethnologist* 6 (4): 791–802.

———. 1980a. "High-Minded High Gods in North America." *Anthropos* 75: 916–19.

———. 1980b. "The Matter of the (Thoughtful) Heart: Centrality, Focality, or Overlap." *Journal of Anthropological Research* 36 (3): 338–42.

———. 1982. "People, Berdaches, and Left-Handed Bears: Human Variation in Native North America." *Journal of Anthropological Research* 38 (3): 274–87.

———. 1983a. "Basin Religion and Theology: A Comparative Study of Power (*Puha*)." *Journal of California and Great Basin Anthropology* 5 (1–2): 66–86.

———. 1983b. "Numic Religion: An Overview of Power in the Great Basin of Native North America." *Anthropos* 78: 337–54.

———. 1988. *Shamanic Odyssey. The Lushootseed Salish Journey to the Land of the Dead*. Menlo Park CA: Ballena Press.

———. 1991. "Delaware Masking." *Man in the Northeast* 41: 105–10.

———. 1992a. *Earthmaker*. New York: Putnam.

———. 1992b. North Pacific Ethno-Astronomy: Tsimshian and Others." In *Earth and Sky: Visions of the Cosmos in Native American Folklore*, edited by Claire Farrer and Ray Williamson. 193–206. Albuquerque: University of New Mexico Press.

———. 1996. "Changing Moons: A History of Caddo Religion." *Plains Anthropologist* 41 (157): 243–59.

———. 1997. *Tsimshian Culture: A Light through the Ages*. Lincoln: University of Nebraska Press.

———. 1999a. "Chehalis Area Traditions: A Summary of Thelma Adamson's 1927 Ethnographic Notes." *Northwest Anthropological Research Notes* 33 (1): 1–72.

———. 1999b. *Lushootseed Culture and the Shamanic Odyssey: An Anchored Radiance*. Lincoln: University of Nebraska Press.

———. 2000. "Indien Personhood II: Baby in the Oven Sparks Being in the World." *American Indian Culture and Research Journal* 24 (3): 155–60.

———. 2001a. "Ashes Ethereal: Cremation in the Americas." *American Indian Culture and Research Journal* 25 (1): 121–37.

———. 2001b. "Instilling the Earth: Explaining Mounds. Commentary." *American Indian Culture and Research Journal* 25 (3): 161–77.

———. 2011. "First Nations Forts, Refuges, and War Lord Champions around the Salish Sea." *Journal of Northwest Anthropology* 45 (1): 71–87.

Miller, Jay, and Vi Hilbert. 1993. "Caring for Control: A Pivot of Salishan Language and Culture." In *American Indian Linguistics and Ethnography in Honor of Laurence C. Thompson*, edited by Anthony Mattina and Timothy Montler. 237–39. Occasional Papers in Linguistics 10. Missoula: University of Montana.

Milner, George R. 1998. *The Cahokia Chiefdom: The Archaeology of a Mississippi Society*. Washington DC: Smithsonian Institution Press.

———. 2004. *The Moundbuilders: Ancient Peoples of Eastern North America*. London: Thames & Hudson.

Mochon, Marion Johnson. 1972. "Language, History, and Prehistory: Mississippian Lexico-Reconstruction." *American Antiquity* 37 (4): 478–503.

Mooney, James. (1891) 1982. *Sacred Formulas of the Cherokee*. Cherokee NC: Cherokee Heritage Books.

———. (1900) 1982. *Myths of the Cherokee*. Cherokee NC: Cherokee Heritage Books.

———. 1932. *The Swimmer Manuscript: Cherokee Sacred Formulas and Medicinal Prescriptions*. Revised, completed, and edited by Frans M. Olbrechts. Bulletin 99. Washington DC: Bureau of American Ethnology.

———. 1989. "Cherokee Mound-Building." *American Anthropologist* 2 (2): 167–71.

Moore, John. 1994. "Ethnoarchaeology of the Lamar People." In *Perspectives on the Southeast: Linguistics, Archaeology, and Ethnohistory*, edited by Patricia Kwachka. 126–41. Southern Anthropological Society Proceedings 27. Athens: University of Georgia Press.

———. 2001. "Ethnogenetic Patterns in Native North America." In *Archaeology, Language, and History: Essays on Culture and Ethnicity*, edited by John Edward Terrell. 31–56. Westport CT: Bergin & Garvey.

Morgan, David W. 1994. "An Analysis of Historic Period Chickasaw Settlement Pattern." MA thesis, University of Alabama, Tuscaloosa.

Morgan, William. 1999. *Precolumbian Architecture in Eastern North America*. Gainesville: University Press of Florida.

Mould, Tom. 2003. *Choctaw Prophesy: A Legacy of the Future*. Tuscaloosa: University of Alabama Press.

———. 2004. *Choctaw Tales*. Jackson: University Press of Mississippi.

Munro, Pamela, and Catherine Willmond. 1994. *Chickasaw: An Analytical Dictionary*. Norman: University of Oklahoma Press.

Nairne, Thomas. 1988. *Muskhogean Journals: The 1708 Expedition to the Mississippi River*. Edited by Alexander Moore. Jackson: University Press of Mississippi.

Newcomb, W. W. 1956. *The Culture and Acculturation of the Delaware Indians*. Anthropological Papers of the Museum of Anthropology 10. Ann Arbor: University of Michigan.

———. 1961. "The Caddo Confederacies." In *The Indians of Texas*, 279–313. Austin: University of Texas Press.

Orr, Kenneth. 1942. "The Eufaula Mound, Oklahoma: Contributions to the Spiro Focus." MA thesis, University of Chicago.

O'Shea, John. 1981. "Social Configurations and the Archaeological Study of Mortuary Practices: A Case Study." In *The Archaeology of Death*, edited by Robert Chapman, Ian Kinnes, and Klavs Randsborg. 39–52. Cambridge, England: Cambridge University Press.

Paige, Amanda, Fuller Bumpers, and Daniel Littlefield. 2010. *Chickasaw Removal*. Ada OK: Chickasaw Press.

Parks, Douglas, and Waldo Wedel. 1985. "Pawnee Geography, Historical and Sacred." *Great Plains Quarterly* 5 (Summer): 143–76.

Pauketat, Timothy R. 2007. *Chiefdoms and Other Archaeological Delusions*. New York: Altamira.

Pesantubbee, Michelene. 2005. *Choctaw Women in a Chaotic World: The Clash of Cultures in the Colonial Southeast*. Albuquerque: University of New Mexico Press.

Peterson, John, ed. 1985. *A Choctaw Source Book*. New York: Garland.

Phillips, Philip. 1970. *Archaeological Survey of the Lower Yazoo Basin, Mississippi, 1949–1955*. Papers of the Peabody Museum of Archaeology and Ethnology 25 Cambridge MA: Harvard University.

Bibliography

Phillips, Philip, James Ford, and James Griffin. 1951. *Archaeological Survey of the Lower Mississippi Alluvial Valley, 1940–1947*. Papers of the Peabody Museum of Archaeology and Ethnology 60 Cambridge MA: Harvard University.

Piker, Joshua. 2004. *Okfuskee: A Creek Indian Town in Colonial America*. Cambridge MA: Harvard University Press.

Plutarch. 1932. *The Lives of the Noble Grecians and Romans*. Translated by John Dryden. Edited by Arthur High Clough. New York: Modern Library.

Pratt, Richard Henry. 1964. *Battlefield and Classroom: Four Decades with the American Indian, 1867–1904*. New Haven CT: Yale University Press.

Prentice, Guy. 1986. "An Analysis of the Symbolism Expressed by the Birger Figurine." *American Antiquity* 51 (2): 239–66.

Pursell, Corin. 2004. "Geographic Distribution and Symbolism of Colored Mound Architecture in the Mississippian Southeast." Paper presented at Joint Meeting of the 50th Midwestern Archaeological Conference and 61st Southeastern Archaeological Conference, St. Louis MO, 20–23 October.

Quattlebaum, Paul. 1956. *The Land Called Chicora*. Gainesville: University Press of Florida.

Radin, Paul. 1911. "The Ritual and Significance of the Winnebago Medicine Dance." *Journal of American Folk-lore* 24 (92): 149–208.

———. (1923) 1990. *The Winnebago Tribe*. Lincoln: University of Nebraska Press.

———. 1945. *The Road of Life and Death*. Bollingen Series 5. New York: Pantheon Books.

———. 1950. *Winnebago Culture as Described by Themselves: The Origin Myth of the Medicine Rite: Three Versions. The Historical Origins of the Medicine Rite*. Memoir 3. Bloomington: Indiana University Publications in Anthropology and Linguistics.

Rankin, Robert. 1996. "On Siouan Chronology." Unpublished manuscript.

———. 2006. "Siouan Tribal Contacts and Dispersions Evidenced by the Terminology for Maize and Other Cultigens." In *Histories of Maize: Multidisciplinary Approaches to the Prehistory, Linguistics, Biogeography, Domestication, and Evolution of Maize*, edited by John E. Staller, Robert H. Tykot, and Bruce F. Benz. 563–75. Amsterdam: Elsevier Academic Press.

———. 2007. "Siouian Tribes of the Ohio Valley: 'Where Did All These Indians Come From?'" American Indien Studies Lecture Series, Ohio State University. 16 May. http://hdl.handle.net/1811/28545.

Rees, Alwyn, and Brinley Rees. 1978. *Celtic Heritage: Ancient Tradition in Ireland and Wales*. London: Thames and Hudson.

Reilly, F. Kent, III, and James F. Garber, eds. 2007. *Ancient Objects and Sacred Realms: Interpretations of Mississippian Iconography*. Austin: University of Texas Press.

Richards, John D., and Melvin L. Fowler, eds. 2003. "A Deep-Time Perspective: Studies in Symbols, Meaning and the Archeological Record. Papers in Honor of Robert L Hall." Special issue of *Wisconsin Archeologist* 84 (1–2).

Robbins, Lester. 1976. "The Persistence of Traditional Religious Practices among Creek Indians." PhD diss., Southern Methodist University.

Romain, William. 2000. *Mysteries of the Hopewell: Astronomers, Geometers, and Magicians of the Eastern Woodlands*. Akron OH: University of Akron Press.

Rouse, Irving. 1992. *The Tainos: Rise and Decline of the People Who Greeted Columbus*. New Haven CT: Yale University Press.

Rowe, Chandler. 1956. *The Effigy Mound Culture of Wisconsin*. Publications in Anthropology 3. Milwaukee WI: Milwaukee Public Museum.

Roy, Susan. 2010. *These Mysterious People: Shaping History and Archaeology in a Northwest Coast Community*. Montreal: McGill-Queen's University Press.

Russell, Sharman Apt. 2001. *When the Land Was Young: Reflections on American Archaeology*. Lincoln: University of Nebraska Press.

Sabo, George, III. 1992. *Paths of Our Children: Historic Indians of Arkansas*. Popular Series 3. Fayetteville: Arkansas Archaeological Survey.

———. 2003. "Dancing into the Past: Colonial Legacies in Modern Caddo Indian Ceremony." *Arkansas Historical Quarterly* 62 (4): 423–45.

Salzer, Robert, and Grace Rajnovich. 2001. *The Gottscall Rockshelter: An Archaeological Mystery*. Maplewood MN: Prairie Smoke Press.

Sam, Archie. 1976. Interview by Charlotte Capers, Olivia Collins, Elbert Hilliard, and H. T. Holmes. 30 August. Mississippi Department of Archives and History, OH83–03.

Saunders, Joe, Reca Jones, Thurman Allen, and Josetta LeBoeuf. N.d. "Ancient Mounds Heritage Area (Owner's Manual)." Baton Rouge: Louisiana Regional Archaeology Program.

Saunders, Joe, Reca Jones, Thurman Allen, Josetta LeBoeuf, and Sunny Meriwether. 2008. *Indians Mounds of Northeast Louisiana: A Driving Trail Guide*. Baton Rouge: Louisiana Division of Archaeology, Ancient Mounds Heritage Area and Trails Advisory Commission.

Saunt, Claudio. 1999. *A New Order of Things: Property, Power, and the Transformation of the Creek Indians, 1733–1816*. Cambridge Studies in North American Indian History. Cambridge, England: Cambridge University Press.

Bibliography

Schambach, Frank. 1996. "Mounds, Embankments, and Ceremonialism in Trans-Mississippi South." In *Mounds, Embankments, and Ceremonialism in the Midsouth*, edited by Robert C. Mainfort and Richard Walling. 36–43. Research Series 46. Fayetteville: Arkansas Archaeological Survey.

Scherman, Katharine. 1981. *The Flowering of Ireland: Saints, Scholars, and Kings*. Boston: Little, Brown.

Schilling, Timothy Michael. 2010. "An Archaeological Model of the Construction of Monks Mound and Implications for the Development of the Cahokian Society (800–1400 AD)." PhD diss., Washington University, St Louis.

Schoolcraft, Henry. 1855. "Origin, History, and Condition of the Chickasaws." In *Information Respecting the History, Condition and Prospects of the Indian Tribes of the United States*, vol. 5, edited by Henry Schoolcraft. 310. Washington DC: Smithsonian Institution.

Schroedl, Gerald. 2000. "Cherokee Ethnohistory and Archaeology from 1540 to 1838." In *Indians of the Greater Southeast: Historical Archaeology and Ethnohistory*, edited by Bonnie McEwan. 204–41. Gainesville: University Press of Florida.

Schultz, Jack. 1999. *The Seminole Baptist Churches of Oklahoma: Maintaining a Traditional Community*. Norman: University of Oklahoma Press.

Shaffer, Lynda Norene. 1992. *Native Americans before 1492: The Moundbuilding Centers of the Eastern Woodlands*. Sources and Studies in World History. Armonk NY: M. E. Sharpe.

Sherfy, Michael J. 2005. "Narrating Black Hawk: Indian Wars, Memory, and Midwestern Identity." PhD diss., University of Illinois, Urbana.

Sherrod, P. Clay, and Martha Ann Rolingson. 1987. *Surveyors of the Ancient Mississippi Valley: Modules and Alignments in Prehistoric Mound Sites*. Research Series 28. Fayetteville: Arkansas Archaeological Survey.

Sherwood, Sarah, and Tristram Kidder. 2011. "The DaVincis of Dirt: Geoarchaeological Perspectives on Native American Mound Building in the Mississippi River Basin." *Journal of Anthropological Archaeology* 30: 69–87.

Shetrone, Henry Clyde. 1930. *The Mound-Builders: A Reconstruction of the Life of a Prehistoric American Race, through Exploration and Interpretation of Their Earth Mounds, Their Burials, and Their Cultural Remains*. New York: D. Appleton.

Silverberg, Robert. 1986. *The Mound Builders*. Athens: Ohio University Press.

Silverblatt, Irene. 1989. "Peru: The Colonial Andes." In *Witchcraft and Sorcery of American Native Peoples*, edited by Deward Walker. 311–22. Moscow: University of Idaho Press.

Skinner, Alanson. 1924. "The Mascoutens or Prairie Potawatomi Indians: Part I, Social Life and Ceremonies." *Bulletin of the Public Museum of the City of Milwaukee* 6 (1): 1–262.

Smith, David Lee. 1997. *Folklore of the Winnebago Tribe*. Norman: University of Oklahoma Press.

Smith, Marvin. 1987. *Archaeology of Aboriginal Culture Change in the Interior Southeast: Depopulation During the Early Historic Period*. Florida Museum of Natural History, Ripley Bulletin Series. Gainesville: University Press of Florida.

Snow, Dean, Charles Gehring, and William Starna, eds. 1996. *In Mohawk Country: Early Narratives about a Native People*. Syracuse NY: Syracuse University Press.

Speck, Frank. 1907. "The Creek Indians of Taskigi Town." *Memoirs of the American Anthropological Association* 2 (2): 100–164.

———. 1942. *The Tutelo Spirit Adoption Ceremony: Reclothing the Living in the Name of the Dead*. Harrisburg: Pennsylvania Historical Commission.

———. (1949) 1995 *Midwinter Rites of the Cayuga Longhouse*. Lincoln NE: Bison Books.

Springer, James Warren, and Stanley Witkowski. 1982. "Siouan Historical Linguistics and Oneota Archaeology." In *Oneota Studies*, edited by Guy Gibbon. 69–83. Publications in Anthropology 1. Minneapolis: University of Minnesota Press.

Squier, Ephraim G. 1851. *The Serpent Symbol and the Worship of Reciprocal Principles of Nature in America*. New York: George F. Putnam.

Squier, Ephraim G., and Edwin Davis. (1848) 1998. *Ancient Monuments of the Mississippi Valley*. Smithsonian Contributions to Knowledge 1. Smithsonian Classics of Anthropology. Washington DC: Smithsonian Institution Press.

Swan, Caleb. 1855. "Topical History: Position and State of Manners and Arts in the Creek, or Muscogee Nation in 1791." In *Information Respecting the History, Condition and Prospects of the Indian Tribes of the United States*, vol. 5, edited by Henry Schoolcraft. 251–83. Philadelphia: J. B. Lippincott.

Swanton, John. (1911) 1998. *Indian Tribes of the Lower Mississippi Valley and Adjacent Coast of the Gulf of Mexico*. Mineola NY: Dover.

———. 1912. *A Dictionary of the Biloxi and Ofo Languages*. Bulletin 47. Washington DC: Bureau of American Ethnology.

———. 1922. "Tokuli of Tulsa." In *American Indian Life, by Several of Its Students*, edited by Elsie Clews Parsons: 127–45. New York: B. W. Huebsch.

———. (1922) 1998. *Early History of the Creek Indians and Their Neighbors*. Gainesville: University Press of Florida.

———. 1928a. "Aboriginal Culture of the Southeast." In *Annual Report* 42, 673–726. Washington DC: Bureau of American Ethnology.

———. 1928b. "Chickasaw." In *Annual Report* 44, 169–273. Washington DC: Bureau of American Ethnology.

———. 1928c. "The Interpretation of Aboriginal Mounds by Means of Creek Indian Customs." In *Annual Report* 1927: 495–506. Washington DC: Smithsonian Institution.

———. 1928d. "Religious Beliefs and Medical Practices of the Creek Indians." In *Annual Report* 42, 473–672. Washington DC: Bureau of American Ethnology.

———. 1928e. "Social Organization and Social Usages of the Indians of the Creek Confederacy." In *Annual Report* 42, 23–472. Washington DC: Bureau of American Ethnology.

———. (1928) 2006. *Chickasaw Society and Religion*. Lincoln: University of Nebraska Press.

———. 1929. *Myths and Tales of the Southeastern Indians*. Bulletin 88. Washington DC: Bureau of American Ethnology.

———. 1931. *Source Material for the Social and Ceremonial Life of the Choctaw Indians*. Bulletin 103. Washington DC: Bureau of American Ethnology.

———. 1932. "Green Corn Dance." *Chronicles of Oklahoma* 10 (11): 170–95.

Taborn, Karen. 2004. "Momis Komet ('We Will Endure'): The Indigenization of Christian Hymn Singing by Creek and Seminole Indians." MA thesis, Hunter College.

Thomas, Cyrus. (1890) 1980. *The Cherokees in Pre-Columbian Times*. Brooklyn NY: AMS Press.

———. (1894) 1985. *Report on the Mound Explorations of the Bureau of Ethnology*. Washington DC: Smithsonian Institution Press.

Thomas, David Hurst. 2000. *Skull Wars: Kennewick Man, Archaeology, and the Battle for Native American Identity*. New York: Basic Books.

Thorne, Tanis. 2003. *The World's Richest Indian: The Scandal over Jackson Barnett's Oil Fortune*. New York: Oxford University Press.

Timberlake, Henry. (1762) 2007. *Memoirs: The Story of a Soldier, Adventurer, and Emissary to the Cherokees, 1756–65*. Edited by Duane King. Cherokee NC: Museum of the Cherokee Indian.

Townsend, Richard. 2004. *Hero, Hawk, and Open Hand: American Indian Art of the Ancient Midwest and South*. New Haven CT: Yale University Press.

Van Tuyl, Charles. 1979. *The Natchez: Annotated Translations from "Histoire de la Louisiane," a Short English-Natchez Dictionary*. Series in Anthropology 4. Oklahoma City: Oklahoma Historical Society.

Vega, Garcilasco de la. 1980. *The Florida of the Inca*. Translated by John Varner and Jeannette Varner. Austin: University of Texas Press.

Volpe, Edmond. 1964. *A Reader's Guide to William Faulkner*. New York: Noonday Press.

Walker, Willard. 1979. *The Natchez: Ethnographic Notes*. Series in Anthropology 4. Oklahoma City: Oklahoma Historical Society.

Warren, Stephen, and Randolph Noe. 2009. "The Greatest Travelers in America,' Shawnee Survival in the Shatter Zone." In *Mapping the Mississippian Shatter Zone: The Colonial Indian Slave Trade and Regional Instability in the American South*, edited by Robbie Ethridge and Sheri Shuck-Hall. 163–87. Lincoln: University of Nebraska Press.

Waselkov, Gregory. 1989. "Indian Maps of the Colonial Southeast." In *Powhatan's Mantle: Indians in the Colonial Southeast*, edited by Peter Wood, Gregory Waselkov, and Thomas Hatley. 292–343. Lincoln: University of Nebraska Press.

Waselkov, Gregory, and Kathryn E. Holland Braund, eds. 1995. *William Bartram on the Southeastern Indians*. Lincoln: University of Nebraska Press.

Waselkov, Gregory, and Marvin Smith. 2000. "Upper Creek Archaeology." In *Indians of the Greater Southeast: Historical Archaeology and Ethnohistory*, edited by Bonnie McEwan. 242–64. Gainesville: University Press of Florida.

Weltfish, Gene. 1977. *The Lost Universe: The Way of Life of the Pawnees*. Lincoln: University of Nebraska Press.

Wermuth, Hans Fritz. 1978. "Crocodilia." *Macropedia* 5: 286–89.

Wesson, Cameron Braxton. 1997. "Households and Hegemony: An Analysis of Historic Creek Culture Change." PhD diss., University of Illinois, Champagne-Urbana.

———. 1999. "Chiefly Power and Food Storage in Southeastern North America." *World Archaeology* 31: 145–65.

White, Nancy Marie, Lynne Sullivan, and Rochelle Marrinan. 1999. *Grit-Tempered: Early Women Archaeologists in the Southeastern United States*. Gainesville: University Press of Florida.

Wickman, Patricia Riles. 1999. *The Tree That Bends: Discourse, Power, and the Survival of the Maskoki People*. Tuscaloosa: University of Alabama Press.

Widmer, Randolph. 1988. *The Evolution of the Calusa*. Tuscaloosa: University of Alabama Press.

———. 2004. "Explaining Sociopolitical Complexity in the Foraging Adaptations of the Southeastern United States: The Role of Demography, Kinship, and Ecology in Sociopolitical Evolution." In *Signs of Power: The Rise of Cultural Complexity in the Southeast*, edited by Jon Gibson and Philip Carr. 234–53. Tuscaloosa: University of Alabama Press.

Willey, Gordon. (1949) 1998. *Archeology of the Florida Gulf Coast*. Gainesville: University Press of Florida.

Bibliography

Williams, Mark, and Gary Shapiro. 1990. *Lamar Archaeology: Mississippian Chiefdoms in the Deep South*. Tuscaloosa: University of Alabama Press.

Williams, Stephen, ed. 1968. *The Waring Papers: The Collected Works of Antonio Waring, Jr.* Vol. 58. Cambridge MA: Harvard University Papers of the Peabody Museum of Archaeology and Ethnology.

Williamson, Ray. 1992. "The Celestial Skiff: An Alabama Myth of the Stars." In *Earth and Sky: Vision of the Cosmos in Native American Folklore*, edited by Ray Williamson and Claire Farrer. 52–66. Albuquerque: University of New Mexico Press.

Wood, Peter, Gregory Waselkov, and M. Thomas Hatley, eds. 1989. *Powhatan's Mantle: Indians in the Colonial Southeast*. Lincoln: University of Nebraska Press.

Worth, John. 1998. *The Timucuan Chiefdoms of Spanish Florida*. Vol. 1: *Assimilation*. Vol. 2: *Resistance and Destruction*. Gainesville: University Press of Florida.

———. 2000. "The Lower Creeks: Origins and Early History." In *Indians of the Greater Southeast: Historical Archaeology and Ethnohistory*, edited by Bonnie McEwan. 265–98. Gainesville: University Press of Florida.

Wright, James Leitch. 1981. *The Only Land They Knew: The Tragic Story of the American Indians in the Old South*. New York: Free Press.

———. 1986. *Creeks and Seminoles: The Destruction and Regeneration of the Muscogulge People*. Lincoln: University of Nebraska Press.

Young, Biloine Whiting, and Melvin Fowler. 2000. *Cahokia: The Great American Metropolis*. Springfield: University of Illinois Press.

Zeisberger, David. 1910. "History of the Northern American Indian." Edited by Archer Butler Hulbert and William Nathaniel Schwarze. Special issue of *Archaeological and Historical Quarterly* 19 (1–2): 1–189.

Zellar, Gary. 2007. *African Creeks: Estelvste and the Creek Nation*. Norman: University of Oklahoma Press.

INDEX

Page numbers in italics refer to illustrations.

Adair, James, 26, 137n5
Adena, 13, 31
Alexander, Linda, 134n3
Alvarado, Luis de Moscoso de, 78
amaranth, xiv
Antaeus, 11
Apalachee, 64, 71, 123
arbors, 108, 125, 151n6, 154n33
archaeologist bias, xi, 5, 133n16
armor (chain mail), 75
artifacts, oversized, 54
assi ('leaf,' herb water), 51, 61, 91, 95, 100, 113, 152n11
atassa (women's wooden knife), 55, 105, 109, 151n7
atoning, xxi, 59
axis mundi, 46

ballast, 134n2
ball game, 61, 86, 93
Barasana, 12
Bartram, John, 29
Bartram, William, 29, 33, 34, 38
Bear Heart ~ Marcellus Williams, 136n18
Big Horn Medicine Wheel, xiv
Biloxi, 141n27
Black Belt (soil), 73

Black Fox, Wiggins, xix
blood: clotted, 81; "crying blood," 68
Blood Run, 30, 139n11
Blount, William ("dirt king"), 72
blowgun, 61, 65
Bluetooth, Harold, 138n9
bluffs, 48
bowl ~ dome, xix, 20
Breath Holder, 118
broken days ~ sticks, 102, 153n24
burials, xi, xx, 2, 23, 31, 39, 40, 48, 50, 55, 78, 95, 122
buzzards, 25, 95, 137n3

Caddo, 43, 132n10, 143n40
Cahokia, xx
Calusa, 71
camps, 108
canoes, 45, 65
Catawbas, 63, 67, 79, 80, 97
Catholics, 71, 129, 148n22
CE 1066 (Battle of Hastings), 8
Chakchiuma, 83
Charleston (SC), 71
Cherokees: ceremonial places, 82; dialects, 81; divisions, 80; pitch, 149n27
chiefdoms, xiv

183

Index

Choctaws: and death, 87; divisions, 85
Chota, 81
chunkey (game), 68, 86, 92
churches, 155n2
clan (matri-), 33, 151n2
Cleopatra, 76
Cloud, Henry Roe ~ Wa-na-xi-lay Hunkah (1884–1950), 137n22
Clovis, xviii, 133n14
Cofitachiqui, 76, 97, 146n16
Communion, ix, xviii, 14, 123, 126
Coosa, 96
copper, 89
cosmos, 6, 17, 47
crawfish, 83, 91
cremains, 45, 123
crops, 44, 57, 65, 66, 85, 93
crystals, 18
curve ~ straight, 18, 42, 44, 58

dances, 115, 122; Buffalo, 107; Crazy, 116; Feather, 104, 112; Gun, 101, 105, 106; Long, 101; Ribbon, 102, 109; Tadpole, 101; Turkey, 101
d'Anghiera, Peter Martyr (1457–1526), 24
deacons, xviii
death, 67
deictic, xiv
Dixie, xiv, xx, 61
Dobu, 129
doctoring, 95
"Drive Away," 73
drum, 15
Duff, Wilson, 132n5
Duncan, Barbara, xix, 149n28
dwarf, 144n49

Earth: Cherokee word, 80; colored soils, 23, 41, 103; Creek word, 50, 80, 90, 143n38, 146n16; Salish etymology, 131n3
Earth Diver, 44
Earthmaker ~ *Ma'una*, 19
earthquakes, 16
Earth/Sky moieties, xx
Effigy Mounds, xix, 30, 38, 58–59
ekvnv (earth), 50
elements (1–4), 20
energy ~ power, 118
Enlighteners ~ *hiya yalgi*, 3
epidemics, 11, 62, 71, 136n14
Eries, 97
Ethridge, Robbie, xxiv
etvlwv ~ *talwa*, ix, 3, 54

Fani Mikko, 27
fast ~ poskita, 70
feasting, 58
Fire, ix, xvi, xvii, 3, 5, 14, 18, 20, 27, 29, 36, 43, 51, 61, 68, 81, 91, 93, 99, 101, 106, 108, 110, 111, 113, 117
fish poisons, 61, 65
Fletcher, Alice, 30, 138n10
Fogelson, Raymond, xii, 132n9, 144n2
Ford, Janet, 132n9
forgetting, 3, 111, 112, 115
Formative Period, 56
Foxes, 82
Frog, 27

Gallatin, Albert, 36, 37
Galloway, Patricia, 150n40
garfish, 69

Index

genders, 2, 7, 13, 17, 29, 49, 66, 91, 93, 114, 122, 126, 153n17
Gentry (Mound A), 42
Gibbs, George, 131n4
Gibson, Jon, 4
Ghost Keeping, 55
Gouge, Earnest, 134n3
grammar, xxi, 35, 63
gratitude, 105, 136n16, 150n34
Greenleaf ~ *Asilanibi*, 154n27
greenwood, 109, 115
Guale, 71
gwa (obeisance), 145n6

Haas, Mary, 64
Hall, Robert, xii, xix, 128
hardships, xv, 145n5
Hawkins, Benjamin, 72, 100
heart, xvii, 25, 117, 118, 143n40
Heckewelder, John, 28
height, 31
Hill, Jean, 118
Hitchcock, Ethan Allen, 106
Hitchiti, 64
Hochungara, 30, 121, 125
Hopewell Road, 43
house (kinship unit), 27, 138n6
Howard, James, xvi, 108
Hudson, Charles, 139n13, 149n24

Ibofvnga ~ High Above, 91; components, 117
Indien, xxv, 134n1, 155n41
Inka, 74, 147n17
IPA ~ International Phonetics Alphabet, 132n11
Irene Mound, 139n13, 139n14

Iroquois, 13, 28, 49, 63, 80, 126, 140n20
Issetibbeha, 36

Jefferson, Thomas, xi, 7, 32, 34
Juricek, John, 137n2

Kasihta (Creek mother town), 51, 98, 100
Kennedy, Roger, 36
Keres, xv, 132n7
Kettle, 122
kin terms, xxvii
Klamath, 120
Koasati, 96, 152n14
Koweta ~ Coweta (Creek mother town), 51, 98, 151n4

LaFlesche, Francis, 31
Lamhatty, 145n4
languages, xvi, 35, 62, 140n23
Lawson, John, 32, 128
left, 29, 39, 40, 110, 112, 135
Lena, Willie, 108
Levi-Strauss, Claude, 131n1
Lizard, 133n13
Logan (Ohio Mingo), 140n20
Lushootseeds, xii, 54, 121, 131n3

Mallam, Clark, 59
Marshall, John, 72
masks, 146n15
matriclan, 33, 151n2
Mauldin, Margaret, 136n17
medicine, 95, 113
Meigs, Return, 72
M'Gillivray, Alexander, 73, 98
mica, 39
microcosm, 2, 6

185

Index

Mi'kmaw, 8
Mind, 10, 117
Mississippi River, 13
"mlm" ~ martin luther moments, xx, 155n1
moieties, 84
moon, 14, 24, 44, 89, 117, 122, 135n11, 137n22
Mooney, James, 30
Moscoso de Alvarado, Luis de (Moscoso), 78
"Mound Builders" (fictitious), 10, 32
mounds, 1, 118; functions of, 56
Mound 72, xx, 144n51
mushrooms, 45
mustee, 11, 63, 79
mvdo ~ thanks, 104

Nanih Waiya, 81, 82, *83*, 124, 150n33
Natchez, xxvi, 27, 31, 38, 62, 67, 69, 72, 85
navels, 4, 26
Nickasaw (Ohio martyr), 40
Nikwasi, xxiv, 51, 81, 143n42, 149n29
Northeast, xiv

observatories, 14, 118
ocher (red), 23, 44, 55
Ohio, 8, 28, 37, 43, 135n9, 142n32
Ole Miss, xix, 132n9, 155n1
Olmec, xviii
Ontario, 58
Ortiz, Juan, 74
Osage, 40, 128
Owls, 82

Pardo, Juan, 146n16
Parkin (site), 77
Pawnee, xxiii, 122, 126, 143n40

Payne, John Howard, 52, 143n44, 153n22
pearls, 76
Pinson Mounds, 133n15
pipes, 44
Pitchlynn, Peter Perkins, 84
plaza, 18, 45, 55, 67, 68, 96, 109, 124, 129, 139n12, 155n2
Plutarch, 11
pole, 25, 53, 83, 92, 108, 114, 124, 141n27, 155n42, 156n6; ball, 66, 93, 108; grave, 87; Pawnee, 122; totem, 131n5, 155n43
pottery, xxvi, 48, 57, 65, 66, 85, 93, 96, 102, 103, 142n33, 150n36, 150n38
powha, xiii, xxv, 17, 134n4
priesthoods, 30, 49, 61, 69, 81
puzzles, xii

Qualla (NC), 9, 80, 81, 134n17, 149n28

ramps, 39, 45, 56, 141n25
Rankin, Robert, 135n9
Red Stick civil war, 72
Red/White moieties, 27, 66, 70, 84, 92

safe (image), xxii, 3, 89, 107, 117, 121, 126, 129, 143n37
San Luis, 64
Saucy Calf, 31
scratcher, 69
SECC ~ Southeastern Ceremonial Complex, 49
seminars, xvii
Serpent Mound, 8, 135n11
shadow, 82, 149n31
Shakespeare, 148n19
shattering, xi, 11

Index

Shawnee, 52, 120, 142n32, 145n4, 151n5
Siouians, 30
skin, xix, 6, 8, 16, 21, 54, 69, 82, 85, 90, 112, 124, 127
slaving, 11, 27, 33, 35, 41, 50, 63, 64, 70, 71, 79, 86, 88, 97, 136n15
Smoker, Roger, xix
snakes, 17, 53, 62, 70, 87, *90*, 123, 135n9, 151n7
Snodgrass, 2
Snowbird (NC), 9
song, 14, 136n18
Soto, Hernando de, 11, 71
souls, 82
Southern Cult, 49
Southwest, 57
Stomp, ix, xvi, xviii, 9, 15, 46, 54, 77, 80, 91, 104, 113, 122, 128, 156n6
Sun(s), xx, 31, 69; Sun Dance, 132n8
sunflowers, xiv
Swanton, John, 132n5

tadjo, 53
Tamaroha, 4, 135n5
Tara, 34, 140n18
Tawasa, 145n4
temples, xvi, 3, 13, 17, 24, 32, 42, 45, 56, 68, 76–77, 87, 124
Thomas, Cyrus, 29, 38

Timberlake, Henry, 80
tubes, 3, 5, 14, 15, 16, 17, 20, 25, 45, 65, 67, 84, 90, 106, 111, 118, 124, 128, 131n5, 132n5, 136n18, 154n31; beads, 145n7; reeds, 136n19, 146n10
Tukabatchee (Red town), 52, 102, 106, 153n25
Tupelo (MS), 26
tysic, xiii, xxv, 83, 114

virgins, 100
vomiting, 155n39

war dogs, 74
war titles, 94, 152n10
Washington, George, xi
Westos, 97
wheelbarrows, 139n14
whistles, 16, 136n17
willows, 109
witches, 95, 133n15
Worth, John, 32

Yadkin River (NC), 39
yahola, 102, 103
Yuchi, 46, 67, 146n12
Yup'ik, xviii, 47

Zeisberger, David, 28

OTHER WORKS BY JAY MILLER

Tribal Trio of the Northwest Coast by Kenneth D. Tollefson (coeditor; *Journal of Northwest Anthropology*, Memoir 10, 2015)

Delaware Integrity: Rituals, Removals, Reforms by Lenape Indiens (CreateSpace, 2015)

Rescues, Rants, and Researches: A Re-View of Jay Miller's Writings on Northwest Indien Cultures (*Journal of Northwest Anthropology*, Memoir 9, 2014)

Honne, the Spirit of the Chehalis (introduction to the Bison Books edition; University of Nebraska Press, 2012)

"The Hoh Tribe in 1949: Richard 'Doc' Daugherty's Ethnographic Notebooks" (editor; *Journal of Northwest Anthropology*, 2010)

Regaining Dr Herman Haeberlin: Early Anthropology and Museology in Puget Sound, 1916–17 (Lushootseed Press, 2005)

Tsimshian Culture: A Light through the Ages (University of Nebraska Press, 1997, paperback 2001)

"Chehalis Area Traditions: A Summary of Thelma Adamson's 1927 Ethnographic Notes" (*Northwest Anthropological Research Notes*, 1999)

Lushootseed Culture and the Shamanic Odyssey: An Anchored Radiance (University of Nebraska Press, 1999)

"Suquamish Traditions" (coauthor; *Northwest Anthropological Research Notes*, 1999)

Writings in Indian History, 1985–1990 (coeditor; University of Oklahoma Press, 1995)

Earthmaker: Tribal Stories from Native North America (Perigree Books, 1992)

Oral Literature (D'Arcy McNickle Center for the History of the American Indian, 1992)

Coyote Stories (introduction and annotation; University of Nebraska Press, 1990)

Mourning Dove: A Salishan Autobiography (editor; University of Nebraska Press, 1990, paperback 1994)

Shamanic Odyssey: A Comparative Study of the Lushootseed (Puget Salish) Journey to the Land of the Dead (Ballena Press, 1988)

The Tsimshian and Their Neighbors of the North Pacific Coast (coeditor; University of Washington Press, 1984)

CPSIA information can be obtained at www.ICGtesting.com
Printed in the USA
BVOW03*0800080416

442545BV00019B/16/P